The Prodigal Diaries

The Amazing Journey of a Modern-day Prodigal

KEN SIMMONS

ISBN 978-1-63525-567-6 (Paperback)
ISBN 978-1-63525-569-0 (Hard Cover)
ISBN 978-1-63525-568-3 (Digital)

Copyright © 2017 by Ken Simmons
All rights reserved. No part of this publication may be reproduced, distributed, or transmitted in any form or by any means, including photocopying, recording, or other electronic or mechanical methods without the prior written permission of the publisher. For permission requests, solicit the publisher via the address below.

Christian Faith Publishing, Inc.
296 Chestnut Street
Meadville, PA 16335
www.christianfaithpublishing.com

Printed in the United States of America

Foreword

Life is a bit like a blank page. I'd stared at this one for what seemed hours. Days. Or was it years? Just blank. Lifeless. Silent.

The television said a shot rang out in Memphis... someone tried to kill a dream. Still, the page is empty.

Another Kennedy is killed. I start, then I stop.

An alien in a funny white suit stepped onto another world and talked about *a giant leap*. Still nothing.

Another president is shot, but I still keep staring at these pages.

Fanatics shouting, "Allahu Akbar" kill thousands and plunge the world into chaos... still nothing.

Ghosts come in to write for me, but they're no better at it than me.

Then one keystroke, one heartbeat at a time... it began to take shape on the page... a word here, a day there, and gradually it filled the page and spilled on over into the next... and then into the next chapter, the next year. More years go by, and I wonder if I'm getting closer to the end or if I'll ever finish it... when a new century, a new millennium started. Y2K turned out to be a big deal about nothing until finally, one day, one day after ten thousand days, I found myself at the last page.

Was this *automatic writing?* You know, that parapsychical phenomena where someone sits down to write, and some unseen power takes over, and they write in a trance. Naw, couldn't be. If it were, then why did it take so long, and did I simply write what was happening, or did I write and then it happened? Was it self-fulfilling prophecy?

Has it really been more than thirty years since I started writing my story? Did I grow old between the first and the last page? I now walk where I used to run, naps have become *something I really look forward to,* and what's this hair business anyway? I've got hair that's stopped growing where it's supposed to grow, and it's now growing where it never grew before—out my nose and my ears—places where it just isn't supposed to grow. My nightstand looks like a shelf at a pharmacy, and to make matters worse, I've discovered that I'm now invisible to young women. I'm not handling this "growing old" thing well at all. I look in the mirror, and I cringe and say, *"Who is this old guy?"*

It's all true, isn't it? I didn't just imagine it, did I? But will anyone believe it—will anyone even care?

--ooOoo--

I suppose most men are born under rather ordinary circumstances and are destined to lead rather ordinary lives... I certainly wasn't much of an exception.

And I wonder just how presumptuous it is of me to think that anyone would want to hear this story, my story, because I think of myself as such an ordinary man. But if I am an ordinary man, even I must admit that I've led somewhat an extraordinary life.

Years later when I was seven, our family moved to Socorro, New Mexico, and I'll never forget the image of seeing a little bird that had been caught in a driving snowstorm. I picked him up and brought him inside to warm him and dried him off as best I could with a towel. He looked really sad—all wet and shivering—somewhat like a drowned rat with feathers. I looked at this pathetic little bird and thought that it was a lot like me—always wanted to fly with the eagles *(or at least with the chicken hawks)*, but I knew that I was a lot more like that little wet bird than any lofty eagle.

I did sense, however, even at that young age, that I was *driven*—although not sure why— to do something or to be somebody even though I didn't have a clue what this meant. Talk about *waxing philosophical*—I guess I wanted to fly with the eagles, *and I was afraid I might end up flapping my wings with the rest of the buzzards.*

And while still on this philosophical bent, later in life I rather imagined I'd someday be called up on some big stage, and with great fanfare, someone would present me with my *"Great One" Award*—*ta-da*—or someone would (drumroll, please) pin my *eagle's wings* on me (ah, such youthful fantasies). I was, at the same time, terrified that someone would discover I was really this scared, wet, and pathetic little sparrow who was pretending to be an eagle.

So if I ever were to accomplish anything that is meaningful, anything that lasts beyond these few blinks we call a lifetime—if I ever do accomplish something significant, and that something might leave a mark on humankind, I felt that it was my insecurities that were the *rocket fuel* in my life and that I have actually been driven more by my fear of failure than anything having to do with my abilities or strength of character.

Now there's a word for you—*character*. My character has been put to the test so many times in my life that I can't imagine being a more successful failure in that regard. In fact, I've failed the character test so many times it has only served to confirm my belief that it was the only thing I was any good at—*failure*. There have been times when I have resolved that my failure has been *absolute!* (Wow, that's really depressing!)

If all I ever *achieve* is to learn that the strength of my character is more important than *achievements* and that instead of having the world salute as I walk by, saying… *"There goes a great man"*… I now know I'd rather have a legacy that says, *"I know that guy… he's an honest man, and his word is true."*

So back to the question of my being presumptuous and questioning why anyone would want to hear my story. If you follow me through these pages, you'll see a picture of a man who accomplished a few things, some that might even seem great by some measurements, but none of those things that happened were because of any inherent or endearing qualities—indeed, they were in spite of my being a severely flawed man. To my way of thinking, the only reason I can see for any of these things happening in my life is that someone tapped me on my shoulder and said, *"Hey, buddy, you're it!"*… and I was willing.

Follow me—even patronize me, if you will—through these pages, and see if you think that someone was merely the invention of a delusional mind fired on by ego and an almost phobic fear of failure. You may not believe or even understand some of the things in this book, but I can promise you one thing—it will be the truth.

Chapter 1

Although my family lineage traces back to one of the *Mayflower* voyages and my maternal grandmother, Kathryn Nance Lyons, can point to a distant cousin John Nance Garner, who served as vice president of the United States under Franklin D. Roosevelt in his first two terms, I was born into a very middle-class family in July 1943 as the second of four children.

Grandmother Lyons had been raised in the gentility of the wealthy South, and I remember how fondly she recalled her colored nanny while living in the beautiful bluegrass country of Kentucky. She said her nanny had been more of a mother to her than her biological mother. But she soon came to know the harsh realities of being a single parent raising five children when her husband, Mervyn Lyons, just walked out one day and never returned. Almost overnight she went from a sheltered and wealthy upbringing to unexpected and drastic poverty. It seemed Grandpa Lyons, an Indian who had migrated down from Canada many years earlier, was a gambler and a drifter. Mom said she never knew which tribe her father was from, just that he was a full-blooded Indian who'd migrated down from Canada, and although he had very light skin, he was also almost completely devoid of any body or facial hair.

After the family was abandoned, they moved to the tiny town of Roy, New Mexico. During the Great Depression there was no welfare system, and she was forced to eke out a meager living by taking in sewing and laundry in order to feed the young Lyons children. Bread was nine cents a loaf—too expensive—so she would bake twenty-one loaves a week from scratch, and she made all the clothes for the children.

The Lyons home had no plumbing, so they had to carry in water from a cistern, which provided their water supply. But one day they discovered that several Gila monsters, those strange-looking venomous beaded lizards found in the desert Southwest, had gotten into the cistern, and one of them had died, poisoning their water supply. Now they were forced to buy water off the truck that came by once a week. Bathing had to be done in a washtub, and trips to the outhouse were often through snow and ice, which meant that a nighttime trip to the outhouse meant having to get completely dressed, only to have to get completely undressed to go back to bed.

The Great Depression hit in 1929, but it didn't seem to affect their lives much one way or another. They were dirt-poor before the Depression, and they were dirt-poor after it… living in the high barren plains of Eastern New Mexico.

Her oldest son, Clayton, was stricken with polio before reaching the age of two, and he was left severely crippled as well as being rendered a deaf-mute. My mother, Myra, was the third of the Lyons children to come along. Even though life during this time was often a desperate struggle for the family, Mom had warm memories of growing up there. She was nine when she began spending her summers at the Brockmans' farm over in the next county, helping out with chores. She also learned to ride horses, bareback, and she trained one horse to kneel down, making it easier for her to climb on. One day the horse threw her off when it came upon a den of rattlesnakes. Unfortunately, her summer visits to the Brockmans soon came to an end when Mr. Brockman, a church deacon, began to take a much-too-keen interest in her blossoming new breasts. Mom was just thirteen.

Mom and Robert Lee Simmons met in the spring of 1938 in Santa Fe, and that night Dad told his buddies, *"That's the girl I'm going to marry."* Later that year they were married in August.

Jobs were scarce everywhere, and one day Dad passed himself off as an experienced heavy equipment operator hoping to get the one job opening for a road crew. That night he and a friend broke into the construction yard, and he practiced all night driving a big Caterpillar road grader. The next morning he was able to convince the foreman he was an experienced operator, and he got the job.

My older brother, Reginald Lee Simmons, was born in Las Vegas, New Mexico, in April 1941, about eight months before the start of World War II, and I was born in the middle of the war in July of 1943. My mother gave birth to twins, a boy and a girl, about fifteen years later, Leslie Allen and Laura Jean, who were born in March on Friday the 13th, 1959.

In the early forties Dad went to work as an aircraft construction foreman for Convair Aircraft in San Diego during World War II. He'd been exempted from military service due to a bad hip and also because he worked as a foreman on one of the crews that built airplanes for the war effort. Mom struggled through the war years like so many other young mothers during that time, and I still remember their stories about gas rationing and the scrambling to gather gas coupons. By today's standards we might have been considered poor, but we never went without, and ours was a warm and loving family atmosphere.

Coronado Island...

Although only two years old, I can remember seeing the sailors coming home to San Diego in the months after the war ended in 1945. At that time we were living in Linda Vista, a suburb of San Diego. Strangely enough, I have vivid memories of the day my brother's dog was run over by a car and killed. Since I was too young to walk, my father was holding me in his arms and with the front screen door held open, and I can still see my Uncle Orland walking out into the street and picking up the dead dog and putting it into a gunnysack (burlap bag). The date on the newspaper clipping, one of those human interest stories about *"Little Boy Loses Dog,"* indicated I was just a little over ten months old at the time of that incident. Strange how some memories stick with you.

Next we moved into government housing on Coronado Island across the bay from San Diego. The only way to get to the mainland at that time was either to take the long drive along the Strand, which was about twenty miles along a thin ribbon of land around San Diego Bay, or to take the ferryboat crossing. I always looked forward to that ferryboat trip—taking the boat full of cars across to San Diego and back, and sometimes if we got to park our car near the front of the boat, Dad would let me sit on the hood of the car as we made the crossing. Today, Coronado is an affluent seaside community with many expensive and beautiful homes and high-priced real estate, but during the war I don't think there was much affluence to go around. By today's standards, we lived in what would probably qualify as a ghetto.

lost innocence...

Living in the government housing, called the projects, provided an all-too-early education for Reggie and me. Once, while playing at the school yard at Glorietta Elementary School, which was just a block away from where we lived on Mullinex Drive, we saw a black couple get into a fight, and the woman beat the man to death with a brick. She was sitting on top of him, straddling his chest, and she just kept wailing on him with that brick. I still have vivid memories of just how bloody it was, and I remember hearing the man's screams—all this within twenty or thirty feet of two very frightened little boys. I can also remember being so scared I didn't want to go back to the playground at the school for a long, long time.

A few weeks later in the group of projects just to the west of us, I saw a gathering of several police officers, and they were interviewing people and taking pictures. Then I saw that it was a dead man they were photographing. He was lying on a stretcher, and I could see he still had an ice pick stuck in his chest. Once the police saw there were young children watching nearby, they covered the man with a sheet and carried him out on a stretcher, but I'll never forget seeing this man who had been murdered—with this wooden-handled ice pick standing upright in his chest and with blood that had trickled down his side and dried. I was five or six when I saw all this blood and death.

Once a neighbor tried to kill my brother Reggie by shooting at him with a high-powered hunting bow, the arrow just missing Reg's head by inches. The man was angry over a scuffle between Reggie and his son. A few weeks later a friend of my dad got in a fight with this same man, and when Dad's friend hit him, the other man fell hitting his head against the curb, killing him. Dad's friend was arrested and charged with manslaughter. These were some of the harsh realities of living in the government housing in those days.

the foundation...

My paternal grandfather, Alvin Simmons, died when I was a small child, so I never had the chance to know him. And since my mother's dad had long ago abandoned the Lyons family, that meant I grew up without ever knowing a grandfather. Alvin Simmons was a Baptist minister, and my parents always spoke of him in the warmest terms as having been a decent and godly man. And so in spite of the mischief little kids learn about, we also learned at an early age the difference between right and wrong, and I think we were given a good moral foundation. It was against that backdrop that the rest of my life began to take shape.

a Norman Rockwell scene...

There's a lot to be said for childhood—it's got a lot going for it. When you're there and in the middle of it and at the risk of trying to paint a Norman Rockwell scene here, it's usually a carefree and adventurous time. It certainly was for me. The biggest problems you have to deal with are, *"Bobby's still mad at me 'cause I hit him in the head with a rock"* or *"Is Santa going to bring me a new bike for Christmas?"*

In San Diego just after the war, my dad worked weekends on the pit crews for some of the midget race car drivers at Balboa Park racetrack. Sometimes I got to go out to the infield with my dad and meet the drivers—drivers like Ed Elder and Bill Vukovich, who (Vukovich), in the early fifties, went on to win the Indy 500 two years in a row, then was killed while leading the race the following year. When Dad took us out to the track with him, it was a real thrill to get to meet the drivers and hear the roar of the engines.

There are sounds and smells from those days that never seem to leave you. They make an indelible impression on your mind no matter how old you are. In later years I heard that they mixed alcohol with their gasoline in their midget race cars, but whatever it was it created an unforgettable smell that instantly brings you back to those memories anytime you get a whiff of that scent again. It's a funny thing about smells—they say that an aroma can trigger a long-forgotten memory quicker than any of our other senses, and I think it's true. But then it's also true that hearing a song or a certain melody can instantly take you back ten, twenty, and even forty years or more.

The "Land of Enchantment"...

From 1950 to 1953 we began working on a new set of childhood memories in the small town of Socorro, New Mexico, which is in the middle of the state, halfway between Albuquerque to the north and Truth or Consequences to the south. Today Socorro is best known for its Very Large Array (VLA) of radio telescopes and the New Mexico Institute of Mining and Technology, a.k.a. School of Mines. Actually, the Very Large Array sits atop a mesa near the edge of a place we knew as Six-Mile Canyon—not sure about the reason for the name the locals had given that canyon, but we always thought it was because it was about six miles out of town.

Six-Mile Canyon has a number of caves, most of them about halfway up the sides of the steep canyon's cliffs, and six or seven boys of our Cub Scout troop had an outing one weekend at the canyon, and I wanted to explore one of the many caves.

Being the first one to scratch my way up the steep cliffside, I was also the first one into the cave. It was pitch-dark inside the cave, and our scoutmaster had the only flashlight. He had entered the cave last, lighting the way for the rest of us with his light, and I'd gone in first. By the time I was inside the cave, he'd gotten distracted by something and left me without the benefit of the light from his flashlight. Here I was, a scrappy eight-year-old boy in a dark cave, and just about the time the scoutmaster finally shone his light in my direction, his beam pointed into the face of an angry mountain lion, and at the same time I heard the terrifying scream *(RRAAOOORRRWWW)* of a mama lion protecting her two cubs less than six feet in front of me. I might have been the first one in the cave, but you can bet your last nickel I was also the first one out, sliding down the cliff on my butt, screaming all the way, followed by six or seven more terrified young boys!

Just above the caves there is a very flat *mesa* (a mountain with a flat, tablelike top) where we located a place where Indians had apparently performed their ceremonial dances. The ground, which was a hard reddish sandstone, had a curious circular indentation about one hundred feet in diameter. Our scout leader explained that the pattern had probably been made by the Indians when they held their dances, and after many, many years their dancing had created an indelible circular pattern in the hard sandstone.

The feeling was indescribable… standing atop that mesa late in the afternoon just before sundown, knowing that native Indians (maybe Apaches, maybe Navajos) had danced by the light of their campfires right here more than one hundred years ago. I could hear them yelping and singing their Indian chants while they skipped to the beat of their drums, and the circular path was still there, forever embedded in the sandstone and red clay.

The other boys must have thought I was crazy, but I danced and hollered in that same circle for what must have been half an hour, wishing I were there with the Indians more than a century earlier, dancing with them around the campfire. It was no wonder they called New Mexico the Land of Enchantment. I'd been told that I was one-quarter Indian and that I had Indian blood in me from my mom's father, and right then at that moment I wished I were Indian through and through. I wanted to ride the ponies into the wind. I wanted to dance around the fire and paint my face with war paint. I could feel it—I could really feel it.

Just as the sun began to drop behind the mountains in the distance, I started to look around for flint, hoping that I might find some arrowheads, and I came upon a hole in the ground on the mesa that was only a few inches wide, not even large enough for me to crawl down into, and so I pulled back some of the rocks to open up the hole a bit, and I uncovered what looked like a small cave or a little room that had been used to store some of their things.

The scoutmaster shone his flashlight into the hole as the other boys lowered me down inside what turned out to be a small room, and when he handed me his flashlight, I could see the room was full of old Indian artifacts including a few weathered and dried out old wooden bows, arrows, and a few arrowheads made of flint and a large heavy stone that was scooped out or indented that was nearly three feet long and about eighteen inches wide, with another smaller and rounder stone on top of it. Our scoutmaster told us this was called a metate (ma-tá-tey), which the Indians used for grinding corn. But the way everything was arranged, our scoutmaster said it looked as though this were a ceremonial place for keeping artifacts, almost as if they were storing their history for someone to discover at a later date.

Living in New Mexico was a continuous adventure for a young boy—*this young boy*—maybe not quite in the same league as Tom Sawyer and Huck Finn, but we did have some real adventures back then. I'm not sure why, but some of those memories are more vivid to me now than what I did *last week!* (They say, this propensity to reminisce so often is a sign of getting older… *oops!*)

Often we'd hike down to the Rio Grande River a few miles away and go fishing with bows and arrows, trying to shoot some catfish or carp; we never seemed to get many catfish though, just mostly those bony, scaly carp. Boy, did we think we were smart kids too, bringing back a bunch of carp and selling them for ten cents apiece to some of the families of braceros who lived on the outskirts of town. These were migrant Mexican families who worked the seasonal crops in the area. After all, a dollar would buy a lot in those days, so even ten cents was a big deal. A bottle of Coke was only four cents, six cents got us a Pepsi (bigger bottle), and the Saturday matinee at the theater downtown was just fourteen cents.

I even got to try my hand at picking cotton. I was all eight years old, but we heard about a cotton field north of town that needed pickers, so Mom and Dad let Reggie and me work in the cotton fields for a few days. Mostly, I remember the long white bag I stuffed the cotton into and then having to drag it behind me, and the more cotton you picked, the heavier it got, with the goal being to fill it with 100 lb. of cotton. I never did manage to fill the bag. And I remember all the little nicks and cuts you get on your fingers from the thorns on the cotton bowls. I'm not sure what our pay was for picking 100 lb. of cotton, but I am sure it wasn't much. As I recall, it might have been two or three dollars—not exactly a scene from "Ol' Man River," but it was fun… and it added to my library of memories.

my horse June…

And I got my first horse when we lived in Socorro. It was a young mare that my uncle gave me, and since he made the gift to me in June, a month before my birthday, I named the horse June. How I came to get that horse is a story all in itself—and one I'll never forget.

My uncle Chester Bishop, who was the husband of my father's sister Marie, had a large ranch in Pagosa Springs, Colorado, which is just north of the New Mexico border, and that year our family went up to his ranch for a few days. His ranch was adjacent to a larger ranch owned by the famous cowboy Red Ryder.

Early one morning, knowing my birthday was coming up in a little more than a month, Uncle Chester saddled up his big buckskin horse, and without saying a word to me, he rode by and one-handedly picked me up and swung me onto the saddle in back of him. It was cold that morning, and he had an old denim jacket draped over his saddle that he handed me over his shoulder. It was much too big for me, but it helped to hold back the bite of the cold air. It seemed like a long ride over a number of hills in what I remember was very mountainous and heavily wooded timber country until we topped out over a ridge and came down into a beautiful green meadow where a small herd of twenty or thirty horses were grazing. I had never seen anything so beautiful—grass greener than I'd ever imagined, surrounded by beautiful pine forests. Uncle Chester, who wasn't known for being much of a talker, still hadn't said a word up to that point.

Finally, he pulled back on the reins, and the horse snorted a few times with that unmistakable sound that only horses can make as it came to a stop just at the top of a ridge, and he simply pointed at the small herd of horses down below us and said, *"Which one do you want?"*

I pointed excitedly at a young mare and said, *"That one,"* and that's how I came to get my birthday horse, June. It was only later that we found out she was only green broke. I'm not sure if Dad even knew what that meant, but she had not been completely saddle broken and was still mostly wild.

A week or so later Uncle Chester loaded June into a trailer and brought her to us in Socorro, which was almost three hundred miles south of Pagosa Springs. We put her out to graze in a field a few hundred yards behind our house.

I can remember sometimes climbing up the cottonwood tree, which was in our side yard, so I could see far enough to get a glimpse of the horse… my very own horse. And later that fall after school I'd run the quarter mile down the dirt road to the corral, which was next to the road where she grazed. June would always come trotting up to me as I stood on the lower rail of the wooden fence because she knew I'd feed her alfalfa or clumps of grass and sometimes wildflowers that I'd picked as I came up to the corral.

Often she'd give me an affectionate nip on my sleeve or on the shoulder of my thick plaid jacket, and her breath made little clouds of vapor from the chilly autumn air, and sometimes she made popping sounds with her lips as she ate the wildflowers. Occasionally I'd climb up on the top rail so I could hop on her back, and she always gave me a gentle ride around the corral. It was as if she knew I was just a kid, and she was being extra careful for my sake. I never did ride her using a saddle—always rode her bareback. Ever since that time, whenever I'm around horses and their distinctive smell, which is like no other smell in the world, I'm instantly taken back to those times, feeding my horse in the corral down the old dirt road outside Socorro. That was an elegantly simple life then, and I find myself longing for it still.

We quickly discovered that Reggie and I were the only ones who could ride June, because she managed to buck off every other experienced rider in Socorro, and ours was known as a horseman's town. Mom called it a *one-horse town*.

Some of the children in the elementary school in Socorro actually rode their horses to the school every day, and the school had put up a hitching post just for that purpose. Some of the kids would shackle their horses (put a short chain on both front legs), which would allow them to walk using short steps—they just couldn't run, and the horses would graze there in our school yard during the school day. That was more than *half a century ago!* How could time have gone by so fast?

boys will be boys…

Yeah, those were the days. Those were also the days for some serious mischief.

It was at the age of nine that I had my first train ride, except that for this particular train ride, I didn't have a ticket, and I wouldn't be sitting in some lounge seat, looking out the window. I, along with a couple of friends, decided to hop a freight car just about a half mile or so north of the train depot at Socorro. The train wasn't moving at the time, so getting aboard wasn't all that difficult. Then I had the bright idea that it might be fun to climb up on top of the freight car. My buddies stayed below inside the empty cargo train as I climbed the ladder up to the top. This was neat, great fun. I walked back and forth on the top of the car, imagining I was some sort of hobo who'd hopped a freight. I even thought about trying to jump from one freight car to the next, but I wasn't quite sure I could jump far enough to land on the other car, so I abruptly hit the brakes. It's a good thing I did because at that time the train lurched forward, almost knocking me off my feet, and it almost caused me to fall down in between the two freight cars. It was then that I thought it might be a good idea to get down from the top. The train was probably moving along at about eight or ten miles an hour, but it was moving faster by the minute… so we jumped, landing on the dirt and gravel alongside the tracks. Someone must have spotted me on top of the train because we soon found ourselves being chased by some men, who probably worked for the Santa Fe. It turned out that was only my first brush with authorities from the Santa Fe Railway.

Reggie and I, along with another boy Mickey, had been playing near the woods in an area north of town known as the bosque (boś-ky), which was a heavily wooded area of mostly cottonwood and oak trees near the Rio Grande River. The Santa Fe Railway tracks ran right through that area, coming down from Albuquerque and on into Socorro just a couple of miles south of where we were at the bosque.

Mickey had a brainstorm. If we pulled up some of the loose railroad spikes and placed them on the tracks, the train would run over them and flatten them and make "daggers" for us—wow, great fun! *(Sounds logical to a nine-year-old boy, right?)*

So the three of us headed southward down the tracks, pulling up any loose spikes we could find and placing them on the tracks. Of course, if one or two spikes were good, then a whole bunch was better, so sometimes we'd place five to six spikes on the tracks, stacking them on top of one another. After all, why make just one dagger at a time?

This was fun! I could already imagine having all these neat daggers to play with.

It wasn't long before a motorized Putt-Putt car came chugging along the tracks, heading south toward Socorro. I remember wondering if the man operating the car was asleep because he was really laid-back, feet propped up, smoking a cigarette, and quite intent on being comfortable. Suddenly, he began to hit some of the spikes, which had been placed about ten to fifteen feet apart on the tracks, and that Putt-Putt car began to bounce violently on the tracks, making loud banging, slamming noises.

The man jumped to his feet just about the time the car hit a larger pile of spikes, and he was thrown off the tracks, and he went flying about thirty feet off the side and down the berm next to the tracks. We could hear him from where we were hiding at the edge of the woods—screamin' and cussin' as he tried to push the Putt-Putt car off the rails, which was now solidly wedged on its side and blocking the tracks.

Soon he was able to call for some help from some Mexican workers in one of the fields nearby, and it took several men to overturn the car and push it out of the way and off the tracks.

Now this guy was no *rocket scientist.* Instead of just clearing the remaining spikes from the track *(duh),* he started running toward the depot in Socorro, which was a couple of miles away, intent on sending a warning to the oncoming Santa Fe train, which was a passenger train steaming southward just a few minutes behind. I couldn't believe it—*he just left the spikes on the rails!*

He didn't make it in time. A few minutes later this huge train came barreling down the tracks, and when it started to hit the spikes, which were placed fairly evenly, one spike at a time, there was a rhythmic and bone-jarring... *BANG-BANG... BANG-BANG-BANG,* and sparks were flying. Since the next batches of spikes were placed with a bunch on one side of the tracks and then a batch on the other side, the train began violently rocking from side to side, and at one point the thrashing nearly tipped some of the cars over, almost derailing the entire train. By this time the engineer had put the train in reverse. I never knew a train could make so much noise, screeching and banging, with sparks flying everywhere. We knew it was time for us to use our shortcut through the woods and *high-tail it outta there… we ran like we had the devil on our tail!* Needless to say, we didn't bother to go back and pick up our daggers.

A couple of days later, having pretty much forgotten our narrow escape, when we returned home from play, Reggie and I were surprised to see two strange men in business suits, sitting in our living room, talking with Mom and Dad, and there was clear tension in the room. It turned out they were special agents from the Santa Fe Railway, investigating the attempted *sabotage* of one of their trains. It seemed one of the Mexican workers had his son with him that day, and the boy knew us from school.

Now, by this time we were sure we would get the whippin' of our lives. Sometimes when it was time to get our whippin', Dad would send us out to the willow tree, which was just on the other side of the big cottonwood tree next to our house, and make us cut off our own switch. It was always with the instructions, *"If you don't get a good one, I will, and you'll wish I hadn't"* or something to that effect. So we always headed out to the willow tree, usually crying all the way, knowing what was in store for us. Dad would always strip off all the leaves on the willow tree branch, all except for the last few leaves at the tip. Then it was, *"Bend over—pants down"*… well, you get the picture.

But this time we were shocked when we found out we weren't going to get a whippin'. Instead, Dad took some long twine, then he drove a number of stakes in our yard, wrapping the twine around each post, and he staked out a makeshift *corral* for us, saying, *"This is your boundary for the next month. Anything beyond this string is off-limits—you got that?"* Even though the boundaries were made of string, only a couple of feet high, it might as well have been fortress walls. Dad was always fair and was always a loving father, but one thing we always knew, and that was not to cross him because his anger was like the *wrath of God* to us. For that whole month we never did cross the barrier except to go somewhere with Mom and Dad.

One of the boys we'd met in school was an Indian boy, named Johnny White Feather, who lived about a mile just north of us. He also had a horse, an old horse, named Geronimo. Sometimes we'd climb up on Geronimo and ride him bareback, running like the wind, but most of the time we thought it was more fun to saddle him up and ride him in the small arena out by the stables. It seemed Geronimo would always buck like crazy when he had a saddle on his back, and we thought it was great fun playing rodeo cowboy, being bucked by this horse. *"Yahoo!"* we'd yell as he bucked, usually sending us face-first into the dirt. It was only later that we learned that Johnny had placed a cocklebur under his saddle, and that's what made him buck so violently.

Dad owned and operated a Texaco gas station in Socorro, and his station was right across the street from the Little Red School House, which was somewhat like a Norman Rockwell painting. Come to think of it, I think it *was a Norman Rockwell painting!* This wasn't the school we went to, but occasionally, we could see where other children had ridden their horses to school and let them loose to graze in the school yard. The Little Red School House was between our house and Dad's station. This was in the early fifties, and television was quite a new thing. In fact, there was only one home in the entire town that had a TV set, and they had a really tall antenna, probably at least thirty feet tall, which was the only way you could get reception from Albuquerque some seventy-six miles to the north.

During this time, there was a TV Western program called *The Range Rider*, and although we'd never seen the program, one day the stars of that TV show came through town and let their horses graze in the school yard, and they paid me a couple of dollars to help feed the horses. That was a thrill that I never forgot.

Socorro was quite a well-known little Western town, and often there would be parades featuring various celebrities, usually Western stars, who came to town, and often Dad would drive them through town in the parade in a convertible from one of the local car dealers, and I would get to ride along with such celebrities as Tex Ritter (the father of the late John Ritter of TV's *Three's Company*).

One spring day, after we'd been there about three years, the Texaco dealer's rep for that area tried to make Dad mix kerosene in with the gasoline to cut costs and boost the profits. Cheating the customers didn't seem to matter to him—this man had quite a reputation for crooked dealings with people. There were two or three other men standing around at the time, and when Dad flatly refused, this man threatened to revoke Dad's dealership. Art Bangerter, who was the grandfather of two of my first cousins on my mother's side and who owned the Studebaker dealership as well as the gift shop next door to the gas station, decked that guy right there in the driveway of the station—knocked him out cold. It was really pretty funny—there was this pompous ass lying there on the concrete driveway while the others just walked away, yelling, *"And you'd better not come back here either"* and so on.

The "Wayward Wanderer"...

Since what was left of Dad's Texaco career was lying unconscious on his service station driveway, it seemed like a good time for us to move on. So Dad sold his dealership, and he decided to look for work in California, but not before we took a nice long vacation.

Dad built a camper, so to speak. He built it out of plywood on the frame of what used to be a pickup truck bed. I think he called it the Wayward Wanderer or something to that effect. Looking back on it all, just naming a little camper like that would be something like naming your rubber raft the RMS *Titanic*.

Anyway, it was fun, and Dad built it well. The wooden side doors opened up to make a table, complete with Coleman lanterns and stove, and inside was a bed that could sleep Mom and Dad or both us boys. When our parents slept in the Wayward Wanderer, we two boys slept outside in sleeping bags, and sometimes we'd switch off, and the two of us boys slept in the camper, and our parents bedded down under the stars.

This vacation went westward from New Mexico, on into Arizona, into California, then Nevada, then back into California, up to Oregon, then Washington where we met some friends near Walla Walla, and then back to California. One night, while on the desert side of the high Sierras, we slept at the foot of Mount Whitney, and the next morning Reggie and I were covered with snow—but what a sight. I'd never seen a mountain so tall. Later when we entered the state of Washington, the countryside near Walla Walla was unlike anything I'd ever seen—mile after mile of rolling green wheat fields, literally as far as the eye could see.

Then on the way back, somewhere in Oregon, we actually saw a tribe of Indians still living in their traditional tepees. I can remember asking Dad to stop so we could visit with them, reflecting on my time on the mesa at Six-Mile Canyon, and wanting to be an Indian. Anyway, Dad didn't stop, and we drove on as I looked out the back window of our '51 Studebaker… watching the Indian children playing with some dogs in a little meadow next to the area where they had all their tepees. It seemed so idyllic. When our vacation ended, we wound up back in California.

Chapter 2

In 1953 we began to write another book in our library of memories in our new life in Long Beach, California—beaches and big-city living. Once, while still living in Socorro, my dad had tried to teach me to swim, and so he pushed me backward into the swimming pool, which was out of town, somewhere near the School of Mines. That swimming pool was memorable in itself. All the water for it was spring fed and was not filtered or chlorinated. At certain times of the year the pool would be filled with thousands of tadpoles, which later became a pool full of baby frogs. And since the water was not chlorinated, the sides of the pool were lined with a thick shiny green blanket of some kind of moss. Often we had to find a long stick and shoo out as many as eight or ten rattlesnakes from the bathroom floor.

Anyway, I nearly drowned when Dad pushed me in the pool backward, and I can still remember Mom pulling me up out of the pool by grabbing a handful of my blond hair. For the longest time after that, I was terrified of the water or, at least, any water more than waist-deep.

a time of discovery...

But when we arrived in Long Beach in the early days of the summer that year, I was determined to get over this fear of the water, so I slowly began to learn to swim at the Plunge, which was a municipal swimming pool near an area of downtown Long Beach known as the Pike, which was the West Coast's equivalent of Coney Island in New York.

My first efforts to learn to swim were when I was ten years old, and by the time I reached my eleventh birthday, I could swim over two miles. Once a friend and I swam out to the breakwater in Long Beach Harbor and back, which took a couple of hours. This young man—who, as I recall, was nineteen or twenty—was an excellent swimmer who frequently made five-mile swims in the canals at Venice, California, so I was fairly confident when he swam out there with me. We were exhausted at the end of the swim because by the time we reached the breakwater, the surf was too rough for us to climb up on the rocks so we could catch some rest, so we made the round-trip without a stop in between. I later learned that the swim out to the breakwater and back was nearly five miles.

That next year we moved to North Long Beach, and our house was right next to the Los Angeles River, which, at that time, hadn't yet been filled with concrete. It was heavily wooded, and in some places it was a lot like a swamp. That was about the closest thing to a jungle that young boys that age could find. It was also the closest thing to woods, which was something I missed since leaving New Mexico.

A few blocks away there was a riding stable, and we'd heard stories about a horse being lost in the river in quicksand. *Yeah, right... quicksand? In the Los Angeles River?* Well, one day I found that quicksand, and I was literally up to my neck in it before my brother and his friend Ronnie Lee pulled me out. We'd been hunting rabbits down at the river with Dad's .22 rifle, and Reggie held Ronnie's hand, and Ronnie stretched out to reach me with the rifle barrel. *Whew! That was close!* That's the strangest (and scariest) feeling, being up to your neck in quicksand and still sinking! I am not sure if Mom was angry or just scared when I came home with mud up to my chin and she found out about my close call in the quicksand. This was the first of several close calls I had in my life.

I had a paper route in those days, and we used to fold and rubber band our papers for the *Long Beach Independent* in front of Dooley's Hardware, which was at the corner of Long Beach Boulevard and West Fifty-first Street, which was the street I lived on (West Fifty-first), and one day we were folding our papers at about five in the morning when we saw this huge flash of light that lit up the whole eastern sky. Later that day we were told it was the flash from an atomic bomb blast that had been tested in the Nevada desert. We saw several more atomic blasts over the next months. Later, I often wondered how many other people had ever seen the blast from an atomic bomb.

It was during those years that I had also discovered a love for reading. I'd become a voracious reader, and by the time I reached my eleventh birthday, I had read Steinbeck's *East of Eden*, *Of Mice and Men*, and *Cannery Row*; Shakespeare's *Hamlet*; Hemingway's *The Old Man and the Sea*; and Tolstoy's *War and Peace*.

Possibly because of that intense passion for learning, which seemed to find expression in all that reading, my sixth-grade teacher entered me into the Greater Long Beach Spelling Bee for ages twelve and under, and I took second place, missing the word *communiqué*. I guessed right when I asked the moderators if it was of French derivation, but since I'd never heard or seen the word, I had no idea how to spell it. So with a big question mark flashing in my mind, I think I ended up with something like *communicay*. Oh well. This soaking up of learning, however, never found its way to mathematics. Math skills eluded me, and I was only an average student in that subject.

the teenage years...

In all the moving around that we did during those years, I consider the times we lived in Brawley the most like home. Brawley is located just south and east a few miles from the Salton Sea, and it's nestled down in the corner of California close to the Mexican border and about sixty miles from Arizona. It's one of the major agricultural areas in the country, receiving the bulk of its water from the Colorado River. This was about the flattest area I'd ever seen, but it was ideal for growing tomatoes, carrots, melons, and sugar beets.

We moved there in 1956. I remember, Mom cried after we arrived because she was absolutely convinced we'd moved to hell. The average summer day was about 118° in the shade, and by July we'd usually had several days well above the 120° mark. Since we had thermometers at both the Wilshire service stations Dad owned, each at the opposite ends of town, and a thermometer at home, all set at eye level in the shade, we could get a pretty accurate reading, and once we got 126° readings at all three locations! The daytimes were hot, all right, but I'll never forget seeing it hit 112° one night—at *midnight!*

But as teenage boys, we always had a way to get cooled off. Usually, it was a short drive out of town to one of the irrigation canals where we'd jump in, clothes and all, for a dip to cool down. Standing out in the hot Brawley sun, it was only a matter of minutes before your clothes were dry, so that wasn't much of a problem.

Oh, and I almost forgot—the crickets. Every summer, usually in late July or August, there'd be a light rain or enough moisture in the air that the cricket larvae would hatch, and they'd come out by the billions. Crickets were everywhere. Businesses had piles of pink formaldehyde powder swept up against their front doors to keep the crickets out while they were closed during the night. Often I'd use gasoline to kill the crickets at Dad's Wilshire stations, pouring a little of it down into the cracks in the concrete, and dozens of crickets would come scrambling out before dying. During cricket season the dead critters would fill a thirty-five-gallon drum every few days at each of Dad's Wilshire stations.

Our home was only one house away from an intersection at West "I" and 2nd streets, and the intersection had a bright streetlight, which attracted thousands of crickets, sometimes even obscuring the light from the streetlight (yes, these crickets *could fly!*). Because there were so many crickets at the intersection the first year we lived there, a car came through the intersection a little too fast, and when he hit the brakes, *he spun out on the crickets and crashed into a parked car.* Sometimes if you walked under one of those streetlights, every step was accompanied with a *crunch, crunch, crunch* on the crickets. They'd crawl up your pant legs—they'd get under your shirt, and women would hold their skirts and dresses tight to their legs so the crickets wouldn't crawl up their dresses. It was terrible—it was a plague of *biblical proportions!* And it was an every-summer event in the Imperial Valley.

During the second half of my eighth-grade year, the teacher apparently liked my reading skills as she had me read aloud various works of literature every day to the whole class for the entire fifth period. For a while it had become something of an embarrassment, meaning that many of the boys gave me a hard time about it, but eventually, it garnered the attention of many of the girls, who often flirted with me after class, so the boys backed off on the teasing.

While still living on West I Street, one day my mother announced she was pregnant. Her pregnancy had begun to show ever so slightly when late one evening she suddenly cried out in pain. She stood up and began to walk out of the living room, but she only got about halfway through the room when she suddenly stopped and cried out again, and then something happened that I'll never forget. A clump of something, covered in thick blotchy blood, fell onto the shiny hardwood floor. Mom had miscarried right there in our living room. Dad quickly rushed her to Pioneers Memorial Hospital in Brawley, and it wasn't long before she learned she was still pregnant—with twins. She had been pregnant with triplets, but when she miscarried the third baby, it probably saved her life as well as the lives of the twins.

It was on a Friday—Friday the 13th—when Mom delivered the twins. I was only fifteen when Mom gave birth to Leslie Allen, who weighed about 5 lb. when he was born, and then a couple of minutes later Laura Jean came into the world, weighing a little more than 3 lb. Both had to remain in the hospital for several weeks with the other premature babies. Later that year I was often seen with my girlfriend as we pushed a double stroller down the street, and many people would say, *"You're so young, and you have twins, no less!"* I proudly replied, *"No, these are my little brother and sister."*

The following year we moved in to a new little home on the other side of town on E. Adler Street. It had been advertised as affordable housing. This was definitely, and literally, the wrong side of the tracks.

But at least the homes were brand-new. Many years later when I visited this same housing development, it had become a sad sight indeed. The homes were run-down, yards were unkempt, and I suppose it was something of a ghetto. But this move also meant I would be living less than a block away from Mary, my girlfriend, who lived on the same street as did the Simmons family. Mary was my first love. We'd met at the high school auditorium, and we went steady for about a year. It was then that I understood what people meant when they talked about falling in love. I had fallen upside down, inside out, and *heels over head*. Did you ever wonder why they said it's *head over heels? Don't we always walk around, head over heels? Hmm.*

Anyway, due to a stupid misunderstanding one day, Mary and I broke up, and I was devastated. As was the case with most teenagers in love, the issue of sex came up, and one day when we began to argue about sex, I told her, *"If I were only interested in sex, there are plenty of other girls out there who would give me what I wanted."*

But Mary only heard, *"There are plenty of other girls out there who'll give me what I want,"* meaning to her that if she didn't give me what I wanted, I'd find someone else who would, which was actually the opposite of what I'd meant.

I've told you all that in order to explain why I drove my car in the opposite direction on that street and ended up saving someone's life.

I was in love, and I was heartbroken. I would sometimes drive east on Adler Street toward Mary's house, which was in the opposite direction of town, but I often drove that way anyway in the hopes I might drive by her house and see her, and due to a strange set of circumstances, my driving in that direction on that day saved a little girl's life.

As I said, I was heading *east* on Adler Street, not *west, toward town*, in order to drive by Mary's house, hoping she was outside so I might get a chance to stop by and talk with her, when I noticed a young Mexican woman standing in the middle of the street, desperately trying to get my attention. I pulled the car up next to her and discovered she was holding a tiny baby, probably only a few weeks old, wrapped in a blanket, and although she spoke no English and my Spanish was very limited, I could see the child had turned blue and was obviously suffocating. I reached across and opened the passenger-side door for her, and we sped off in the other direction heading across town toward the hospital. During the summer that year, I'd learned CPR in my lifesaving classes at the high school swimming pool, so I began to try to communicate to her how she could help the baby breathe. We raced through town as I flashed my lights and honked the horn, often at speeds well over 70 mph.

By the time we reached Pioneers Memorial Hospital, the baby hadn't breathed on its own for more than twenty minutes. We rushed in to the hospital and took the child into the ER where the doctors worked frantically to save the baby's life. When I spoke with the ER physician, he told me that had we gotten there another minute or two later, the child wouldn't have survived. Often I've looked back and wondered how this baby turned out. The following day an article appeared in the *Brawley News* about how I'd raced through town to save this child. I hope she's been able to live a good, full life.

"Little Panama"...

We had something of a desert rat pack, which included some of my best friends in high school—John Millerburg, Gordie Burger, Tom Jones, Mike King, and me. Occasionally, we'd head out for one of our favorite summertime activities, which was canal skiing. That's right, skiing down a canal *behind a pickup truck!*

There was one location we dubbed Little Panama since it had a drop-off over a six-foot spillway about every quarter of a mile, and there were at least six or seven spillways reminding us of the Panama Canal. That was great fun—flying over the spillway and landing onto the white foaming water below often at speeds over 50 mph. There was a smooth dirt road that ran alongside the canal, and the other side of the road was bordered by a drainage ditch, which was always filled with a foot or two of thick gooey black mud.

Since we were being towed by a 100 ft. rope and being pulled by a pickup truck, there was almost no limit to how fast we could go. This canal was only about fifteen feet wide and just four feet deep. Once I reached 60 mph before I let go of the rope, and I remember falling headfirst into the waist-deep water, skis still on, when the force of the water tossed me into a complete flip in the air, landing on my butt on one of the hard rocks next to the bank. That, along with all the beer drinking we did, it's a wonder any of us lived to tell about it.

One day at Little Panama was particularly memorable because we captured on 8 mm film the most spectacular episode for one of those *And They Walked Away* TV shows you could imagine. John Millerburg was skiing down Little Panama when he wiped out at 72 mph in the most awesome wreck you could have imagined. When he fell, hitting the water at such a high speed, he flipped head over heels, clearing the bank of the canal, and bounced into the air, flying completely over the road where the pickup was driving and landing in the drainage ditch on the other side of the road. We were certain he'd been killed. A few minutes later out came John. His shorts were ripped off, and he was covered in sticky black mud from head to foot. And Gordie had filmed the whole thing.

John later went on to do some significant work in motion picture graphics, including doing some major special effects for such films as *Star Trek: the Motion Picture* and a number of notable television commercials. He also made an appearance as a musician in the movie *You Light Up My Life*. John was quite an accomplished singer and musician. One day several years later John showed me some original drawings of some of the most notable and lasting examples of his work, which were all the opening logos for Universal Pictures—particularly, the one where the Universal logo slowly came around and circled the globe. John also did many of the Paramount Pictures opening logos. His seemingly endless motion picture credits read like the Who's Who in motion picture graphics. Here are a few samples of graphic art that have made it into our pop culture:

cooling off in Julian...

Another way to cool off was to take the hour-and-a-half drive to the mountain community of Julian, which was west of the Imperial Valley between the Salton Sea and San Diego. Julian was a great getaway.

Julian has an annual festival and parade called Apple Days, and it was during this festival that my friends got their little dachshund drunk on beer. It was pretty comical seeing this wiener dog, with its short, little legs, stumbling around. It was also the first time I got drunk. I was fifteen.

There was a dance at the town hall the last night of the festivities, and someone talked me into drinking vodka and 7 Up.

"Hey! This isn't bad. Let me try another one," and after several stiff drinks, it suddenly hit me. I couldn't stand up! *I can't stand up, and here comes this police officer, walking right toward me!*

Julian's sidewalks were mostly boardwalks at that time, and I tried to act calmly as the officer approached. I leaned up against a post next to a building, hoping to keep from falling down or, worse, vomiting. I could just see it now—the telephone call to my parents to come and get their kid out of jail in Julian *for public drunkenness!*

I saw the officer's handcuffs on his belt, and I imagined they would soon be locked tight around my wrists in just a minute. I was already sick to my stomach, but the thought of being arrested and being dragged off to jail, kicking and screaming, just made it worse.

Oh no! I stepped to the side of the boardwalk and I could no longer hold it in. "*BLWOOEEAAUURRGH!*" just as the cop came up to me. Well, that was all it took! The officer took one look at me, and... "*BLWOOEEAAUURRGH!!!*" as he joined me in the most awful stinking "pukeathon" you could imagine! *It turned out that he was drunker than I was!*

I'm not trying to glamorize any of the things I did as a kid. Most of it were really stupid and dangerous. I'm just telling you the way it was. This was the first of many crazy episodes, and I was becoming something of a hell-raiser.

Drinking played a big role in our lives during those years, and we often drank during and after school. I even had one high school teacher who would slip out of class and join me for a beer and a cigarette behind the woodshop building. He also had gotten a bad reputation for putting the pretty girls in the front of his class so he could look down their blouses.

close calls with the law...

By this time many of my friends had ended up in trouble with the law. One night we'd been drinking, and we broke into the concession building in Brawley where one of the Dodgers' baseball farm teams held their spring training. We stole some money and a few cases of cigarettes, and as we were leaving, heading down a dirt road next to an irrigation canal near the ballpark, headlights in front and in back of us suddenly turned on, and the police shouted out on their bullhorns for us to raise our hands. Instead we all scattered, and in the confusion, I managed to slip into the canal with my nose just barely above water, hiding among the reeds and cattails. All my friends were caught and arrested, but I got away, and none of them informed on me. And they all went to juvenile hall. I was never caught.

I knew that some of my friends were involved in stealing cars, and one night they offered me a ride in a stolen '51 Ford. Since I wanted to go to the movies that afternoon, I said, *"Sure, just let me off in front of the Brawley Theatre."* They dropped me off at the corner on Main Street next to the theater, and they hadn't gone more than one hundred feet or so after letting me out before they were pulled over and arrested. Off they went, back to juvenile hall.

One night at a party one of my friends got quite drunk and pulled his switchblade out, threatening several of the other kids. Since we weren't exactly invited to this party, we thought we'd better be cool about it and leave. As soon as we got him out of the party and into the car, we took him to the edge of town, beat him up, and threw him into a canal. This was our way of sobering him up as well as teaching him a lesson. Apparently, a neighbor heard the commotion and called the police, because we were soon surrounded by police cars. Everybody was arrested and went to juvenile hall… *except me.* I kept getting out of these jams, and I had no idea why.

Once before class, we got drunk and drove a couple of dune buggies onto the school yard, spinning *brodies,* tearing up the grass, and hanging off the sides of the dune buggies as we guzzled beer. They threatened us with suspension, but since it was before school had started and since the only people who'd seen us were other students who wouldn't identify us, they dropped the suspension threats. They only suspected that I was one of those in the dune buggy, but no one ever ratted me out. It never occurred to us there was anything wrong with what we were doing. We just thought this was good, rowdy fun.

As well as owning service stations, Dad had been a deputy sheriff when we were living in New Mexico, and he still had a police light, which plugged into his car's cigarette lighter, that he kept up in the hall closet. It didn't take us long to find that police light and to imagine some wicked ways to put it to use.

Cruising Main Street in the late fifties in Brawley was probably much the same throughout America during that time. Everyone, and I mean *everyone,* went cruising every Friday and Saturday night. They polished up their wheels—including hot rods and classics from the thirties, forties, and fifties—and with radios blasting out rock 'n' roll music, they cruised Main Street from one end to the other—everyone wanted to be seen, and they wanted to see everyone else. My slightly custom '56 Ford was lookin' good—custom paint job, lowered just a little in the front, and jacked up just a little in the back—when one night a particular kid jumped out of his car, which was ahead of me, and kicked my car in the fender as I went by. He didn't manage to dent it, but I did have to later buff out the scuff marks from his shoe. That did it. No one's gonna get away with kickin' my car. I jumped out of my car and ran over to him, got right in his face, and said, *"Let's get it on, you blankety, blank"* (you fill in the blanks). We decided to take the fight out into the country.

At least five or six other carloads of guys followed us out to a road in the country where we usually went to drag race, but this night we weren't thinking about racing. They called it fight fever—when it looked like a fight was about to start, all the guys would begin shouting, *"Fight! Fight! Fight!"* This guy was about 6'4", and on a good day I might stretch to 5'9", but I was *cranked off!*

I had a reputation for being a lover, not a fighter. In the high school newspaper, they had written that my car was a "motel on wheels." But no one's gonna get away with slammin' his foot into my car. Anyway, we squared off, and he took a swing at me, I ducked and made him miss, and I countered with a right to the gut, followed by a left and then a killer uppercut to his chin, and his feet actually left the ground as he landed on his back. He was just lying there on the ground, moaning, *"I can't see, I can't see!"* The fight was over. Actually, I had gotten lucky—really lucky. But from then on no one ever thought of picking a fight with me. Since he wasn't able to get behind the wheel, one of my friends hopped in his car, and we loaded him into my car and drove him back to town. But that wasn't the end of it.

Later he actually told one of his friends at school that he'd won the fight, and even though all my friends knew it wasn't true, it started the rumor that he'd kicked my butt—go figure.

dangerous pranks...

One of our favorite pranks was to cruise Main Street on a Friday or Saturday night and pick out the car of someone we knew—someone we wanted to harass, and we'd trail them for a while, then we'd switch on Dad's red police light. *You did what?* My dad had been a deputy sheriff in New Mexico, and he still had his portable flashing red light. So when we really wanted to have fun, I'd sneak the red light out of his closet, and we'd go lookin' for trouble.

We often used a friend's car, which was an old dark Ford, and at night it could easily be mistaken for a police car. We'd pull up behind some unsuspecting victim, set the flashing red light on the roof, and plug it into the cigarette lighter socket, and bingo, we were *the man.* The driver, thinking he was being pulled over by the police, immediately began tossing beer cans and marijuana cigarettes out the windows. Then we'd drive by, laughing, waving, and sometimes flipping him off.

I don't remember just how many times we pulled this prank, but it was one time too many. And flipping him off just added insult to injury. The results were usually the same. As I said, they weren't too happy to have to toss out their beer cans, wine bottles, marijuana cigarettes, and so on. But as with the old adage of reaping what you sow, we had sowed to the wind, and we were about to reap the whirlwind.

It was late on a Saturday night when we tried this trick on a carload of Mexican lowriders, who were all in their twenties and thirties. These guys were real tough *pachucos*, and when they started chasing us all over town, it soon wasn't nearly so funny. Bob, who was older and out of high school, was driving, and after being chased all over town by these guys, he got cornered in a dead end next to the railroad tracks. These Mexican men piled out of their car and walked up to us, and one of them, who appeared to be their leader, flipped open his switchblade and held it right to Bob's throat, pushing it just hard enough to bring a trickle of blood. Of course, we were brave (macho) and really stood up to them—*are you kidding?* No, instead we became very humble and apologetic at that time, and we managed to weasel our way out of this really close call, escaping with our lives. I think I made a feeble attempt at prayer just about then. That was the last time we used Dad's police light. We put it back into the closet and left it there—for good.

the Mexicali brawl...

One partying and drinking episode stood out in particular as it turned out to be a classic. Again, it's a wonder any of us made it to our eighteenth birthdays, and let me make one thing perfectly clear... we were flirting with real danger with all that drinking and carousing. We either didn't know or didn't care about the dangers of teenage drinking. But what's done was done. Any one of these episodes could have had deadly consequences, but that was the last thing on our minds. On the other hand some of it were really comical, and if you can't look back at it and laugh a little, well, maybe we should all lighten up a bit.

hair, teeth, and eyeballs all over the floor...

Mexicali was about twenty-five miles east of Brawley and just across the Mexican border. We'd just left a Brawley–El Centro football game in which Brawley had just beaten our El Centro rivals. About seven or eight of us piled into a big old '51 Buick and headed down to Mexicali for some wild celebrating, but when we got to our favorite bar, which was well inside Mexico and about fifteen or twenty blocks from the US border, a group of the El Centro guys were already there.

If you mixed lots of booze, loud music, and dancing—in a Mexicali bar—along with several rowdy Brawley boys in the same bar with eight or ten El Centro boys, you had the makings of a real old-time chair-smashing, bottle-breaking, and mirror-crashing brawl.

I don't exactly know what started it, but I was dancing with this Mexican girl (one of my friends later told me she was a prostitute) when the next thing I knew, someone took a swing at me. I ducked, he missed, and my return punch knocked him to the floor. It wasn't long before one of my friends and I picked up this El Centro kid and threw him over the bar and into the mirror, crashing a whole bunch of bottles of booze and, of course, smashing the mirror into a thousand pieces. Two El Centro boys picked up one of our buddies and smashed him onto the top of a small table, breaking it into pieces, and it was serious bedlam—you know, one of those *"hair, teeth, and eyeballs all over the floor"* scenes.

Anyway, I heard the bartender screaming in Spanish on the telephone for the police to come, and so we all piled into the old Buick, which was nearly scraping the asphalt from the weight of all of us, and we headed back toward the US border. We didn't even get to the end of the block before I saw a Mexican police officer on foot, blowing his whistle and waving his nightstick at us as he ran in our direction. When we rounded the next corner, we noticed we had two more Mexican policemen on our tail, and both were chasing us and blowing their whistles as they ran down the street.

During the mile-or-so mad dash to the border, we'd picked up three or four Mexican police cars in hot pursuit with sirens screaming and red lights flashing, and we had that old Buick *huffin'* and *puffin'* for the border as fast as it could go. I don't remember who was driving, but he was drunk. We all were pretty well drunk.

When we were about one hundred yards from the border, we all started to celebrate our escape... a little too soon. Too drunk to make the last turn, we slammed into one of those concrete wheel stops, which launched the car into the air and up onto a concrete abutment, which was about eighteen inches high and which was in front of each of the border stations, and our bumper ran up on top of it, hopelessly lodging our car. We were really stuck and still on the *Mexican side of the border!* I'll never forget what followed because it was just like a scene right out of the movies.

We all got out of the car and began to try to push it off the curb, and the Mexican police cars were getting really close. We still couldn't make it budge, so three of the US Border Patrol officers stepped across the border onto the Mexico side and helped us push it off—just in time to cross the border and just as the Mexican police cars arrived on the scene, screaming obscenities in Spanish. All of us, including the US Border Patrol officers, decided to do our part for international relations, so we responded by giving the Mexican police a salute—a one-finger salute.

When I was a sophomore in high school, I became the assistant circulation manager of the *Brawley News*, which was a small-town newspaper with a circulation of only about three thousand five hundred. But as a fourteen-year-old kid, I had a lot of responsibility with twenty carrier boys and two adult car-route carriers. And I had to keep the books, make bank deposits, and pay all the carriers. I later learned that my having a responsible position with the newspaper was part of the reason I escaped so many brushes with the law. I was a young kid with an otherwise good reputation working for the newspaper, and I was well-known. Nobody really believed (at least, the police didn't) that this good kid (me) could have had anything to do with rowdy, drunken parties, brawling, and stolen cars.

By the time I was sixteen, the newspaper had hired a secretary/bookkeeper for me, and she resented the fact that this young kid was her supervisor, especially since she was also the boss's girlfriend. This was at a time they made me interim circulation manager for a short period while they looked for a replacement when our manager quit… but I soon saw the handwriting on the wall because my secretary was making things pretty difficult, what with her being the general manager's fiancée, and here she was with this sixteen-year-old kid as her boss. I soon decided to learn typesetting back in the newspaper's printshop.

In those days everything was printed with hot type, which meant using melted lead, and they used 40 lb. "pigs," which were about 4' long lead castings with an opening for a hook at one end, which were then slowly lowered into hot metal pots and melted again to form into "slugs," which made up a line of type on machines called Linotype machines as well as being used for casts for making lead molds that made up much of the print advertising for the newspaper.

I was already a fast typist, having set the California high school typing record at 124 wpm on an old-fashioned manual typewriter. Some guys had magnificent football trophies at the school; I had a dinky little trophy for typing—*whoop-de-do!* Over the next ten or twelve years I would sometimes fall back on this skill, working as a typesetter in various newspapers.

Later I went to work for the *Garden Grove Evening News*, in Garden Grove, California. It was a union shop, so I needed to join the International Typographical Union (ITU).

I really hated typesetting as I found it incredibly boring. But it was a skill that came in handy later when I had a young family to support. The TTS machine was very similar to a typewriter except that it spit out a string of tape with coded holes punched in it, much like a ticker tape. Then they fed this roll of yellow coded tape into one of the Linotype machines—in effect, running it automatically. And by the time I was in my early twenties, the manufacturers of the Fairchild Teletypesetter (TTS) machines we used had told me I was the world's fastest typesetter, and they had these machines in newspapers and printshops around the world.

Once after our typesetting had become computerized, I learned that my fastest typesetting speed was 188 wpm, and I had been able to average just over 100 wpm over an entire seven-hour shift. The computer was able to indicate how fast I was setting type as it was their way of measuring a TTS operator's daily output. The computer they used, which justified the lines of type (made them line up in an even column), was about the size of a large refrigerator and probably weighed half a ton. It had considerably less computer capacity than a modern cell phone today.

The reason I'm telling you this (my typing speed) is that it soon became a real point of contention with the union. They repeatedly tried to fine me because they said I was so fast that I was putting at least two other union members out of work, but I always appealed the matter, and so their fines never stuck. The computer indicated my daily tally sheet (output) was as much as one hundred sixty thousand keyboard strokes for a day's shift, and the union only required typesetters to do a minimum of forty thousand strokes, so you can see why they felt I was keeping other members from working.

My explanation was, *"I signed on to do my best, and if that's faster than some of the others, too bad—live with it. I'm not going to do less than my best just to satisfy you."* But because of my greater production levels, the newspaper management secretly paid me under the table every week, nearly doubling my salary. Luckily, the union never found out about that arrangement.

I never did get used to it when a group of schoolchildren on some sort of field trip, often up to fifteen or twenty, came through. They made a special point of watching me on the TTS machine, all looking over my shoulder, with their teacher commenting, *"Oh, look—look how fast he can type. Don't you kids wish you could type that fast?"* Often I wanted to shout out, *"Forget about it, kids. It's the most boring job in the world!"*

I'm getting a little ahead of myself. So skipping back a few years, while I was still in Brawley, I also became a radio announcer at KROP, which was the only radio station in Brawley. This was *small-town radio*. It played a mix of easy-listening and classical music, which was a strange combination, particularly since the Imperial Valley was primarily cattle-and-farming country, and the listeners were mostly adults preferring Country and Western music as the young people were into rock 'n' roll.

Actually, I got my start at that radio station because one of the announcers, who also handled the play-by-play announcements for our local high school's football games, forgot that his microphone was still on during a spectacular touchdown run by one of our fastest players, and this announcer stood up and shouted, *"Look at that black son of a —— run,"* completely unaware that it went out over the air. Needless to say, he was fired, and that's how I got my start in radio.

the "DJ"...

As boring as was the format at KROP, the rock 'n' roll top-forty format at KAMP in El Centro, some eighteen miles south of Brawley, was exciting. I got my start there during my first year at Imperial Valley College, and I soon had the number one time slot and the number one ratings as a rock-and-roll DJ. Although we got a real boost in our ratings since there we had more than one hundred thousand listeners across the border in Mexicali, this was small-time radio in a small-time city, *but I loved it*—I thought I was really in my element.

But my first day on the air was one I'll never forget. One of the gimmicks they used at the rock 'n' roll station was a telegraph key that they used to punctuate between the news stories with a "*Dot, dada dot dot, dash, dash, dash*" (which I thought was a bit amateurish), but anyway, we were expected to use it.

Apparently, no one had ever noticed that when the telegraph key had been anchored next to one of the turntables, it created an electrical short circuit, and when my chin touched the big microphone in the broadcast booth, it completed the circuit—*BAM!* It was as though Joe Louis had hit me on the chin with a knockout punch, and the next thing I knew, I was lying on the floor unconscious. I was alone in the broadcast booth, so I didn't know how long I was out, but when I finally came to I had no idea what had happened. I regained my composure, gathered up the news copy, and resumed the newscast when a few minutes later, *BAM!* It happened again, and finally, I knew where that right cross had come from. From then on I made certain that if my chin touched the microphone, my hand was *nowhere near that telegraph key!*

It wasn't long before there were girls everywhere, and it got so bad that I had to be ushered into the local theater through the back entrance because I would be recognized and mobbed by screaming teenage girls.

"I know who you are... you're Ken Simmons," a girl behind the candy counter screamed out, and the next thing I knew, I was surrounded by squealing teenage girls who wanted just to get a look at me—to touch me or try to kiss me.

Even on that small scale, I found out about young groupies. Some girls would come to the radio station on Saturdays and stand in line. You could simply take your pick... well, you can imagine the rest.

There was something of a competition between me and one of the other DJs because we were always trying to make each other crack up (lose composure) on the air. And there were a number of my college female friends who were all too willing to sometimes come by the radio station and try to break me up during a newscast. They often came into the broadcast booth and began to kiss me all over, rubbing their hands all over, and then they would put their hands where they didn't belong… you get the picture—all for a laugh, just to get me to crack up on the air.

This other disc jockey I mentioned was frequently coming by and disengaging the turntable, causing the record to slowly wind down to a garbled growl. Another one of his tricks would be to sneak up behind me while I was reading the news and set my news copy on fire. There I was, trying to put out the fire while calmly reading the AP or UPI wire copy. And yet nobody had been able to make me lose it on the air—nobody, that is, until one particular Saturday afternoon.

Our radio station was on the second floor in downtown El Centro at Sixth and Main. The broadcast booth was in the extreme corner of the building, so I could look out the window and see into the cars as they drove by, and someone was always trying to drive by and try to get our attention—try to get us to react or comment about them on the air. It was an in thing for people to cruise by the corner of Sixth and Main and honk or wave and sometimes moon us, and sometimes guys would drive by in a convertible with their girlfriend, with their hand down her blouse, just in order to get us to make some comment about it on the air. Usually, they'd hear something like, *"Hey, hey, hey… you know that's naughty. Does her mother know where your hand is right now?"*

So this guy Mike, who was also DJ, but carried the title program manager (making him my boss), decided he was *going* to get me to crack up during a newscast—one way or another. It was almost expected that in some way he'd try to make me lose it. The disengaging of my turntable hadn't worked although I usually had to come up with some kind of funny quip to the audience about why the record slowed to a low, garbled growl. I actually lost track of how many times he crept up behind me and set my news copy on fire during a news broadcast, but that still hadn't worked. He'd never been able to get me to crack up on the air.

In front of the broadcast booth, just beyond the DJ's microphone, there was a large window, and on the other side of the window was the newsroom with a desk pushed up next to the wall and right up next to the window.

I was right in the middle of a serious newscast when Mike stood up on the desk that was just on the other side of the glass window in front me and also in front of the window that was in view from the traffic below, and he turned around, bent over, and *dropped his drawers.* Yup, he mooned me in front of God and everybody, including the cars below at the intersection.

Here was this fa—oops—*swollen* man standing up on a desk right in front of the window in the broadcast booth, in full view of the people as they drove by at 6th and Main. Try as I might, I began to crack up. Every time I tried to compose myself and settle down to reading the news again, he'd drop his pants once more, and I'd start to lose it all over again… anybody driving by could also see this—this *swollen* guy standing on a desk in front of the window with his pants down around his ankles. I think *raunchy* would be a good description.

I couldn't continue the newscast. I laughed nonstop and uncontrollably until I finally realized my microphone was still on, and that did it. Cars were driving by, honking, and I was absolutely worthless for the rest of the newscast. I had to put on an LP album and forget about any ideas of continuing my radio show for at least another ten or fifteen minutes.

As I said earlier, this was only a small-time market (even though we had some one hundred thousand listeners across the border in Mexicali, Mexico), but my brief flirtation with small-town celebrity was unforgettable. When the radio station was sold to out-of-state buyers, they came in with a whole new staff of their own, and all of us were soon job hunting. But it was memorable while it lasted. Several years later I would get back into radio in a larger market in Florida, first as an announcer, then as news director.

But in the meantime, I moved to Ontario, and I was able to get work as a typesetter at the *Ontario Daily Report.*

Bear with me if you will, and hit the Rewind button for a moment. Hopefully, it will begin to make sense.

I was married at eighteen, and by the time I turned twenty-one, I already had two children, Tamarah Lee and Jeffrey Addam, and I was going through a rather ugly divorce.

I had met Carolyn Odle when she was a sophomore at Brawley High shortly after breaking up with Mary, the girl I mentioned earlier, who was my first love. I hadn't gotten over Mary yet, and here I was with a pregnant girlfriend and getting married. Now, less than three years later, Carolyn and I had separated, and she filed for divorce.

I remember sitting alone in our home, in the Red Hill area of Upland, California, which we had just bought with the help of Carolyn's father, and I was working on my third six-pack by that time, literally crying in my beer. My life was in shambles. My wife had moved out and filed for divorce. I'd also just lost my job at the *Daily Report* newspaper in Ontario because when she moved out, she'd written a number of hot checks for her rent on an apartment, and because of those bad checks, I had my wages garnished, and because the newspaper had a policy of mandatory termination when any employee had their wages attached, I was jobless. And there was a good chance I'd lose the children in the divorce. Due to my typing skills, I'd managed to earn a living in the newspaper print media. Now that looked like it was all headed down the toilet. Carolyn found the routine of married life drudgery. She was too young. We were both too young.

Chapter 3

After what turned out to be an ugly divorce, I moved in with my parents, who had moved to Garden Grove, California, and I helped out my dad with his two Gulf service stations, both on Harbor Boulevard about a mile south of Disneyland. I'd been reading the Bible, still looking for answers, and I even attended a Billy Graham Crusade in Los Angeles. Something I'd read in the Bible would soon come back to hit me, literally *right in the face.*

"turn the other cheek"...

It was on a Saturday afternoon, and I was sweeping off the front driveways at the northernmost one of Dad's gas stations on Harbor Boulevard and Chapman Avenue when a former employee of Dad's came by. I knew him to be somewhat of a tough guy with a reputation as a troublemaker, and I also knew he carried a gun in his VW van. Somehow I rather expected trouble when he drove up.

When he got out of his van, I could sense that he was very agitated, and I also wondered if he might have been high on some kind of drugs. This guy was really cranked! When I greeted him with, *"What can I do for you?"* he shouted, *"Your dad owes me some money, and I came here to get it."* If I tried to say anything at all, he would scream, *"Give me my —— money!"*

He then threatened to kill me and my dad if we tried to stop him from getting *"his money."*

I tried to calm him down, and I said, *"I'm sure that if you have any money coming to you, my father will pay you... he's a fair man"* or something to that effect, but he just became more agitated.

The next thing I knew, he took a big swing at me. I dodged, and he just barely missed my chin. Just then some of the Bible scriptures I'd been reading flashed before my mind—about turning the other cheek. I thought about it for a (brief) moment, but after he took another swing at me and I made him miss again, I said to myself, *Nope, no way—I'm not turnin' the other cheek,* and I hit him as hard as I could, knocking him to the ground. He was quite a bit bigger than me, but he'd made me angry, and at that point I didn't care how big he was.

Actually, I could have ended the fight with the next few blows because after he got back up, I hit him again, three or four times in a row, and by that time, he was literally out cold on his feet. But he'd made me mad... *really mad!* After all, he'd threatened to kill both me and my father, and so as he was falling down, already out cold on his feet, I hit him again very hard just for good measure. Well, that was all it took—not for him, but for me! Sure, he was awfully bloody, and it would take a few weeks for those ugly cuts and bruises to go away, but I ended up in the hospital with a broken right hand!

God, if you're real...

Remember all those questions I'd been asking, such as, *"God, if you are real..."* and so on? I had been at the hospital for hours, trying to have the broken bone in my hand set so that it could be put in a cast. The doctor was a diminutive Japanese man named Dr. Yamamoto, and I recall him struggling so hard pulling on the little finger of my right hand then quickly trying to wrap it so it would set. Then he'd rush me down to the X-ray room, and each time the bones wouldn't set. He called it an unstable fracture. He tried this literally ten or twelve times, each time repeating the procedure of wrapping and then rushing me to X-ray, and I actually remember him taking off his shoe and putting his foot to my chest so that he could get leverage to pull harder, but to no avail. It just wouldn't remain set.

Dr. Yamamoto scheduled me for surgery on my hand and said that an orthopedic surgeon was going to have to drill through the bones and wire it together. This was at a time when I wanted to go back to typesetting since I could earn better money at the newspaper than I could reading electric meters for Southern California Edison, which was what I'd been doing for the past few months, helping my dad out at the service station on the weekends.

So the morning of the surgery, I insisted Dr. Yamamoto order another X-ray. I'd just been praying another of those *"God, if you're real"* prayers, and I was going to put it to the test. At first the doctor protested, saying that we'd already had ten or twelve X-rays, and the insurance wouldn't pay for any more. Of course, by now you've probably gotten the impression that I'm a bit stubborn, so I said to the doctor, *"No X-ray, no surgery,"* so I prevailed. Dr. Yamamoto said, *"OK… it's your money,"* and we had one more X-ray just before scheduling me for the surgery a week or so later.

The day of the surgery they wheeled me down to the operating room. By this time he'd forgotten about the last X-ray, so there was no mention of it to the orthopedic surgeon. They had shaved my arm up to my armpit *(for surgery on my hand—never did figure that one out)*, and they brought another small table up next to the operating table, strapped my arm onto the smaller table, numbed my whole right arm, and made an *X* with iodine on my hand where the incision was to be made. They'd given me local anesthesia, but other than that I was completely awake and lucid.

Next, the surgeon stepped over to the stainless-steel sterilizer on the wall and removed the surgical instruments. Then he braced his right hand, and he actually had just touched the scalpel to the *X* mark to begin the incision when the radiologist rushed in with the X-rays, shouting, *"Stop! Doctor, I don't think you want to operate on this hand. Take a look at these X-rays."* The unstable fracture was now completely stable, and the X-ray negatives showed it had almost completely healed. The doctors shook their heads, and they sent me home. This, of course, really set me to thinking. By this time I thought I truly wanted *to believe*.

Over the next few days I met a young woman who was to become my second wife. Karen McClure also lived in Garden Grove, and I met her at a movie theater, and she was with someone I presumed to be her boyfriend. I thought I was being pretty slick by lining up a date with a girl while her boyfriend was at the candy counter. I later discovered it was her brother whom she was with, and I realized I hadn't been so clever after all.

I tried to impress her by taking her sailing on our first date, but I was not much of a sailor, and the rented boat was not much of a sailboat either (not very impressive—me or the sailboat). But I was impressed with Karen. She was a slender brunette, and she was very beautiful. We recovered from the sailing fiasco and continued to date for a while, and we quickly fell in love. My divorce from Carolyn was still pending, but when we got the go-ahead from my attorney, we were married on Christmas Eve 1966 at the Garden Grove Community Church, which was later to become the Crystal Cathedral where Dr. Robert Schuller was pastor.

her best foot forward…

Our first child, which was my third, was Kimberly Jean. I'll never forget bringing Karen into the delivery room. I put on one of those green hospital gowns, and when they moved Karen onto one of the delivery tables and pulled the sheet back, there was this little foot sticking out. That has got to be *one of the strangest sights you can imagine* (a little *too much* visual imagery, huh)! Anyway, I thought I'd be tough and stick around for the delivery. But this tough guy was overcome with sympathy pains. I almost passed out. They helped me out of the room, and I spent the next twenty minutes trying not to pass out from the *stink of those awful smelling salts they were waving in front of my nose!*

Before Kimmy was born, we had rented a three-bedroom nice little house in Santa Ana, which was right next to the tennis courts at Santa Ana College. I'd had a custody battle with Carolyn over Tammy and Jeff, but I was finally able to prevail, and the judge awarded me custody, which was fairly unusual since fathers were seldom given sole custody. Karen already had a son, Scott, who was not quite two years old.

That's about the time when I went to work for the *Garden Grove Evening News*, and since this was the first union shop I'd worked for, I had to join the International Typographical Union (ITU).

Yes, things were looking up. I had a good job although typesetting was about the most boring occupation imaginable, but the prospects for the future were promising.

So now it was a case of *"hers, mine, and ours,"* and the five of us began our journey into *"Happily Ever After"*.

Chapter 4

This was the time in my life when I'd begun to ask the usual questions, you know—*"If there is a God"* and *"God, if you're real"*… that sort of thing. I had made some gestures of faith earlier as a child, but this was the first time I had begun to seriously look for some answers, and I had even joined some friends and gone to a Billy Graham meeting in Los Angeles where I went forward and answered an altar call, still not quite sure of all that it meant, but sincere in wanting to try and find out.

where's the faith?...

Now go ahead and hit the Pause button. I want to make some clear distinctions here. My story has little, if anything, to do with *religion*, nor has *religion* ever had much of an impact on my life. I've never thought very highly of religion.

When I started my search for some answers and I began looking into the issue of faith, I was really shocked. What I learned was that faith, compared to what we see in today's religious world, is often two very, *very* different things. When I began to look at examples in the Bible, I soon discovered that what I had come to know as religion and what the Bible described as real faith *had little in common!* In fact, as I saw it, there was very little, *if any*, resemblance between the two.

We'll hit the Play button and resume in a little while, but for now keep it on Pause.

I began to read through the first four books of the New Testament in the Bible—Matthew, Mark, Luke, and John—and then on into the Book of Acts. This was *powerful stuff!* Most of us are familiar with many of the miracles during Christ's life, but I was absolutely astonished to discover that some of his disciples had similar and equally amazing miracles occur during their lifetimes. They (the disciples) healed the sick, cast out demons, and even raised the dead. These things could be expected from the Son of God... but not mortal men, and I wasn't even sure I believed it! In fact, I was pretty dubious about the whole thing.

But according to these scriptural accounts, many of the people at that time sold all their possessions and gave the money to the disciples so they could carry on their work. *Wow.* That's a far cry from passing the collection plate on Sunday and dropping in a buck or two if you can spare it out of your beer money.

And one couple, a man named Ananias and his wife, Sapphira, sold all their belongings so they could kick in some money for the disciples' work too. But there was a difference. They decided to lie about how much money they got for their rummage sale, and they kept back some for themselves for that proverbial rainy day (compared to some of the sins you hear about in today's churches, that was pretty mild stuff!). Anyway, Peter, who was one of Jesus's disciples, knew about their scheme to lie about the money, and when he busted Ananias about it and asked him why he'd lied, *the man fell over dead! Wow, nothing like that ever happened in any church I'd ever been in!* If that were how things worked in today's religious circles, *they'd have to build a whole bunch of new cemeteries!*

A while later Sapphira, Ananias's wife, came to Peter, not knowing how her husband had just keeled over after being caught in a big lie, and Peter confronted her as well, saying, *"When you sold your goods that money was yours, and while it was yours you could have done anything you wanted with it. Instead, you conspired with your husband to lie about it to us and to the Holy Spirit. Listen to the footsteps of those that just buried your husband because they're coming to carry you away as well!"* (Acts 5:1–5)... and she fell dead right there on the spot too. Talk about tough love! God really wanted to get his point across, huh! Any names come to mind in today's religious circles? *Another big wow!*

And they cast out *demons* from people. What? *Demons?* Aw, c'mon. What kind of superstitious mumbo jumbo is that? That was all pretty spooky to me, and I wasn't quite sure what to make of it. Most of these people ended up being put to death for their faith. I read that Peter, not feeling worthy of being hanged on a cross in the same manner as Jesus, insisted on bring crucified upside down.

These early Christians were leading lives that certainly didn't resemble anything I knew about Christians or modern-day Christianity. Most everything I'd seen was just more *playing church.* Who knew that Peter *actually* walked on water? It was only after he started to think a little too much about it that he began to freak out, and he started to sink… but he *did walk on water!* That is, if I were to believe what is said in the Bible.

And raising people from the dead? *You've got to be kidding!* And yet that's what the scriptures clearly said. Either they were lying about it, or these things really happened, and I had to find out if this was true or if it was all a lie.

These people, men and women alike, led remarkable and sometimes miraculous lives, and many of them were put to death in some horrible ways over their belief that Jesus was the Messiah, the Christ, the one who had been promised according to the old Hebrew prophets.

Many have suggested that the apostles simply lied about the miracles they'd seen and experienced, especially about Jesus rising from the dead on the third day. Think about that one for a minute. Would you allow yourself to be tortured to death… *over something you knew was a lie? Crucified for something you knew to be untrue?* I sure wouldn't die a horrible death over something I knew was a lie. If someone were going to torture me to death over something like that and I knew it was a lie, *I'd cough it up in a New York minute!* All but one of Jesus's disciples were either tortured, crucified, dismembered, or stoned to death. It would be unimaginable that they would suffer like this over a lie. These people were intense and absolutely passionate about their faith, and I'd never seen anything like that, *nor had I ever known anyone who was even remotely interested in that kind of total faith!* This was absolutely foreign to me and foreign to any experience I'd ever had.

Put to death? Are you kidding? We won't even come back to that *church* if we can't find a good parking spot, and we'll go to another *church* next Sunday if they have a better choir or if their pastor gives us a message that's more pleasing or *user-friendly*. It's like going to the movies—you look through the ads to see who's got the best show. Many people go to church the same way. There's no commitment to anyone, and if some other church is putting on a better show that Sunday, we'll go there instead.

Ah yes, and *going to church*—now there's a subject. I learned that Church isn't something you can *go to*. The Church doesn't have an address. The Church is not a building! Either you're in it, or you're not. Either you're part of it, or you're not. Don't get me started.

I just couldn't seem to bridge the gap—this enormous chasm that seemed to be the difference between this kind of original Christianity and what I saw in today's modern religion. If that kind of faith and dedication that was evidenced in the early Church was punishable by death, then our punishment for being a Christian today *wouldn't be grounds for a parking ticket!*

Up until that time, our religion had been a one-hour-on-Sunday thing—you know, sit down, stand up, sing page 157, and pass the plate... we all love one another *so* much, but don't even think about cutting me off when I'm trying to get out of the parking lot. And if you did, it was, *"Hey, you bleeping idiot, watch out where you're going."* After all, the Colts and the Cowboys are playing today, so get out of my way!

You've got religious nutjob wackos blowing themselves up, along with everyone around them, trying to get in line so they can molest seventy-two innocent virgins throughout eternity, and yet the people I saw who called themselves Christians wouldn't go out of their way to help anybody—what gives with that?

playing church...

And it seemed everybody was judging and criticizing! There were Baptists, Methodists, Presbyterians, Episcopalians, Catholics, Pentecostals… who was right? Was anybody right?

Somehow I just saw all these denominations as *divisions*, and it didn't seem to ring true with the kind of lives the early Christians lived, who went from house to house, breaking bread together and strengthening one another in the faith, and they had such powerful faith that *"fear came upon everyone."* Does the faith in today's Church strike fear in anyone? *Yeah, right.*

Was everybody just *playing church?* If there were any similarities between what I felt was true (early) Christianity and today's religion, even the Christian religion, it seemed to be in name only. At one point I decided I wanted no part of it because none of it seemed real. As children, little girls played with dolls, and little boys played cowboys… and now as adults, the world seemed to be playing church, and I'd decided I wanted nothing to do with it. Let's clarify something about "going to church". As I said, "the church" is not something you can "attend". You're either part of it, or not. However, that's not to say that Christians should not gather together to worship, and most evangelical Christians do so on Sunday. That's something I encourage in the strongest way. It's just that if you're gathering together with other believers, please understand that you're not "going to church". Jesus said… *"I will build my church and the gates of hell shall not prevail against it"*(Matthew 16:18). And yet, we all know that church (buildings) are sometimes destroyed by natural disasters, and occasionally haters of Christianity sometimes burn them down. *"Don't you realize that all of you together are the temple of God and that the Spirit of God lives in you?"*(I Corinthians 3:16 NLT). We are the church, and that church is not made with bricks and mortar and *that church* will live forever.

Does that mean that Jesus was wrong in saying that the gates of hell would not prevail against it? No, it just means that the church (building) at Tenth and Main was destroyed. It's just a building.

I'm an intense kind of person. Whatever it was, I'd always been intense about it. Whether it was music, work, fun, love, romance, or sex... whatever the subject, I was always passionate about it, but if I couldn't have this kind of intense and passionate faith, then I would pass on it. Sorry, it's just not for me.

Oh, I almost forgot. You can hit the Play button now.

Several months went by, and I ended up moving to my parents' home on Harbor Boulevard in Garden Grove just a little more than a mile south of Disneyland. Just as in Brawley, Dad had two gas stations. Both were Gulf stations on Harbor Boulevard about four blocks apart. He ran the stations, and Mom kept the books for the businesses. Before, when we still lived in Red Hill in Upland, I often worked weekends for Dad at the service stations, and after Carolyn and I split up, I moved in with them. I began to work there full-time. After school I had worked at both of Dad's Wilshire stations when we lived in Brawley, learning such things as lube jobs and brake jobs, fixing flats, and so on, and so doing the same thing in Garden Grove wasn't much different.

This was back in the day when gas was 25¢ a gallon, and when someone pulled up to the gas pumps, you washed their windshield, checked their water and oil, and sometimes checked the air in their tires.

What's next is pretty funny, but you'll have to hit the Rewind button again... for just a little.

While still in Brawley I recall one hilarious incident. There was a family of wealthy tomato farmers in Niland, which was about fifteen miles to the north of Brawley, and these farmers, all named Singh, were from India. One sweltering hot day that must have been at least 118°, one of these farmers came in with his big black Cadillac. The car barely made it up the driveway because it was coughing and sputtering and lurching forward. The man spoke little English, and when he asked Dad to check it out, my father lifted the hood of the car and began to test the throttle lever of the carburetor, and then he pulled spark plug wires off one at a time, checking for a problem. A few minutes later my father approached the man and said, *"I'm afraid you've got a short in your car's electrical system."*

The man had a puzzled look on his face, then a few seconds later he pulled out his wallet to see how much money he had on him, and while he was leafing through his wallet, in his thick Indian accent he asked, *"How much you charge to make eet longer?"*

I could barely control the laughter, so I turned and hid my face from him as I walked toward the office. *How much you charge to make eet longer?*

Okay, you can hit Play again.

After moving in with Mom and Dad in Garden Grove, I felt my life was falling apart and that I was just groping for some answers. I kept trying to make sense of my life, but nothing was fitting into place. I made a few feeble attempts at prayer, but still I got nowhere. I missed having some order in my life.

Although I'd been granted custody of my children, one day I got a call from Carolyn, and she said she was bringing them back to me. She actually said, *"Being a mother is too much—it's like being a vegetable."* Carolyn was only sixteen (I was eighteen) when we married, and I knew that she was just overwhelmed and in way over her head. For her to have two children by the time she was eighteen was just too much, and I knew it was the frustration in her that was speaking, but I was also looking forward to having the children back with me.

Tammy was about three, and Jeff wasn't quite two years old at that time, and when we were all together at home with Mom and Dad, life began to take on some sense of normalcy. My parents took to the idea of having their grandkids in the home, and Les and Laura, my younger twin brother and sister, liked the idea of helping out with them from time to time.

About a year passed when Carolyn called again and asked if she could come over to see the children. She explained that her father would be with her, and I said, *"Sure, come on over."* During the visit, while I was in the kitchen, talking with Carolyn's father, Lee Odle,

Carolyn whisked the children out the door and into the car, and I saw them speeding down Harbor Boulevard with Tammy and Jeff looking out the rear window with a frightened look on their face, wondering what was happening.

It was several more months before I learned where she had gone and where she had taken my two children. Carolyn had moved up the coast to Monterey, which was about a six-hour drive from Garden Grove and two hours outside of San Francisco. The only reason I had any idea where she had moved with the children was that I got a call from the district attorney's office, saying that Carolyn was demanding that I begin making child support payments.

So I formulated a plan. I told the district attorney I wanted to begin making payments but that I needed an address to send them to. Apparently, at that time, fathers didn't make their support payments to some government agency, but sent them directly to the spouse, so they gave me the address, which was up north in Monterey.

I filled up the car at Dad's station, and he then loaned me his credit card for me to use for the rest of the trip. I drove the six hours to Monterey, and I pulled up to the address I got from the DA's office at a little after midnight, and I waited—and I waited. I watched the apartments from some distance, looking through a pair of binoculars. I didn't want her to spot me and then take off with the kids.

I assumed she would leave the apartment at around eight in the morning to go to work, but when nine rolled around, I knew something was wrong. I walked up to the apartment building and inquired with the manager, who told me she'd moved out a week earlier. I was at a loss as to how to locate my children. I had to go to plan B, *except that I didn't have a plan B.*

At that point I was quite discouraged, and I began to wonder if I'd made the trip for nothing. Then it occurred to me that she probably hadn't had time to locate a full-time babysitter while she worked, so maybe she'd placed the children in a day care center somewhere in the city.

Immediately I went to a store and changed the remaining few dollars I had on me for a pocketful of dimes, and I headed for a nearby phone booth. I began calling the day care centers listed in the Monterey phone book one by one. I called and kept calling, but nothing. None of them had any record of my children being there. My pocketful of dimes had dwindled, and now I found myself with quite literally the last dime in my pocket when I finally reached a center that was my last resort and likely my last chance to locate my children.

A stern Germanic-sounding woman was on the phone, and when I explained to her that I was their father and that I had both their birth certificates with me, she relented and told me they were there. When I arrived, this imposing German woman, who was at least six feet tall and who easily topped out at 220 lb., stood in front of me in an obvious attempt to block me from getting to the playground. I stepped from side to side trying to get a glance around her broad expanses, and I managed to get a glimpse of Tammy. I stood my ground, and she pressed forward and up against me with her massive expanse of a chest, and in a gruff voice she said, *"You vill not get passt me. I vill call her moder befoar you can see zees little onez. You doant haff my purrmishun."*

I'd never struck a woman, but I growled to her in a deep and very authoritative voice as I waved the children's birth certificates in her face, and in a loud voice I barked out, *"Woman, you may be as big as a mountain, but these are my children, and if you don't get out of my way right now, I'm going to roll over you like a Sherman tank!"*

I think she understood the "Sherman tank" reference because that's what the American GIs used when they rolled over the German army in World War II. She stepped aside in a huff, and when I saw my two little ones out in the playground, I picked them up and held them in my arms, and with tears running down my face, I rushed to the car and headed home. They were thrilled to see their daddy.

I found the key...

Back home, at some point I decided I was going to find out if this God thing was real—or not. I was tired of pussyfooting around—*I wanted to know!*

Somewhere along the way I think I found the key. These people (the early Church) *really believed.* I read and reread the Book of Acts, then read it again. These people *believed.* And if they were going to be stoned to death or crucified for it, they'd better *believe!*

And if that's the case (they *believed*), it must hold true that maybe we don't really *believe.* At least, I didn't. And I didn't know anyone else who did—not like those in the early Church. There was nothing that I'd seen in life or that I'd seen in modern religion that showed any signs, any reality, that Christ was the real thing—the Christ, the Son of the living God. I couldn't find anything in religion that would make Jesus out to be anything more than just another prophet or holy man. And if that was all he was, I was back to square one—for all intents and purposes it was no different from Buddhism or Hinduism, and that wasn't what I was looking for.

These were some rather harsh and uncompromising views, and I admit to being very critical of what I saw around me. Nonetheless, that's the way I felt during this period of my life because I'd yet to find anything real. And yet even with this completely negative attitude toward people who called themselves Christians and toward the institutions who called themselves the Church, I kept coming back to the fact that those early Christians really believed—*they lived their faith...* I couldn't shake it off, and it *haunted* me.

Chapter 5

During this time I said that I had begun seriously seeking some answers. I just wasn't sure I knew which questions to ask.

Karen and I had attended Melodyland Christian Center, which was across Harbor Boulevard from Disneyland, and the pastor Ralph Wilkerson had talked about a book entitled *The Cross and the Switchblade* by David Wilkerson and that David Wilkerson (unrelated to Ralph) was going to be speaking at Melodyland in a month or two. He began to tell us about this little skinny preacher from some hick small town in the Midwest, who had taken his message of Jesus to the mean streets of New York, and he was having some amazing results.

I picked up a copy of the book, and I read it through at least three times. Ralph Wilkerson was right. Here was this little *nobody* of a preacher who had left his small-town church to go to places like the Bronx and Bedford-Stuyvesant, places that were infested with drugs, gangs, and prostitution. These were the real ghettos, where the black gangs hated the Puerto Rican gangs, and a little white boy preacher hadn't a chance in hell to even survive, let alone make a difference. But he *was* making a difference, and it really captured my imagination.

There were the stories of boys like Nicky Cruz and Sonny Arguinzoni, who were the worst of the worst, and their lives had been changed by Dave Wilkerson's simple message, *"Son, Jesus loves you."*

I later got a copy of a record album that Nicky Cruz had recorded, which was the story of his life—his testimony, if you will—and his passionate voice loudly cried out in Spanish (he hadn't learned English well enough as yet) when David Wilkerson told him, *"Cristo te ama, Cristo te ama"* (*"Jesus loves you, Jesus loves you"* in Spanish), which were the words young David Wilkerson had told him when he had run out of answers—he simply had nothing else he could tell Nicky, no magical solutions, just, *"Son, Jesus loves you,"* and it haunted Nicky. It haunted his dreams, and it haunted him when he was awake—those simple words from that skinny preacher man, *"Jesus loves you."*

I read on, over and over again, the accounts of heroin addicts who had been healed of their addictions, many of them not even having to go through the agony of heroin withdrawals, simply because of this preacher's faith and that he cared enough to believe and pray for them.

Here it was... *here it was! My search was over!* I finally discovered someone, someone in this crazy, sick, religious "play church" world, who was *living their faith just like the early Christians! Here it was!* Here was someone to whom Christianity wasn't the "one hour on Sunday" thing... you know, "sit down, stand up, sing page 182, and pass the plate" kind of thing that leaves you wondering, *Is this all there is to it?*

I just had to find out more about these kinds of people... people like David Wilkerson and the others at Teen Challenge. I wanted to see if what I had been reading could really be true.

I went back to Melodyland to hear David Wilkerson, and he told a compelling story about how he felt called by the Lord to go to New York and work among the gangbangers and the drug pushers. I also heard him tell about his own journey, seeking answers to some of the same questions I'd been asking, and he wondered if church life in that small Midwestern town was all there was to this business of faith, because if faith was real and it could work in small-town America, it had to be just as real in the ghettos in New York as well. If it's real, it's got to be real to kids like Nicky Cruz and Sonny and all the others; otherwise, it's just playing church.

He was saying the same things I'd been saying! If it's real... let's do it! If it's not real, then let's forget about the whole thing. He also talked about being so frightened... and yet the Holy Spirit had given him boldness and courage when he needed it. He even talked about being filled with the Holy Spirit. I'd always thought that was just some old King James English way of saying you were *filled with goodness* or something like that. Yet here was this small Midwestern preacher literally facing death every day on the streets of New York because he was filled with the Holy Spirit and with power! I wasn't sure what this guy was on, but I knew he was *on to something.*

I can't pin it down to the day or the hour because with me it was more a work in progress, a continued act of submission, but I answered several altar calls during the series of meetings with Wilkerson, each time determined to really find this kind of *early-Church* Christianity and each time submitting more and more of my life and my will to Christ. I was tired of this empty, dead-end life I'd been living.

One of the first things I noticed was that I had less and less of a desire to do things I knew to be wrong (sin), and when I did those things, I felt really bad about it—not the kind of guilt society puts on you and not the kind of guilt the psychiatrists talk about and then try to talk you out of it, but the kind of guilt that comes from conviction of the Holy Spirit. And I also began to *want* to read the Bible. It was difficult at first, and I had to struggle through much of it, but I wanted to learn more about this thing, being filled with the Holy Spirit, even though this conjured up images of Holy Rollers and people swinging from chandeliers.

Once, when I was fifteen or so and living in Brawley, a friend took me to a Pentecostal church where the people were running around and shouting, shaking, and gyrating, and some were even rolling on the floor, and every once in a while someone would shout out, *"Shandala matalah balulah"* or something like that, and I thought that these people were absolutely out of their *lunatic minds!* So I thought, if that's what this Holy Spirit stuff is all about, *forget it.*

Yet I kept coming back to what Wilkerson said about having the power in his life to be bold for Jesus and to be fearless for him in the face of such danger and having the faith and the power to pray for young men and women who were hooked on heroin, and they had no withdrawals… miraculous kind of faith. I remembered from my

Baptist days as a youth, hearing the Great Commission over and over. They shouted from the pulpit our marching orders, *"Go ye into all the world, and preach the gospel to every creature"* (Mark 16:15, KJV).

Now, we'd always been told that these were the last words Jesus uttered before *"he was received up into heaven, and sat on the right hand of God"*—not exactly. Can you imagine how irate the world would be if for years we'd only been told half of Lincoln's Gettysburg Address or half of Martin Luther King's *"I Have a Dream"* speech and the other half had been left off because someone decided it might possibly offend someone or because it wasn't politically correct? I was *really ticked off!*

Here are the last words Jesus uttered before his ascension… or, as Paul Harvey would say, *"And now… the rest of the story."*

> *And he said unto them, Go ye into all the world, and preach the gospel to every creature. He that believeth and is baptized shall be saved; but he that believeth not shall be damned. And these signs shall follow them that believe; In my name shall they cast out devils; they shall speak with new tongues; They shall take up serpents, and if they drink any deadly thing, it shall not hurt them; they shall lay hands on the sick, and they shall recover. So then after the Lord had spoken unto them, he was received up into heaven, and sat on the right hand of God.* (Mark 16:15–19, KJV)

I decided then and there that if this was what it took to be able to live the Christian faith as the early Church lived it, I had to have it. I wasn't sure about this *tongues* business, but I knew I had to be filled with the Holy Spirit. As I said before, *"If this is real, then let's do it… if it's not, then let's forget all about it."*

By this time I knew that I was now a believer… a *Christian*. I knew that Jesus Christ had come into my life and that he was the Son of the living God, and I knew that he had become my personal Savior, and he'd forgiven me for all the wild, crazy, sinful things I'd done. And by this time I knew that just as Jesus had told the thief on the cross next to him when he asked, *"Remember me when you come into your Kingdom,"* and Jesus replied, *"Truly I say to you, today you will be with me in paradise"* (Luke 23:42–43, NKJV), if my life were to be suddenly ended like blowing out a candle as it could have been so easily cut short earlier in my life because of all the partying and drinking and driving drunk, I knew that if I died, I would be with him in paradise.

But I also knew that I needed the *power*… the *power* to overcome sin in my life… and the *power to* live boldly for Christ like the early Church had lived and like people such as David Wilkerson and those at Teen Challenge. I still had the same struggles with the same temptations, but now I had a helper to overcome them.

I also read in the Book of Acts, where the people were all gathered together in an upper room shortly after the death and resurrection of Christ:

> *And when the day of Pentecost was fully come, they were all with one accord in one place.*
>
> *And suddenly there came a sound from heaven as of a rushing mighty wind, and it filled all the house where they were sitting.*
>
> *And there appeared unto them cloven tongues like as of fire, and it sat upon each of them.*
>
> *And they were all filled with the Holy Spirit, and began to speak with other tongues, as the Spirit gave them utterance.* (Acts 2:1–4, KJV)

Then the apostle Peter went out and, on that same day, preached with boldness, and three thousand people were saved. Wow! Wasn't this the same Peter who just a few weeks earlier denied even knowing Jesus to save his own neck? The scripture says in verse 13 that others mocked them, saying, *"These men are full of new wine,"* but Peter went on to explain to these men that this was merely the fulfillment of what had been spoken long ago by the prophet Joel about the outpouring of the Holy Spirit, saying, *"And it shall come to pass afterward that I will pour out My Spirit on all flesh; Your sons and your daughters shall prophesy, your old men shall dream dreams, your young men shall see visions. And also on my menservants and on My maid-servants I will pour out My Spirit in those days"* (Joel 2:28–29; Acts 2:17–18, KJV).

Now, Peter had some new kind of *holy boldness,* and he defiantly preached the gospel, healing the sick, casting out demons, and even, yes, *raising the dead.* Peter said to a woman named Tabitha, who had become sick and then died, *"Tabitha, arise. And she opened her eyes, and when she saw Peter she sat up"* (Acts 9:36–42, KJV). This was the early Church in action, and what I saw in the pages of *The Cross and the Switchblade* was the closest thing I'd ever seen to that kind of real faith.

Over the next several months I began to earnestly seek this baptism of the Holy Spirit, staying up late in the evenings in front of the fireplace, fervently praying that God would pour out his Spirit on me. I saw in the scriptures that when people were really serious about wanting God to intervene in some way, they fasted. So I fasted. And I prayed... and prayed. Nothing happened.

Orange County Teen Challenge...

Meanwhile, I had met a man named Les Warren, who was the circulation manager at the *Garden Grove Evening News,* where I had recently gone to work as a typesetter, and he, along with people like George and Betty Wakeling and Don Matison and Max Rapoport, was trying to get a local Teen Challenge started in Orange County.

George was a drugstore manager in Santa Ana, and he too was seeking this baptism in the Spirit. He and his wife, Betty, had opened up their home in Tustin for meetings, and it was there that I met Don Matison, who was the director of the center for the first few months.

We met in George and Betty's home at least once a week, and it seemed every week more people were added to our group, and we kept hearing reports of more and more being saved, many of whom had been seriously addicted to drugs.

One such young man was Bill Green, who was brought to the Wakeling home after he'd been found in a drug stupor, literally hiding out in the *doghouse* at his parents' home. I later learned that Bill Green was one of the most heavily addicted people I'd ever known—he had become what's known as a *needle freak* because of his addiction to the drugs and his love for the needle. Bill told me he'd sometimes injected cough syrup and even small quantities of gasoline when he'd been out of heroin. And his love of the needle turned to an obsession—an obsession for the rush an addict got whenever the drug hit the brain. Sometimes he even used a partially thawed Popsicle so that it was very cold and mushy, and then he'd inject it intravenously because the cold liquid would give him a rush, a heady jolt when it hit his brain.

And yet Bill was one of the most gifted musicians I'd ever met. Later, after he'd come to the Lord, I heard Bill play one of his compositions on the piano before about three thousand people at Melodyland Christian Center in Anaheim, and there wasn't a dry eye in the place.

Here's what made that performance unique. No one had announced that Bill would be playing as he was simply asked to provide background music as people filled in to the auditorium and took their seats. Bill had what was termed an anointing on his music. It was quite literally a gift from God, and it was so powerful that when he played—played this amazing and powerful music he'd composed—the grand piano began to vibrate and shake so that it began to inch its way across the stage… it moved so that he had to keep scooting the piano bench forward to keep up with it. Imagine music this powerful, totally unaccompanied and without lyrics, without any previous introduction, moving an audience to the point of standing and cheering and weeping.

Larry Reed stepped right out of some crime novel and right into our lives. Larry had been a heroin addict for sixteen years and had also spent sixteen years in San Quentin for his various drug-related crimes. Larry was tough. He was big, he was rough, and he was tough. Larry also loved Jesus… in fact, I'd never seen anyone so passionate about his love for his Lord and master. Larry was the kind of guy that if you saw him, you might want to hide your wallet or walk across the street. That was, until he got close—close enough for him to give you a hug, and when he did so, he sometimes had a tear in his eye, telling you, *"Jesus loves you, man."*

During that time the flower children frequently staged love-ins, where they would play their acid rock music and frolic in the sunshine, usually high on pot or LSD. And Irvine Park, which is located in the foothills in the eastern part of Orange County, was often the scene of these events.

One weekend we decided to stage a Christian "praise-in" at Irvine Park, and many people from both Orange County and Los Angeles Teen Challenge came there to share Jesus's love with the flower children. Larry Reed was there, along with many other recently converted former addicts and drug dealers. Once the sound system was set up, our praise-in started out with one of our Christian musical groups but was soon followed by the testimonies of the ex-addicts. When Larry Reed took the microphone, everything went quiet… then he began, in his rough mannerisms and booming voice, *"For sixteen years I shot heroin into my veins… and anything that wasn't nailed down, I stole. I stole to support my habit! I used to run up and down the big yard in San Quentin with all the other convicts… and we were lost! Everyone was fighting and killing and…"* Larry Reed's testimony went on for about ten minutes, and then in a booming voice he finished up with, *"Then one day JESUS came into my life. And* JESUS *set me free. It was* JESUS *who filled me with his Holy Spirit and* SET ME ON FIRE FOR HIM.*"*

His big, powerful voice echoed through the park as young people everywhere stopped to hear this prison-hardened man tell about the tender love of Christ. Many souls were saved as the young people fanned out, witnessing privately and praying with anyone who was touched by the message.

Next, a group of us from Teen Challenge went to Griffith Park in Los Angeles. It was a similar scene, with thousands of young people, mostly hippies and dopers, and hundreds of tough bikers, all doing their thing, which were sex, drugs, and rock and roll.

Max Rapoport and his wife, Sandee, were also there. Max had been a very successful businessman, but he had also been deeply involved in drugs, particularly marijuana and LSD, and I can remember Max relating stories of getting high with attorneys and judges during those days prior to his conversion.

Originally from Rhode Island, Max had been born a Jew but abandoned by his parents at age three and was raised by relatives as a Catholic in a tenement house in Providence, which was directly over a bar. Max often recalled the fights and even killings in that bar below their apartment. His dramatic conversion to Christ brought him a passion and power that were rare. He was about thirty-three or thirty-four at the time, and Sandee was twenty-three, and she had been a dancer and a model. She too had a powerful testimony, and she was able to reach many young people for Christ.

That day at Griffith Park, I suddenly noticed that Max and Sandee had been surrounded by a group of bikers, Hells Angels types, who had been making obscene gestures at Sandee, and they defiantly began to close ranks in a circle around the two of them. They'd seen Max and Sandee praying for a young boy, and several of them pulled out knives and began to come toward both of them. I was just a few yards away when one of the group, who was slapping a motorcycle chain against his hand, poured wine into his mouth and down the front of his pants and then all over the top of his head, and then as he was pouring it into his mouth again, he spit out a mouthful of it all over Max, spraying him with it so that Max was covered and dripping with red wine.

He then said to Max, *"You don't get it, do you? It's real simple... I'm gonna wrap this chain around your neck, and we're gonna kill you. You're gonna die, right here today."*

As they drew in closer, an anointing came over Max, and he began to preach to them with *boldness* and *power,* saying, *"Yes, you could do that... you could kill me, but if you do, I'll just go to be with my Lord and Savior, Jesus, a little sooner... but you will spend an eternity in the fires of hell, roasting over the flames and turning over and over like a pig on a spit... on the other hand, you could give your lives to Jesus right now, and you can know the love and joy that Sandee and I have found."*

You could *feel* the Holy Spirit reaching out and touching these men, one by one... and one by one they began to drop their knives and chains. It wasn't long before Max and Sandee were standing with several of these men, holding their hands and praying for Jesus to reveal himself to them and to come into their lives.

It had only been a few months earlier, before Max's dramatic conversion, that he'd been at Griffith Park, tripping on LSD.

"I was on this really heavy acid trip, and I suddenly got this idea that I needed to get back to Orange County right away and that if I could really concentrate, I could transport myself there... the next thing I knew, I was literally running down the middle of the freeway, causing quite a traffic jam... and then I ran down an off-ramp, and I saw a building, a Christian Science Reading Room, and in my hallucination I thought that if I could just get to the other side of this glass door, I'd be in Orange County... I'd be transported or astral projected there. I ran right through that glass door, and I cut myself up pretty badly... I was covered with blood. When the police got there, I was nearing the peak of my acid trip, but in my delusions they looked like demons... and so I fought with them in a terrible rage, and I even kicked two or three of them in the face.

> *"I had thought I could project myself to Orange County, but instead I had projected myself straight to hell… because it wasn't until after the police had subdued me and handcuffed me backward, facedown in the back of the police car… well, it was then that I peaked on this acid trip, and it was like being in the pits of hell itself, and I was screaming like a madman. If there was anything good that ever came out of my taking LSD, it was that I realized that there was a devil because I saw his demons, and I knew that if there was a devil, then there must be a God."*

Max later said that at the time of his conversion, he had met the Lord in a very real and powerful way, and when the Lord had come to him, he fell to the ground, being blinded by his light, and then the Lord spoke to him and said, *"Get up… I want you to go and preach my Word."* Since his conversion Max has ministered the good news of Jesus Christ to much of the world, including several countries in Asia, Africa, Europe, and all over the United States.

rivers of "living water"…

One night, after I had spent months seeking this baptism in the Holy Spirit, I went with the Orange County Teen Challenge group to a small Assembly of God church in Orange, California. The pastor was Peter Caruso. Larry Reed was scheduled to speak that night. As I mentioned earlier, Larry was pretty rough around the edges, having been a heroin addict for sixteen years and an ex-convict who had served sixteen years of hard time in San Quentin. He was loud, and his voice and mannerisms were definitely from someone who was *street tough* and hardened by a life of crime and drugs, but when he spoke, you *knew* that this man *knew Jesus*. As I said earlier, he had a gentleness and compassion that belied his tough outward exterior.

Afterward, I came up to Larry and began to explain to him how long I'd been seeking this baptism in the Holy Spirit… and how I wasn't sure about this "speaking in tongues" business… and how I wasn't sure about… Larry just smiled (interrupting all my questions) and placed his hand on my head and began to pray for me.

I'll try as best I can to explain what happened next, but it's almost unexplainable. Maybe you recall that I said in the beginning of this book, *"You may not believe or even understand some of the things in this book, but I can promise you I will tell you the truth."*

When Larry Reed laid his hands on my head, something began to happen. Something *physical* began to happen. It felt like something was bubbling... like a fountain was bubbling inside my belly. I remembered briefly looking down at my stomach and wondering what was happening. It was like the scripture said, *"Out of his belly shall flow rivers of living water"* (John 7:38, KJV).

And at the same time, it was as though I were being flooded with light. My entire being was being flooded with light, and suddenly, even when my eyes were open, all I could see was light, and when they were closed, there was nothing but light. I had never felt such peace and joy in all my life, and I began to weep, and at the same time this living water within me was rising up and continued to rise up until it filled my chest, and just when I thought I'd burst, my arms reached upward, and I began to praise God: I was praising God for loving me and forgiving me, I was praising God for his Son, Jesus, and as I was being filled and overcome with praise, suddenly, I began to speak in a language I'd never learned and I'd never before spoken... all this while still being blinded with light.

I collapsed to the floor, weeping and praising God and speaking in this strange language. This was *real.* This had not been conjured up or imagined. God reached down and touched me... *and I knew it!* Here I was, this hell-raising, boozing, fornicating, and brawling sinner, who had been touched by the hand of God, and he had filled me with his Holy Spirit! For some ten or fifteen minutes while lying there flat on my back, *I saw nothing but light! If my eyes were closed, I saw only light, and if my eyes were open—nothing but light!*

Also, while I was lying on the floor, the Holy Spirit was moving over me in waves—one wave after another, after another, and another again—and it was then that God showed me the most incredible thing.

God revealed to me that the same Holy Spirit who had entered the tomb where the dead body of Jesus had been lain was now moving over me, in wave after wave, and breathing on me and quickening me just as that same Holy Spirit breathed on the dead body of Jesus and quickened him and raised him from the dead. It was incredible, and I couldn't contain myself laughing and weeping for joy.

Later that evening I rushed home and told Karen about this experience. I'm not certain if she understood much of it that night; I was babbling on so excitedly about what had happened. But immediately, something else happened. Not next week or next month, but immediately, I began to have an insatiable desire for the Word. And just as suddenly, the Bible seemed to leap off the pages to me… and *I understood it… for the first time I really understood it!* Not only did I understand it (with my mind), but I also had spiritual revelation pouring out to me, page after page. I understood about being *quickened* by the Holy Spirit. I understood about holy boldness and the anointing. I understood about Jesus being quite literally transformed and how he was *transfigured* right before the disciples' eyes and how he could have gone to meet the Father then, right then and there escaping the agony of the cross, but instead he endured the cross and the shame that went with it. He literally became sin so that you and I and everyone in the world would not have to stand before God and hear the words, *"Guilty!"*

Something else equally astonishing began to happen to me. I was being *led* by the Holy Spirit… everywhere I went I seemed to be *led* to help someone and to minister to someone, and everywhere I went people were being saved and filled with the Holy Spirit, and others were being set free. *And* I began to speak for Christ with boldness! I remember going with Les Warren and several other Christian men to one of the chapels at the California Institution for Men, and I began to talk to all the inmates there about the love of Jesus and how he loved them and could *set them free* even while they were behind bars! Everyone in that room that night came forward and accepted Christ as their Savior. Call it jailhouse conversions if you want to, but these men were weeping before the Lord and repenting of their sins.

This was *me* talking—the same guy who was such a hell-raiser and who got into bar fights in Mexicali and had all-night drunken parties. Yeah, this was *me*... and yet it wasn't me because I was a new man. Scriptures say, *"Therefore if any man be in Christ he is a new creature: old things are passed away; behold, all things are become new"* (2 Cor. 5:17, KJV).

Dr. Robert Schuller...*

During this same period of time I started attending the Garden Grove Community Church (later the Crystal Cathedral), where the Reverend Dr. Robert Schuller was pastor. It wasn't long before Rev. Schuller and I had struck up something of a friendship, and soon he asked me to teach a Sunday school class of high school students, which rather surprised me since I was such a new Christian with so little experience.

Just a few weeks before Larry Reed prayed for me and I was baptized in the Holy Spirit, I had been teaching the class of high school students, and we came across several passages in the gospels where it referenced the casting out of demons. One of the students had asked me, *"What's all this business about casting out demons? It seems that just about everywhere Jesus went he was healing people and casting out demons!"*

And of course, being the expert I was *(not)*, I responded with an answer even though I didn't have a clue. My absurd response went something like this:

"Well, Jesus, being a contemporary man of his day, simply went along with the myths and superstitions of the time" and blah, blah, blah.

Remember, this was in response to a specific question about the passages in which the demon threw this poor boy to the ground, and he was foaming at the mouth, and Jesus rebuked the unclean spirit and healed the child and returned him again to his father (see Luke 9:38–42). I should have kept my mouth shut because I certainly didn't know what I was talking about, and what I had just told the students in the class was spiritual *hogwash!*

a demon is manifested...

However, a few weeks after my experience of being filled with the Holy Spirit, Rev. Schuller asked me to speak to a group that was made up of young adults, mostly in their twenties, who were from the Garden Grove Community Church. It was on a Friday night, and there were about thirty people at this meeting, which was in one of the couples' homes, and as I began to speak, I once again felt an unusual anointing, meaning that I felt the Holy Spirit's presence in a very real and tangible way. And as I spoke, his presence became very evident to everyone in the room… there was a sense of awe, and everyone looked around the room wide-eyed as if to say, *"Do you feel it too?"* A quiet hush and a sense of fear fell on everyone there.

Remember, these people were from Rev. Schuller's church—not exactly a hotbed of wild-eyed Pentecostals—and although they called this a prayer meeting, it was more of a social gathering.

As I spoke, suddenly, a well-dressed quiet young man, who had been sitting on a couch in the back of the room, stood up and began to ask me a reasonable and intelligent question, but while he was speaking, he was interrupted midsentence, and he began to… *howl* and to *wail at the top of his lungs…* this otherwise quiet and shy young man *was howling like a wolf!*

Next, he was thrown to the ground and began to shudder and convulse and drool out his mouth, all while he continued to howl at the top of his voice. And yet even during the violent convulsions, a chilling deep, guttural voice was speaking from this young man's mouth, saying, *"You can't have him—I've been in here sixteen years"* and spouting off all sorts of vile things. Everyone in the room was terrified, including me, and everyone's eyes were as wide as saucers. You could sense a fear come on everyone there… we were all terrified. It was so very violent as the demons within thrashed him about. For a moment I thought it would kill him; such was the violence.

Then suddenly, it was as though scriptures were being scrolled through my mind as on a ticker tape, and I saw the passages about the boy who was brought to Jesus by his father, having an unclean spirit, and the demons within thrashed the boy around so that the father feared it would kill his son. Suddenly, I knew that my religious babble a few weeks earlier, about Jesus going along with the superstitions of his time, was spiritual nonsense, and I knew what had to be done.

Although just moments earlier I had been so scared that I almost ran out of the place, suddenly, I felt authority come over me like a warm blanket, along with a sense of peace and a holy boldness that filled my being. It was an anointing, somewhat like the pouring of warm oil over my head as they did when they anointed the prophets in the Old Testament, and I walked over to him and said with absolute authority, *"Demon… I command you in the name of Jesus to come out of him now!"* That was when the spirit in him growled in a devilish voice.

"I'm not coming out… I've been in here for sixteen years, and I'm not coming out."

This young man was terrified as he screamed out in horror. Yet at the same time two voices were coming out of him—one howling like a wolf and the other, a demonic growling male voice claiming possession of him.

Once again, I responded with, *"I command you in the name of Jesus Christ to leave him… come out of him NOW!"*

The young man *screamed* out in a loud voice, then he leaped to his feet, and then with a violent shudder, he collapsed onto the floor followed by a violent convulsion as if hell itself had left him. *He had been set free!* He began to weep an uncontrollable weeping, which soon turned to unrestrained joy as he asked Jesus to come into his life and to be his Lord. Never before had I seen someone so overcome with joy because *he had been set free!* I tried to imagine being tormented for all those years and then finally being *set free!*

There was a sense of awe and fear on everyone there, and many dropped to their knees, weeping. I was amazed that something so vile and ugly as a demon being manifested could turn into something so incredibly beautiful because he was no longer in bondage.

It was also then that I determined never to answer a question about which I knew nothing, especially when it came to spiritual matters. Regardless of what I had previously believed, the spirit world was real—*demons were real.*

The following morning I received a call at about eight thirty. The call was from Rev. Schuller, who asked that I meet him at his office at the Garden Grove Community Church. Not knowing what to expect, I obliged, and I drove the six or eight miles to the church and met with him. When I got there, his office was otherwise empty, and he said to me, *"Ken, come on in. There's something I want to talk to you about. I've been hearing reports about strange things going on at that meeting last night."*

He then pointed to the Tower of Power, a twelve-story edifice that had just been built and was nearing completion, and he said, *"Ken, I like what I've built here, and I don't want anything going on that will jeopardize that, and I think it best if you and your family found another church."*

Without asking for an explanation about what had happened the night before, he'd made up his mind. I would have loved to have had a chance to explain that none of this was anything I'd conjured up or sought. It just happened. If it had happened a few weeks earlier, I was sure I wouldn't have believed it myself. I simply replied, *"You're probably right, and I think I've accomplished what God sent me here for,"* and I walked out of his office.

I never questioned Rev. Schuller's faith or his methods. I just knew that I never asked for this experience with the young man and the demon—this *deliverance*, if you will—to happen, and I only wished Rev. Schuller had been there to witness it. I believed it might have changed his life forever as it did mine because he would have seen the power of God at work firsthand.

I did know that when Rev. Schuller started out, it was his zeal for God that moved the people and created such a large following. He began by going door-to-door in Garden Grove, telling people about his drive-in church (which was actually located in a drive-in theater). He would tell people, *"You can come as you are, bring the whole family with you. You don't even have to get out of your car,"* and on Sunday mornings he would preach from atop the roof of the snack bar, and his congregation quickly grew to one of the largest in California and was known as the Garden Grove Community Church. Later his weekly broadcasts, *The Hour of Power,* were televised to the entire nation.

*Dr. Schuller died in April of 2015 of esophageal cancer.

Chapter 6

The year 1967 was at the height of the hippie culture. *"Flower power"* and *"Make love, not war"* were the slogans of the day. Drug use was rampant, and there seemed to be no stigma attached to turning on, which was more of a way of life than just bumper-sticker slogans in those days. Huntington Beach, California, was a mecca for the drug-and-hippie culture at that time.

On any given Friday or Saturday night, just as the sun went down, the surfers with their woodies and surfboards seemed to disappear, and out came the flower children. Thousands of them roamed the streets, high on LSD, and the smell of pot filled the air as you walked down Pacific Coast Highway.

I remember one Friday night when a car screeched to a stop next to the curb right next to me, and the driver had passed out with his outfit (needle) still stuck in his arm, and the surgical tubing still wrapped around his bicep with his head just nodded off against the steering wheel. This man had actually been *driving while shooting up!* Young girls, some thirteen- and fourteen-year-old runaways, were sleeping in cars and vans and sleeping with anyone who would put them up for the night—just for a joint, some acid, or maybe a little bit of food and a place to sleep.

We'd managed to rent a large older white wood-frame building for the Teen Challenge Center, which was on Chapman Avenue in Anaheim, and Max and his wife, Sandee, were living in the garage, which had been converted to a makeshift apartment at the center. Max became the director of the center after Don Matison had left.

Max was a Larry Reed with more polish and sophistication. And he was bold for Jesus. Well-dressed and neatly groomed, I can still remember him unafraid to corner anyone there on the streets of Huntington Beach and telling them, *"Jesus loves you, and he wants to save you... but if you don't accept him, you're gonna roast like a chestnut!"*

None of us had an overabundance of wisdom in those days, but we had plenty of zeal, and we had love for the people we were trying to reach. Max was leading many young people to Christ, and our Teen Challenge coffeehouse, which we had opened just weeks before, was always filled to overflowing with literally hundreds of young people—so much so that we got weekly threats from the fire department that they'd close us down if we didn't put a stop to the overcrowding. Incidentally, the name of that coffeehouse was the Ultimate, Eternal Trip (sorry, I didn't pick the name).

Sometimes we'd have Andraé Crouch & the Disciples sing at the coffeehouse, then they'd hit the streets with us, witnessing to the crowds of dopers and hippies. Later Andrae Crouch frequently sang on national television for Christmas specials during the eighties.

One night Andrae Crouch and I were walking over to a head shop called the Magic Mushroom since we frequently met young people in there and talked to them about Jesus. As we walked into this shop, where they specialized in selling drug paraphernalia, I was about to take a drink from the cup of soda I was holding when Andrae grabbed it out of my hand, reached inside, and pulled out a wedge of acid (LSD). He'd seen someone drop it in there just seconds before.

We also held many meetings at a beautiful home owned by a couple in Laguna Beach. On a clear day you could see Catalina Island from their living room window. Laguna Beach was a haven for flower children in those days, with thousands of them living in the nearby canyons, camping out and living out of Volkswagen "flower power" vans. And many were brought in off the streets, and some churches began as an offshoot of that work. One night in particular stands out.

This was only the second or third meeting we'd held at that home, and there was a real spirit of anticipation.

I remember praying that night for God to make me an instrument he could use for his glory, and as I was praying, I began to notice an intense burning on the palms of my hands. This was really intense, and yet strangely, it was not painful, but it was startlingly real. *It was as if my hands were literally on fire—without any pain!* It would be some time before I would learn the significance of that night and the burning of my hands.

Meanwhile, we also had weekly meetings at the Teen Challenge Center, where Max was usually the speaker, but one night a man named Dick Mills was the guest speaker. Dick is well-known around the world for his prophetic gifts and the word of knowledge. This is one of the gifts of the Holy Spirit as outlined in the New Testament (see First Corinthians 12:4–11) in which someone will receive knowledge in a supernatural revelation that is usually specific to or about someone who is present. There is a supernatural but demonic equivalent to this, called a spirit of divination or soothsaying, more commonly known as fortune-telling, because for each God-given supernatural gift, there is an otherworldly counterfeit.

So that night at the Teen Challenge Center, Dick Mills pointed me out of the crowd, walked over to me, and said, *"Young man, God's going to be sending you clear across the country, and I see you ministering to thousands, and many will be saved. God has his hand on you, and he has anointed you for a great work. Get your affairs in order because you'll be leaving soon."*

That night I went home, and I had a vision in which I was standing chest deep in a river, and I was baptizing young people who'd given their lives to Christ. When I woke up from this visionlike state, it continued without interruption. The vision was so vivid and so specific. I saw trees along a riverbank heavily laden with Spanish moss, and the banks were filled with hundreds, maybe thousands, of people watching as the new Christians went down into the water. And as they came up out of the water, the Spirit of the Lord descended upon them, and with a heavenly glow about them, they lifted their hands and began to praise God. This dream went on for a long time, and each new convert came down into the river to be baptized, and the crowds of onlookers were amazed at the scene.

    I wasn't exactly sure what to make of this vision, but this seemed to be the confirmation I needed… God had called me to do a work in Florida.

Chapter 7

I began to make preparations for the move, and within weeks we were all packed up. Everything we owned was crowded into a U-Haul trailer and into our '62 Chevy sedan. I'd given my notice at the newspaper, and Karen had given advance warning to her sister who lived in Plant City, Florida, that we'd be (all six of us) descending upon her and her family for a few days until we found a place to live.

So we were off. The tongue of the trailer was so heavy I actually had to use a jack in order to hook it up to the trailer hitch, and the weight of it made the hitch start to bend and droop as soon as I removed the jack. But it only bent so far, and then it seemed OK. I worried about that hitch for the first few hundred miles or so, but since it didn't seem to get any worse, I began to forget about it. Now, this trailer had a full upright piano in it, a refrigerator, couch, and table and all our beds. I actually drew out a diagram and scaled each piece of furniture, and so I had every article assigned an exact spot. And it all fit although I had to shove the remaining blankets and pillows into the trailer with a broom handle. The back door of the trailer had a distinct bulge to it by the time I finished stuffing it.

Driving more than two thousand five hundred miles, from the Pacific Ocean to the Atlantic, with four small children in the car, would have seemed a nightmare, but strangely enough, the kids never once asked, *"Daddy, how soon will we be there?"* or *"Daddy, how many more miles is it?"*

We'd just passed New Orleans, and we came through a little town called Mandeville, Louisiana, when a drunk driver crossed the road in front of us, and like a deer caught in the headlights, he saw us, panicked, and froze in place. About an hour earlier I'd heard a voice—not with my ears, but from deep inside me—and over the years that's how the Spirit of the Lord would speak to me, and that day he said to me, *"Satan knows why you're going to Florida, and he will try to stop you. Don't be afraid because I will be with you,"* and this message was repeated before reaching Mandeville.

It was a terrible wreck or would have been except that *I didn't feel the impact or hear the crash at all!* It was, quite honestly, as though I were going through it in silent, slow motion. I hit the brakes as hard as I could, but there was no stopping these five tons of car and U-Haul heading down the road.

The front of the car was pushed up nearly to the windshield, and parts of the engine were in the front-seat compartment. The driver of the other car was so drunk he didn't really know what had happened, but he wasn't hurt. And no one in our car was hurt either. Scotty ended up with a little bump on his forehead, but miraculously, no one was injured. Our car, of course, was a total loss.

The sheriff soon arrived, and as it turned out, he was the nephew of the drunk driver. He helped us out of the car and then graciously offered to put us up in his home for the night until we could go down to the car dealership the next day and buy another car. We agreed, and so we went to his family home and spent the night. We learned that next morning that his hospitality, along with buying us a vehicle to replace my wrecked '62 Chevy, was in exchange for my not pressing charges against his uncle for drunk driving.

He drove us into town where he took us to a local used-car lot, which was owned by a friend of his, and he bought us a '63 Ford, nine-passenger wagon. It had *lots* of room and seemed to run fairly well, so the deal was made, and we packed up and left. Meanwhile, the bulge that had been in the back of the U-Haul was now in the front of the trailer, and it bulged out several inches. All our belongings had been driven to the front of the trailer by the force of the impact, and the bulge in the front made it look like we were pulling an *Airstream* trailer instead of a wooden U-Haul.

Late that afternoon we were heading into Tallahassee, Florida, when the transmission on the Ford wagon just gave out, with smoke pouring out from under the car and the smell of burned transmission fluid in the air. It was a goner.

We called Karen's sister and brother-in-law, and they agreed to come and gather Karen and the children and drive them on to Plant City while I stayed behind and had the transmission repaired. The only problem was, we were down to our last few dollars. Karen's (twin) sister, Sharon Garrison, called an old friend, who was also a state assemblyman in Tallahassee, and he was kind enough to pay for the transmission repairs, so by midmorning the next day I was back on the road, at least for a while.

Within twenty miles or so, I noticed the station wagon was seriously overheating. I pulled into a little country gas station, and within seconds after getting out of the car, there was this loud *BOOM!* The left rear tire had simply exploded while I was sitting there parked in front of the gas station. It seemed the transmission shop had engaged the parking brake, and since the brake light didn't work, the parking brake didn't work well enough for me to notice it slowing down the car, but it did work well enough to heat the rear brake drums to the point of *melting the wheel brake cylinders* and, of course, blowing out the tire.

I had $10.25 left, and I needed a tire. I talked them into putting one on for me for $6. And I needed gasoline. I put the last $4 in the tank, which brought it to nearly a full tank of gas, and I spent fifteen cents on a soda. I had an almost bald, used tire on the left rear and not nearly enough gasoline, and I had no brakes (except for a little slowing with the emergency brake) because of the melting of the wheel cylinders and the loss of all the hydraulic fluid.

Yes, sir, I was headed to Central Florida to serve the Lord—with no brakes, not enough gas, bald tires, 10¢ in my pocket, and… *light-*

ning! Soon there were thunder and lightning, and there was lightning everywhere!

Within ten miles of leaving the gas station, lightning was striking *right in front of my car*. I mean, BOOM, BOOM, BOOM—lightning everywhere. Six or eight times I literally was swerving down the road to avoid the lightning strikes, and each time it was a blinding flash and a ball of fire hitting within a few feet of the car. I was tempted to get out of the car and start screaming… but I didn't. What was going on? Hadn't I heard from God that he wanted me to go to Florida to start a work for him? What's this all about? *The transmission goes out, the car overheats, the tire blows out, and* now there's thunder and lightning? And the lightning was trying to hit my car—not once, but again and again and again! *Huh? What is going on?*

Then it hit me, and I began to laugh. Once it started to sink in, I really started to laugh, and finally, I had to get out of the car; I was laughing so hard. There I was, standing in the pouring rain, laughing my foolish head off. I said, *"Thank you, Jesus."*

You see, I remembered the warning I'd gotten earlier—that the devil knew why I was going to Florida, that he didn't like it one bit, and that he was going to try to stop me. Well, that message I'd heard had been repeated. This was the next catastrophe—avoided.

"Satan, you're all show! And you're kinda funny, at that! Is that the best you've got? Come on, Devil, gimme your best shot. God told me I'm going to Lakeland. You can't stop me… and you don't scare me!"

You see, I figured out that all this was God throwing a monkey wrench into the devil's timetable… he probably had another head-on collision with a drunk planned for me just up the road a bit.

From then on I had to take the time to approach each traffic light from a considerable distance because the emergency brake would only slow me down a little, and for the last one hundred miles or so, the gas gauge was below empty… I coasted on into Plant City, *broke, on fumes, and with no brakes!*

Chapter 8

After staying a few weeks in Plant City with the Garrisons, we located a house for rent on Oppitz Lane in Lakeland, just off South Florida Avenue, and quickly settled in. The landlord simply couldn't figure out why he was agreeing to rent us this home without any deposit and agreeing to let me pay him after the first month—not before. I soon got work as a typesetter at the *Tampa Tribune* through my Typographical Union membership.

Shortly after settling in at our new home, we began to look for a church home. I soon began to hear good things about Rev. Karl Strader at the First Assembly of God church on E. Main Street, near Lake Bonny, in Lakeland. Theirs was a congregation of three hundred to four hundred, and although it was a Pentecostal church, Pastor Strader was a man ahead of his time.

My first visit to First Assembly was on a Sunday evening, and I decided to check things out. As I recall, the service began at about seven, so I got there a little before the service began. As I mingled around, a young couple approached me, and the woman said, *"I know you."*

I told her that wasn't possible because I was new in town. In fact I'd just arrived from California. She persisted, *"I know you. I recognize you from a vision I had two nights ago. God showed me that you were coming to Florida to begin a great work here, and I also saw spiritual warfare in the heavens over your coming here."*

About that time another lady, in her thirties, overheard the conversation, and she cried out, *"I had the same vision Thursday night. I saw you too. You're the same man in my vision."*

This was surreal—almost *spooky*. Here were two ladies I'd never seen and who'd never seen me, and they recognized me from a vision they received from God. From that moment on I never questioned the wisdom of coming to Florida.

We'd started having meetings in the home of a local doctor in Lakeland, and right away our meetings were packed with young people I'd brought in off the streets. I'd been working as a typesetter at the *Tampa Tribune* for a few months when one day I had a severe case of strep throat, and I was too sick to go to work. I put a call in to the union boss, explaining about the strep throat, but that night I managed to make it to the meeting in the doctor's home not only because the doctor said he had some medicine for me, but also because I specifically wanted prayer for healing of the strep throat. However, someone (I never learned who) saw me going to the meeting that night and called the union boss, informing him that I'd been at a meeting instead of at work at the *Tribune*. As was the case in California a few years earlier at the *Garden Grove Evening News* when the union repeatedly tried to fine me because of my fast typesetting speeds, I began to get the same complaints at the *Tampa Tribune*. They continued to warn that if I'd only slow down because my greater production was knocking others out of a job, the call I received the next day wasn't a huge surprise. It went something like this:

"So you're too sick to come in to work, but not sick enough to be out and about, eh? Well, try this on for size—you're fired."

I'd already been catching quite a lot of heat at the newspaper for my Christianity because I wouldn't join in and become one of the gang, going out to lunch with them and joining in with their dirty jokes and all, so when I got the news I'd been canned, I wasn't surprised. I'd never heard of the *union* ever firing one of its members, especially a skilled journeyman with several years' experience and several years of steadily paying my union dues, but I was fired.

The day I got the news I'd been fired was on a Sunday—July 26, 1969. I remember the date because just one week earlier I'd been at work at the *Tampa Tribune*, and in the proofreader's room there was a television set up on the wall, and everyone in the printshop watched that night as Neil Armstrong stepped out onto the surface of another world and said, *"One small step for (a) man, one giant leap for mankind."*

A few weeks later I took five members of my team to Ybor City, which was a rough ghetto in a suburb of Tampa, and we began witnessing to anyone willing to listen. This was a gang-infested neighborhood, and I sensed we were never far from danger. Twice that night officers in a patrol car stopped to warn us of the dangers, and the third time they stopped us and warned that one of their informants had heard that someone in a nearby black gang was going to drive by and open fire on us. At that time I'd never heard of drive-by shootings, but we came close to being victims of one that night. We'd witnessed to many, and one young black man had knelt with us in prayer to receive Jesus, so I felt we'd accomplished what we'd set out to do, and so we left.

Right away I started to go out onto the streets of Lakeland on Friday and Saturday nights talking to the scores of young people who congregated in front of a hamburger joint on South Florida Avenue, and I soon learned there were so many young people involved in drugs. Getting high was just as big a problem there as it was back in California. This wasn't the far-out *flower power* crowds of Huntington Beach or Haight-Ashbury; this was Lakeland, Florida, in the middle of the Bible Belt.

I wasn't some Bible-waving fanatic standing on the street corner, screaming hellfire and brimstone, but I simply met with the young people, usually three or four at a time, and told them about Jesus and his love and how he could change their lives.

It wasn't long before many young people began to come to the Lord, having dramatic conversions, and the word spread quickly. Soon I was followed by reporters and newspaper photographers almost every time I was out there on the streets, and very quickly my work began to frequent the front page of the *Lakeland Ledger*, and instead of it being negative publicity, which you'd expect, it was all quite positive. This newspaper was published by John R. Harrison, who was also a vice president of the *New York Times*. Later I came to know Jack Harrison, and I believe we shared a friendship and mutual respect for each other.

And it wasn't long before I was surrounded by Christians who were eager to get involved and help in this work. We also found a group of mature Christians who wanted to serve on our board of directors, and soon we hired an attorney to draw up the papers for a nonprofit corporation. I was not sure these men had ever encountered anyone like me before. I wasn't their idea of a traditional preacher, and I didn't fit into their mold of Pentecostal or Evangelical or whatever. They didn't know how to put a label on me, but they knew that I was bold for Jesus, and I was out there getting things done. That was the beginning of what we called Youth Challenge.

I located an empty building, which had previously been a biker bar hangout, and soon opened it up as the Dove coffeehouse (the dove being one of the symbols of the early Church). I was also not a bad amateur sign painter, and I painted a large red-white-and-blue sign on the side of the building, about eight to ten feet tall, that said, *"You've got a lot to live… Jesus… has a lot to give,"* and this was modeled after the Pepsi logo, with Jesus being in the middle, where "Pepsi" would have been. It was somewhat corny, but it was catchy, and it looked good, like it was painted by a professional.

A few months later I received an invitation to speak at an Assembly of God Church in Clearwater, which was across Tampa Bay, about an hour's drive away from Lakeland. I had sent advance teams of some of my young converts over to Clearwater on Saturday to begin witnessing to young people in the area, and they spent the night in one of the homes of a church member, so when I arrived that Sunday morning, the church was packed, and many of those in attendance were street people, dopers, and gangbangers. All these were young people who had been scooped up from the streets and local hangouts, and all of them got saved that morning. One of them was dramatically set free from some heavy demonic activity. I was always amazed and somewhat in awe when these things happened because I knew that I'd had little to do with it—the Holy Spirit had done all the work for me, so I was certainly not about to take credit for it.

So I was a bit bewildered when I got a call from the pastor the following Monday, and he began railing against me and generally tearing me down. When I asked why, he said, *"Because I heard you were a divorced man, and I've never let anyone ever preach from my pulpit who was divorced. If I'd have known that, I would never have invited you."*

Once again I saw that religion had reared its ugly head and tried to undo the work of the Holy Spirit, so without any attempt to defend myself in this man's eyes, the following morning I simply returned the offering I'd received. I sent the money back and never heard from him again, but I sensed that the results would be long-lasting and would benefit his congregation and the surrounding community.

That experience, among others, made me sometimes wonder about the wisdom of all this—of my striking out on my own and heading off to Florida. I had quit my good-paying job with the newspaper in California, I didn't have the backing of any group or denomination, and within a few months of my getting the job as teletypesetter operator and Linotype operator at the *Tampa Tribune*, I got fired. I was getting some firsthand lessons on how to live by faith.

Soon, the Dove was filled with young people, most of them off the streets. Some were dopers, others were just criminal types, and many were just recreational drug users. Then of course, there were those who came in just because of the curiosity factor. After having been open for a few weeks, a young man named Wayne Friedt, who had been a major drug pusher to the locals in the Lakeland area, came in, and he introduced himself to me. Wayne was a new believer, not one of my converts, but he'd recently had a dramatic conversion. Earlier, Wayne had reached his low point, a point where so many had to reach before coming to the end of themselves, and several times he'd tried to work up enough courage to commit suicide. Many times he told of putting a gun to his head, but each time something stopped him from pulling the trigger. Once, in final desperation, he said, *"I'm just not going to think about it. I'm going to get high and then pick up the gun and pull the trigger."* Each time God intervened.

As I said, Wayne was also a major drug dealer in that area. He usually managed to keep a step ahead of the law because he didn't fit the usual profile as one of the stoner types. Wayne was always well-dressed and had a clean-cut appearance. But he finally got busted, and he managed to find himself in jail, and while he was locked up, he met a man in there, and they struck up a conversation. Wayne told him about his struggles and his thoughts of suicide, and the cellmate kept telling him, "Yeah, but what if you're wrong? What if there really is a hell?"

Wayne soon submitted to the tugging at his heart, and God reached down and gloriously saved him... while he was on his Harley-Davidson motorcycle. He now pastors a church in North Lakeland called the Believers' Fellowship and has been faithfully serving God all these years.

But shortly after Wayne came to the Lord, he got a call from one of the local churches about a young man in jail, and they (the church) had felt led to bail him out. Wayne said he would take the money needed to get him out of jail, but the help would be conditional—only if the young man would promise to come to the Dove coffeehouse on Friday and Saturday nights and to go to church on Sundays and if he would agree to these conditions for the month or so he would have remained in jail... that would be the price for his freedom.

So Wayne bailed a young sandy-haired Danny Jones out of jail and brought him to the Dove. Although Danny resisted, soon afterward Danny was saved and filled with the Holy Spirit, and he too has been serving God since then. Wayne and Danny were a vital part of our team over the next few years.

Bill Green comes to Florida…

Shortly after establishing the ministry in Lakeland, I contacted Bill Green, the former heroin addict from Santa Ana who had been found in a drug stupor and hiding out in his parents' doghouse, and I asked if he was in a position to leave California and join me in our work in Florida. A few weeks later I picked Bill up from the airport in Tampa and brought him back to our home on Oppitz Lane. Bill worked with me as the invitations came in for me to speak in local churches, and this continued off and on for the next several years, with Bill ministering at the piano followed by my speaking.

To my knowledge Bill never went back to using heroin, but I knew that staying free of his addictions had always been a struggle, and I also knew that he loved the Lord. This was one of the questions for which I'd never found an answer—how some of the addicts had such a complete and instantaneous deliverance from their addictions while for others it was a continuous struggle.

Meanwhile, his music continued with an amazing anointing. Most of his music were all his own compositions, and it was never used as background for any of the ministry. His was a unique gift that God used to touch people's hearts. I was the speaker, and Bill played the piano, and time after time he would play one of his compositions, and these musical masterpieces never had any explanation as to their meaning or background; he simply played, and the audience was usually moved to tears or to standing ovations or both.

I had never felt that I had been called to provide Christian entertainment—you know, to bring out the crowds and put on a good show. To me, if it wasn't used to minister to people's needs and to touch their hearts and lives, it was superfluous and a distraction. Although there is definitely a place for Christian entertainment, I believe that's fine so long as that's the way it's presented in the first place. So much of Christianity had turned into being just another form of show business, and that simply wasn't the road I'd been called to travel.

But we had been blessed with so many talented Christian musicians and singers throughout our work there—people like Bill Green and Paul Luttrell who had a special musical gift for singing and playing the guitar. Then there was Grace Carter who had the voice of an angel and who could move your heart to tears with her singing. Grace was only fifteen or sixteen when she first came to work with us in our ministry, but she had a talent that was well beyond her years and an anointing that could have come only from God. And there were young men like Randy Horton and Charlie who could have easily had careers as professional entertainers but who were with us every weekend ministering at the Dove instead.

One Saturday night after the meetings at the Dove coffeehouse, I was heading home on Highway 92 when I felt the Lord urging me to continue on into Plant City, and just after coming to the first stoplight in Plant City, I felt the Lord telling me, *"Turn right at the next intersection."*

Since this was a very strong signal I felt coming from the Lord, I obeyed, wondering what was going on. After driving a couple of blocks, I felt the Lord again, saying, *"Turn right,"* so I did so. Then about halfway down the block, I again felt the Lord, this time saying, *"Stop and go up to that house."* That house was in the middle of the block, and as many homes in the South had large screened-in front porches, this home's front-porch light was on, and a shirtless young man stood next to the door. As I got out of my car and walked toward him, he said, *"What took you so long?"*

As I approached and introduced myself, he explained he'd decided to commit suicide that night, and he'd called out to God in desperation, that if God was real, and if he knew who he was and what he was going through, to send someone to him that night, *"Otherwise, I'm going to kill myself."*

Isn't it amazing how God knows everything about us and that he's even numbered the hairs on our head? The young man surrendered to the Lord that night right there on his front porch. He soon came to our meetings at the coffeehouse, and he was one of the ones I baptized in Lake Morton.

a reporter looks for a "gotcha" story...

During that time we also rented a two-story white wood-frame house that our young people called the Jesus House. This was an older home, but it had plenty of room, and there were times when we would receive young parolees who were conditionally released to us from one of the youth prisons.

One day a reporter from the *Lakeland Ledger* newspaper called me up and told me of a story she intended to run regarding the Jesus House, so I went to the *Ledger* to meet with her. Apparently, this female reporter had actually crawled under the house, dragging herself through the dirt and cobwebs, all in an effort to have a "gotcha" story about *those hypocritical Christians* staying at the Jesus House. She located some half-empty liquor bottles that were apparently hidden there by one of the young people staying at the center. You could actually see the glee in her eye as she told of this find and how she had intended to expose us. The world takes delight in finding fault with Christians because it tends to justify their own lives, lives without faith, and it tends to validate their criticisms of Christianity.

Of course, what she had found was absolutely true. We did have troubled youths staying at the center, and many were struggling to find their way. Finding bottles of booze under the house didn't surprise me in the least. But the point was, the world (and the world's system) loves to find blemishes on the faces of Christians and loves to point them out when they do. That's just the god of this world's way.

When the publisher of the newspaper, John Harrison, heard about the story she intended to run, he canceled it. I think he realized it had little news value, and it would only underscore the fact that we were working with troubled youths. But the point was, the reporter wanted to dig up some dirt on local Christians. It makes people of the world feel good when they can uncover something like this, and they take particular delight in doing so. They're eager to point the finger and shout, *"Hypocrite!"* Are they right? Sometimes. None of us are worthy to even call out his name. It's just that the world cannot understand his grace and mercy. I am certain that at some point after writing my story, someone's going to want to point the finger at me, saying, *"Hypocrite!"*

God had his hand on Bill Davis…

One Friday night we'd had an unusually large group at the coffeehouse, and we had a large crowd gathered inside and also another large crowd gathered outside next to the building where I had a stage constructed. We often had Christian musical groups perform, and many would give their testimonies of how the Lord had changed their lives, and the young people always enjoyed it. I think they also liked the bonfires and the hot dogs and marshmallows. I was speaking to a crowd inside the Dove while another Christian musical group played a mixture of soft Christian rock that night on the stage outside.

I didn't notice it, but a young man had driven by and noticed the Jesus (Pepsi) sign and stopped for a while, then pulled off. I later learned he did this three times, each time sitting in his car, tempted to come in, and then each time driving off, muttering to himself, *"Naw, that's not for me—that's for those sissy Christians!"*

By that time, the band had stopped playing, and most of the people had come inside when Bill Davis entered the door. I then began to get a word of knowledge about him, and I began to tell him things about his life.

Let's hit the Rewind button for a minute and go back a few years to Bill's life in 1969.

Bill had been a thief and a burglar, and he'd been deeply involved in drugs, especially heroin, and he was *hooked*. When heroin sinks its teeth into someone, it seems their lives revolve around scoring more dope at any cost. A few years earlier he'd gone to the Sunset Strip in Hollywood where he tried to pull off an armed robbery of a mom-and-pop grocery store. When Bill pointed his gun at the elderly man behind the counter, the man simply said, *"Young man, I'm not going to give you my money. But I do want to tell you that Jesus loves you, and I love you too."*

Frustrated and angry, Bill stormed out of the store empty-handed, mumbling to himself. Still mad about the foiled robbery, it was only a matter of minutes before someone came up to him and *robbed* him *at gunpoint, taking his gun and what little money he had left.*

He was still high from drugs he'd taken earlier that evening when he noticed a building where a number of young people were coming and going. Thinking this was some kind of a head shop (a doper hangout), Bill went inside and headed upstairs into a dark room where he could hide from himself and from everyone else.

About that time a man came up to Bill and said to him, *"Young man, God's got his hands on your life."* He went on to say, *"God said that 'in the last days He'd pour out of His spirit upon all flesh, and His sons and daughters would prophesy, that young men would see visions and old men would dream dreams'* [see Acts 2:17–21]... *son, that's you. God's called you."*

It turned out that the *head shop* Bill had tried to escape in was actually a Christian coffeehouse, and the man who spoke to him was Arthur Blessitt, who became famous for walking thousands of miles around the world, carrying a wooden cross, even witnessing to such world leaders as Fidel Castro.

By this time Bill was really flipping out, and he ran out of the building, not knowing what to make of what'd just happened.

It wasn't long before Bill was arrested. With a number of outstanding felony warrants, he faced some serious jail time. While awaiting trial he found himself locked up in the Los Angeles County Jail. In the adjoining cell was another young man, also a druggie, named Charles Manson, who was awaiting trial for the Tate-Labianca murders that shocked the world. During the weeks leading up to his court hearing, Bill and Charlie struck up something of a friendship, and Manson even put a tattoo of a spider on Bill's ankle. When Bill's arraignment came up, he was shocked to hear that the charges against him had been dropped. This wasn't the last time Bill would hear a judge say, *"Son, I don't know why I'm doing this. God must have his hand on you because all the charges have been dropped."*

Bill's parents lived in Auburndale, Florida, so when he returned to Florida, where he'd been raised, he began to take to his old habits of burglarizing homes and businesses all over Lakeland and the surrounding areas. He'd learned many of his burglary and safecracking skills from an inmate in prison called Slick Willy, and during his time locked up, he committed dozens of burglaries of homes and businesses in the Lakeland area.

Lakeland is in Polk County, Florida, and there was a certain judge who got the nickname *the Hanging Judge* for his reputation for being tough on criminals… especially when he was wearing his red tie! And the last thing you wanted was to come into Judge Amidon's courtroom when he was wearing that red tie! You see, Bill had applied for a job a few days earlier, and when he was burglarizing this particular home, the job application fell out of his pocket and landed on the floor. The home he was burglarizing was the home of a church deacon where Judge Amidon was also one of the church elders. But once again, he heard the judge tell him, *"Son, I don't know why I'm doing this, but I'm going to let you off with time served. But I don't want to ever see you back in my courtroom."*

For some reason, no one picked up on the fact he had other outstanding warrants, and so Bill was free again.

Yet just as surely as if Judge Amidon had sentenced him to prison, he was still a prisoner to his life and to his heroin addiction.

This hard-as-nails judge let Bill off easy, and soon he was back out on the streets. During this time his heroin habit continued to take its toll. He knew he was sick, but when he began spitting up blood, he got a sense of just how bad his condition had gotten.

He managed to make it to a hospital in Winter Haven, and after performing a number of tests, the doctors hooked him up to electrodes so they could monitor his condition. Soon one of the physicians came in to the emergency room and informed him that if they didn't operate immediately, he would likely be dead within twenty-four hours. Bill's heroin addiction was worse than ever, and he was hemorrhaging and bleeding out both ends.

That seemed to be the last straw. He felt his life was already pretty much in the toilet, so when he got the news that he was dying, he sat up on the gurney, ripped out the IVs from his arms, and said, *"I'll be damned if I'm going to lie here and die on some operating table."*

He then headed off for Tampa where he knew he could score some heroin. When he arrived, his friend who had the heroin wasn't home, so he broke in, and he stole three bags of heroin along with an outfit (syringe and surgical tubing). He decided he was going to drive to Auburndale, park in front of his mom and dad's home, and overdose on the heroin. This wasn't as it seemed though—certainly not a way to get back at his parents. Bill just didn't want them to be saddled with an expensive ambulance bill. He just wanted to *check out of his miserable life and OD.* To him his life was over.

This was where things got interesting. In order for him to drive from Tampa back to Auburndale, Bill had to drive on Highway 92, and this route took him right past my Christian coffeehouse in Lakeland. So as he drove by, he saw a crowd gathered around a bonfire outside the coffeehouse, where a group was playing Christian music; after seeing the crowds and seeing the Jesus (Pepsi) sign, he thought about it and then drove off. Three times Bill sat there, thought about it for a while, and then said, *"Naw, that's not for me"* and drove off, but each time he found he was drawn back there, and he didn't know why. The third time, he got out of the car and walked up to the front door at the Dove coffeehouse, made it through the crowd that had gathered outside, and came through the door. I noticed Bill right away, and when he stood there, I received a supernatural word of knowledge from the Lord, and that's when I said to him, *"Son, God's got his hand on your life. I know because tonight you were going to take your life."* I then went on to say, *"But God said that 'in the last days I will pour out of my spirit upon all flesh, and your young men shall see visions, your old men shall dream dreams, and on my servants and on my handmaidens I will pour out of my spirit and they shall prophesy'"* (see Acts 2:17–21). Without knowing it, I'd told him the same thing and even quoted to him the same scriptures that he'd heard a few years earlier when he went into Arthur Blessitt's coffeehouse in Hollywood.

With a stunned look on his face, he walked over to me, and without hesitation, he dropped to his knees and began to weep and cry out to God. You could almost feel the weight of the world and years of crime, prison, and addiction lifting off him. I led him in prayer, and within minutes, Bill's weeping and repenting began to turn to joy—Bill was being set free! Right then and there, Bill was being saved by the same God who had his hands on him for all these years. And within moments, Bill was baptized in the Holy Spirit, speaking in a heavenly language and praising God. Bill later said he couldn't understand why he was speaking *Greek!* I tried not to be jealous because Bill had received, within minutes, what I'd prayed and fasted for a year and a half before receiving. Wow! God touched Bill—big time, right then and there.

This went on for several minutes before he eventually rose to his feet. The next thing I noticed was that he had a surprised look on his face. He began to move his hands over his body and over his stomach area as if to check himself out, and as if in disbelief, he said, *"I don't know what's happening, but I think I've been healed—I think I'm healed."*

I said, *"Healed... healed of what?"*

He then told me about being in the hospital a few hours earlier and getting the news that he was dying from internal bleeding because of his heroin habit.

Without my knowing about it or praying for it, Bill received an instantaneous healing.

Soon he was shouting, *"No, I know I'm healed. I'm healed."*

By this time several of us had been standing around Bill, giving him hugs of encouragement, and I told him he should go back to the doctor to confirm this new diagnosis.

So that same night Bill returned to the hospital where he saw the same doctor who'd told him earlier that day that he would be dead within a matter of hours if they didn't operate immediately. Bill said to the doctor, *"Hey, Doc. I don't need that surgery."*

The doctor said, *"Why not?"*

Bill replied, *"Because I got healed."*

"Healed... who healed you?" the doctor asked.

"Jesus. Jesus healed me, Doc," Bill shouted out.

"Oy vey," the doctor cried out. *Oy vey... Bill's doctor was a Jew!*

Bill told his incredible story to the Jewish doctor, and the astonished physician had to know more about this, so Bill brought him to the coffeehouse the next night, where the doctor accepted Christ as Savior... the *Jewish* doctor found Christ as his long-awaited Messiah! *(Yes! Yes! Yes!)*

Bill never looked back, and after working with me at Youth Challenge for a while, he went on to start a large and thriving church in Tampa... a church filled with over one thousand young people seeking a real life with the Son of God, and today Bill Davis has a worldwide ministry, often preaching throughout Europe, Asia, and Africa. Through Bill's ministry and his compelling testimony, it's estimated that at least five hundred thousand people have given their lives to Christ. A few years later the 700 Club ran a reenactment of Bill Davis's conversion on national television, which was broadcast in thirty countries, and a similar documentary reenactment was run on Dutch TV, and not only Holland heard his story; it was carried throughout all of Europe.

Soon after that, Bill led a man named Lowell Dudding to the Lord, and it wasn't long before Lowell was the pastor of a thriving church of young people in Brandon, Florida. I still hear reports of the ripple effect from those days and how many people are still coming to the Lord as the results of those outpourings of God.

You might question this idea of pastoring when, obviously, these young men had not gone to any seminary. You see, we get back to the premise of the way the early Church functioned. No one told Jesus's followers that they couldn't be pastors or apostles or evangelists or that they had to go to four years of divinity school at the Holy Church of the Whatever! They just did it, and they were ordained by God. God chooses whom he will, and if you wait for man to put his stamp of approval on what you do, you'll probably miss out on what God's doing.

I was licensed for the ministry by the United Evangelical Churches, but not because I had passed any courses. They recognized that I had a calling from God and that his calling was all that I needed. This simply meant that they recognized and confirmed what God had already done in me. And the only reason for the formality of papers was so that I wouldn't be hassled in getting into the prisons to bring the message of Christ. I certainly didn't want to be called Reverend because the title implied that I was somehow to be revered…

Chapter 9

It was 1972, and our group from Youth Challenge began to go to weekly rock concerts held in Lowry Park in Tampa. The Hillsborough River runs through the park, and it has a unique natural scenic beauty. This rock festival usually had anywhere from fifteen hundred to five thousand people, sometimes more, and it was the scene of loud acid rock music and getting high. Each Sunday we would travel to the park, and right in the middle of the rock festival, we put up a large wooden cross made up of railroad ties. This was the same cross we kept on the stage at the Dove coffeehouse.

Our message was simple:

"Jesus is real… and he's Son of the living God. He loves you and wants to give you life. We didn't come here to preach or condemn. We came here to show you how to have life, and that's through Jesus."

Immediately we began to see results. Some of the most-hardened dopers there were softening up, and several had asked to receive Jesus as Savior. Much like the hippie scene in Huntington Beach, the drugs were everywhere, and the smell of marijuana filled the air. Sales of heroin were made right out in the open, and many of them danced around with visions of mushrooms in their head, high on LSD. It truly was a scene—sex, drugs, and rock 'n' roll.

By the third Sunday that we'd been coming to the rock festival, one of the members of the rock band summoned me to the microphone, and I got the sense he wanted me to get up on the stage to see if I'd make a fool of myself. He demanded, *"You keep saying Jesus is real… come on up here on the stage and prove it,"* and when I jumped up on the stage, he handed me the microphone.

As was the case with most rock festivals of that time, this one was also known for its open use of drugs, and occasionally, you could see someone shooting up heroin, and it seemed pot smoking was everywhere, so much so that you could get high just walking around because the pot smoke filled the air. Some were having sex in sleeping bags during the concerts, but when I took the microphone, all went quiet. The Holy Spirit seemed to descend on the crowd like a love blanket for some five thousand or so people. Then I began, *"Just as real as I'm standing here... Jesus Christ, the Son of the living God, is here. He's real, and he's here. We didn't come here to talk to you about religion—religion never saved anyone, and religion never helped me. We're here to talk about Jesus. If you're quiet and listen to your heart, you'll feel him. He's got your heart in his hands right now. I know you feel it. You can feel your heart beating, pounding in your chest. Call on Buddha, call on Allah—nothing happens! Call on the Hindu gods, and nothing happens! But CALL ON JESUS, and he will touch you on the inside, and you'll know it's him! Just when I said that, some of you felt your heart skip a beat. Some of you felt a lump in your throat. That's the Spirit calling you to him. Jesus loves you. Did you hear me? Jesus loves you. He didn't come here to condemn you, and we sure didn't come here to talk about church or religion, but to love you and share Jesus with you. Some of you feel him right now... and in your heart you know it's him! The word of God says, 'The words that I speak to you are Spirit, and they are life,' and if you act on those words, you will RECEIVE LIFE! If you just surrender to him, every one of you can be saved."* Then I said, "Many here have had their lives touched by Jesus. Dopers, pushers, prostitutes. It doesn't matter. Whatever you've done, Jesus already took the rap for you so you'd never have to stand before God and hear the word, 'Guilty!' We're going down to the river and baptize those of you who have given your lives to Jesus."

As I jumped down from the stage and began to walk the one hundred yards or so to the river, I heard a commotion behind me, and after walking some distance, I turned around, and to my amazement, everyone—*everyone*—was leaving the rock festival and going down to the river. The entire rock festival emptied out and followed me to the river to watch the baptisms.

By this time there was a line of young people waiting to be baptized.

The first was a young man, Lucky, who'd lost both his legs in Vietnam; he struggled down the bank of the river to me, and as I lowered him into the water, when he came up out of the water, it was as if the heavens opened up, and the Holy Spirit poured out an endless river of love over him. He lifted his face toward heaven and spontaneously began to praise God. It was then that I looked up, and to my astonishment, I remembered my vision that was being played before my eyes exactly as I'd seen it nearly three years earlier as though in instant replay:

"I saw trees along a riverbank heavily laden with Spanish moss, and the banks were filled with hundreds, maybe thousands, of people watching as the new Christians went down into the water. And as they came up out of the water, the Spirit of the Lord descended upon them, and with a heavenly glow about them, they lifted their hands and began to praise God. This dream went on for a long time, and each new convert came down into the river to be baptized, and the crowds of onlookers were amazed at the scene."

Even down to the leaves on the oak trees and the Spanish moss, everything was the same. This was the literal fulfillment of that vision. When I went home later that evening, I fell to my knees and wept. God had told me what was going to happen years earlier, and it happened exactly as he said it would.

We continued to go to the rock festivals every weekend for several months, and on one particular day there was a riot at the rock festival.

We had been there witnessing and leading many to Christ when I suddenly heard shots ring out. I looked up and saw a young man running as fast as he could run, pointing a gun in his outstretched arm. He caught up with another young man, and he wrestled him to the ground. This was no longer the peaceful flower-power hippies of the late sixties. Flower power had turned ugly. This all happened within fifty feet or so from where I was standing in the river, baptizing people. He sat on the guy, and then he pointed the gun directly at his face... his white-knuckled fist was shaking, and I could tell he desperately wanted to pull the trigger. This was one of the young men who'd tried to beat him to death a few minutes earlier when he'd attempted to make an arrest, and his rage almost overtook him. But instead he rolled the man over, handcuffed him, and placed him under arrest. He was an undercover narcotics officer.

When the police van pulled off with the prisoner inside, an angry mob tried to stop the van. They were pushing it violently back and forth in an attempt to flip it over, rocking it from side to side. Again gunshots rang out... *bang, bang... bang, bang, bang,* and soon it sounded like machine gunfire. There were local members of the Hessians motorcycle gang roaring off on their Harleys while they turned around and shot at the police, and there must have been thirty or forty gunshots that day—bikers firing at the police, and the police firing back. Amazingly, no one was hit by all the bullets flying around.

Meanwhile throughout this riot, throughout all the gunfire and confusion, I continued with the baptisms in the river. It was then that I noticed a young man wearing what looked like army fatigues, standing on the bank of the river.

After I finished the last baptism, I climbed up the muddy riverbank and walked over to him. By this time a police helicopter, along with eight or ten police cars, had arrived, and the mayor had also just arrived by helicopter along with several of the media outlets with their television crews. This had been an ugly and dangerous riot, and the story hit the national news.

I approached this young man who was standing on the bank, and when I got near, I could see tears welled up in his eyes. Throughout the riot, with the crowd trying to kill the undercover cop, through all the gunshots, the screams, and the roar of the motorcycles, he had been standing on the banks of the river, waiting for me, and he had been quietly weeping during the entire time. It was then that I recognized him as I'd seen him several times in the crowd at the rock festival, and I later learned he was a major heroin dealer at the rock festival. He struggled to take in what was happening to him as he asked me, *"What do I have to do?"* as he tried to hold back the tears. I quietly led him to the Lord and then baptized him too. When he emerged from the water, he was overcome with joy. *He was set free!*

This young man went on to enroll in Southeastern Bible College in Lakeland, and I later heard that he graduated and was still serving God. I saw him a couple of years later at a printshop when I was having some of our Youth Challenge newsletters printed up, and he reminded me of that day when he had given his life to Jesus… in the middle of a riot.

The last day of the rock festivals was possibly the most memorable and remarkable of all. Each Sunday we went out there telling the people that Jesus loved them and that Jesus was real. And each Sunday we had many converted, and many were baptized.

fire from heaven…

On this particular day it was overcast, and thunderclouds were looming overhead. The wooden stage that had been constructed for the rock festival bands was huge, easily seventy-five feet long, and it was located directly under and in front of several unusually large oak trees, with the tree branches serving as a backdrop or canopy overhanging the stage.

One rock band had just finished playing, and another was setting up their equipment on the stage when it began to sprinkle. Obviously, rain meant trouble for all their electronic gear, and the leader of the group was visibly angered over the prospect of rain. It started to sprinkle a little more, and in an act of sheer defiance he grabbed the microphone, and with his other hand he began to shake his fist and point up at the sky, shouting in a loud voice, *"You've been telling us Jesus is real, and I'm sick of it. Well, if God's bleep--ing real, give us a sign!* GIVE US A SIGN! *If God's so bleep--ing real, make him stop this bleep--ing* RAIN.*"*

With his fist still clinched and shaking defiantly toward the sky, still screaming out at God, thousands of people saw lightning strike directly in front of him within just a few feet of the front of the stage, and with it came a ball of fire and a blinding flash of light! The young man ran down the length of the stage and jumped off it, screaming hysterically, running as fast as he could for parts unknown. There were newspaper reporters there that day to record the event as well. The crowd saw it all.

Not only did his defiance *not* stop the rain, but it also rained so hard it flooded the park and washed away the stage. When I left, as I was driving away, I looked back and saw the stage floating away down the Hillsborough River. To my knowledge Hillsborough State Park never hosted another rock festival.

Chapter 10

I had continued to receive a great deal of publicity, most of it favorable, in the local newspaper, the *Lakeland Ledger*. Often an article would appear on the front page, and a few times articles and pictures of me and my work appeared on the entire front page of the "Lifestyle" section of the paper. I had never asked for the publicity—it just happened. It was through this publicity that many doors began to open—in the prisons and in the schools—all this in spite of the fact I had a little ministry in a tiny coffeehouse that used to be a juke joint for bikers, but it was having a real impact.

My work was called Youth Challenge,
but one reporter got it wrong and called us Teen Challenge.

God miraculously opened up the schools to us in Central Florida, and we were able to come in and share our testimony of what Jesus Christ had done in our lives. This was a stunning and wonderful development. Because of all the media coverage, the word had spread, and somehow the invitation for us to come into the schools and share our stories unexpectedly opened up to us. So not only were we taking our team into the jails and prisons and out onto the streets, but also now the previously lock-tight doors of the school system suddenly swung wide open for us. We went to numerous high schools and a few junior highs as well, and the team I had gathered was eager to share their stories with the students.

the miracle at a high school...
We'd received a request for our team to come to a high school in Dade City, Florida, for a voluntary assembly in which all the students were invited to come in, or they could simply mill about the campus as free time since the remainder of classes had been canceled for the day. This particular assembly didn't seem to be any different from any of the others... at least not at first.

Our usual program or routine in the high schools would be that the principal would introduce me, then I would introduce each of the young men or women who would give their testimony of how Christ had freed them from drugs and crime. And after the last of our team spoke, I would usually wrap it up, commenting about the work, where we were located, and how they might get involved if they were interested.

This day the assembly hall was filled with hundreds of students, and more kept coming in. Soon it was a standing-room-only crowd with eight or ten students standing at the back of the assembly hall and up against the walls on the sides, and it was overflowing out into the foyer. The assembly was scheduled for an hour, but this day we were running a little long, and one of our speakers was still giving his testimony when the bell rang, indicating the period was up. I looked over at the principal, and instead of giving me the signal to wrap it up, he motioned to me with his hands, mouthing the words, *"Keep going, don't stop."* I later learned that the principal was a Christian.

Every time I expected a cutoff signal from the principal, he would just smile and signal me to continue. It was truly amazing because the students were taking in every word as more and more students filed in. That day something was different: the anointing of the Holy Spirit was so tangible—*you could feel his presence.* Although we knew we couldn't tell the students, *"You need Jesus"* or *"You need to get saved,"* because if we did something like that, we'd never be invited back to another school, but we were free to tell them what Christ had done in our lives.

So for the better part of the remaining hour I was able to preach Jesus with a powerful anointing, and I could sense that God was moving in the crowd of young people. I was a fairly good preacher even though I'd never considered myself to be a *great preacher*, but one of the earmarks of my ministry seemed to be that when I ministered, *the people felt his presence*, and that day everyone in the auditorium was sensing it.

By now two class period bells had gone off... meaning that we were now two hours into this voluntary assembly program that was originally scheduled for just one hour, and the principal still nodded approval. Also by this time there were double the number of people standing against the walls and in the back of the auditorium. Under any other circumstances, at a time like this I would give an altar call, but again I knew that if I did that, we would never be asked to come to another school, and yet I also knew that God was speaking to their hearts in a powerful way. I simply didn't know what to do next.

Then I heard that still small voice say to me that I should stop, be quiet, and pray. I continued on for a minute, not certain if this was truly the voice of the Holy Spirit or just my imagination, and then I heard it again, this time much clearer...

"Stop, be quiet, and pray."

So I stopped speaking midsentence and announced to the auditorium full of high school students, *"God's doing something special right now... I don't know exactly what's happening, but I don't think God's finished yet. He wants me to stop what I'm doing and pray, so I'm simply going to obey God. You do whatever you want to do... but I'm going to pray."*

I bowed my head and began to pray silently. At first I was feeling pretty awkward because for the longest time nothing was happening.

Had I really heard from God? I asked myself—still nothing. Here I was, standing alone in the middle of this big and otherwise empty stage, and still more students had been quietly filing into the auditorium. What was probably only a minute or two seemed like an eternity of silence. This was awkward—*really awkward!* Again I questioned if I had really heard God about stopping to pray, or was it just my imagination? No one made a sound, and the silence was deafening.

And then something began to happen. In a faraway part of the auditorium I heard someone begin to weep... then another... and soon others were crying, and it began to sound like half the student body were in tears, weeping. This went on for a while, and then I looked up and saw the most amazing sight I'd ever seen. Without my saying another word dozens of young people were rushing, some running, toward the front of the auditorium... *weeping!* And when they reached the front, many fell to their knees and began to cry openly. Within minutes the front of the auditorium was filled with weeping high school students on their knees, surrendering their lives to Jesus. I still can't go back to that time and that scene without tears coming to my eyes.

We were in many high schools all over Central Florida, and the doors continued to open for us to tell our story.

One Friday we had an assembly at Kathleen High School, which was on the north end of Lakeland, and Wayne Friedt once again gave his testimony, and with power and conviction, he said the following:

"'There's no hell because there's no God'... That's what Satan said to me one night as I was about to commit suicide. I was out of jail on bond,

facing eleven felony charges that could have added up to one hundred years in prison. I was reaching for a pistol to blow my brains out when God stopped me with a vision. Suddenly, I was reliving an experience that I had in jail six months before. At that time I was going to cut my wrists with a razor blade and die in the night in my cell. Although no one knew what I was going to do, a convict of nine years started saying to another inmate, 'You know... you've got eternity out there, just as far as your mind can comprehend, and then your life, just a vapor, gone in a flash, and then eternity again. And it goes on and on and on, and there's no end. Now I don't know if the Bible is true or not,' he said, 'but if there's just one chance in a thousand that it is, a man would be an absolute fool to take his own life, knowing that the Bible says he would spend an eternity in hell'

"*I stood to my feet and lifted my hands to God and said, 'God, if you are there, I'm going to find you! And if you're not, I'm going to find that out too. But one way or another, I'm going to know. Either you are really real or you're not!' Shortly afterward Jesus Christ came into my heart and changed my life. It wasn't in church or with a preacher, but on my Harley-Davidson motorcycle when I was born again. And you too can know that God is really real!*" Wayne had been a major drug dealer in Central Florida.

There were many young people who gathered outside afterward, and several gave their hearts to Christ. Two of the boys, however, weren't buying any of this Jesus stuff, and they mocked and made gestures as we spoke to several of the others outside the auditorium. I said to them, "*Quit playing around. If you want to find out if God is real, come to our coffeehouse and find out.*" Then some of our team told them how to get to the Dove coffeehouse.

That evening several of the guys from the high school arrived at the coffeehouse, including the scoffers who had poked fun at our young people earlier following the assembly.

Meanwhile, a young boy who was crippled had come to the Dove, and he had to wear a special shoe that was built up a few inches on one of his feet. Wayne felt led by the Spirit to pray for this boy to be healed, but because of the mocking going on by the young men, he shouted to them, *"If you saw God heal this boy right now, right before your eyes, would you believe then?"*

One of them said he would, but the other one (the one who was so defiant earlier) said that he wouldn't believe even if he saw it.

We had a large wooden cross, the same one we'd taken so many times to the rock festivals, on the stage at the Dove, and Wayne seated the young man on a chair in front of the cross. We then asked the boys who had been mocking to come close, and just to let them know it was not *us* doing this, *but God,* we told them *they* would be the ones to put their hands on the crippled boy as we stood back some twenty feet away and prayed.

"I want us to pray… but I want us all to pray with our eyes open so you can see what happens with your own eyes when God heals this boy. Don't close your eyes, I want you to watch because God is going to heal this boy," Wayne said boldly.

Then we began to pray… to pray for this young boy and to pray that God would reveal himself and his power to these young men. Right in front of their eyes God miraculously touched that young boy's leg… *it was being healed, a visible healing, even as they looked on, and the boy's leg was completely straightened.* The leg that was several inches shorter than the other was now straight, and it not only straightened, but it also grew out right in front of their eyes.

"Now do you believe?" Wayne yelled out. *"Now do you believe?"*

One of the boys was so moved he fell to his knees. The other boy ran out the door and out into the street, screaming out, *"I saw it, but I don't believe it… I saw it, but I don't believe it!"* as he ran down the street, still screaming in disbelief. He was nearly hit by one of the cars as he frantically ran down the street.

Due to all the newspaper coverage of our activities, I was flooded with requests to speak—in churches, schools, and prisons. We made a regular monthly pilgrimage to the North Florida Youth Development Center in Marianna, Florida, which was basically a prison for boys. This was nearly a six-hour drive up to the Florida panhandle, but the long drive was always worth it because we saw many young men come to Christ there, and a few were released by the State of Florida to stay at the Jesus House, which was an older two-story wood-frame we had rented where some of the young people could stay, receive counseling, and get their lives straightened out.

One of those requests came from a prominent local Baptist church. Having had my earlier upbringing as a Baptist, I usually felt comfortable speaking to them.

This particular church, although not a particularly large congregation, was somewhat affluent, and many of the women often wore their Sunday best, sporting beautiful hats and fashionable attire, and most of the men were equally well-dressed. I knew this because when I first arrived in Lakeland, I had attended one of their services, and so when the invitation came for me to speak there, I was looking forward to it.

I'd had a little more than two weeks to prepare for the services at this lovely church, which looked like it had come out of one of those travel brochures, and although I never wrote out a sermon, I usually had something of an outline prepared beforehand. But as the time drew closer, I still had nothing. It was always my practice to pray and ask the Holy Spirit to lead me and let me know what it was that he wanted me to share, but when I prayed for some direction, I got nothing. Finally, the day arrived, and still I had nothing prepared ahead of time. So I simply prayed, *"Lord, show me what to do, and show me what to say to these people."*

As I sat up front on the platform next to the pastor that morning, I looked out at the crowd of about two hundred to two hundred fifty, and I saw a large sign, a message, just above the doors that entered into the sanctuary, which read, *"Go into all the world, and preach the gospel,"* which was a partial quote from the sixteenth chapter in the Book of Mark.

Suddenly, I knew what I was supposed to speak about that morning. I had the message I'd been waiting for, but I was also a bit unsettled about it.

With my earlier Baptist background, I knew that this was Jesus's marching orders for the Church, often referred to as the great commission—to go into all the world and spread the good news. Jesus had made that declaration after he'd risen from the dead and just before he ascended into heaven to be with his Father. But I also knew that this was only part of the quote about what Jesus said before he left.

I leaned over and whispered into the pastor's ear and explained to him that I had struggled with what I would be speaking on, but just then I knew that God wanted me to speak on Mark 16:15 that morning. As I held the passages in front of him, passages that I'd heavily underlined earlier in my Bible, I could tell he was familiar with it. This pastor, who was a distinguished middle-aged man, looked at me with a little hesitation, then looked back at the well-marked passages in front of him, and after a brief hesitation, he said, *"Well, I guess if you're sure that's what God wants you to speak about..."* as I sensed his discomfort even as he somewhat reluctantly gave me the go-ahead. I felt he was uncomfortable because these passages in the Bible are considered by many to be controversial as many in today's modern world don't believe that God still performs miracles, and they believe that the works of the Holy Spirit mentioned in those passages no longer apply today. As many Baptists put it, the gifts of the Holy Spirit died out with the apostles. But I knew firsthand that Jesus has never changed and that he is the same yesterday, today, and forever. I had seen firsthand the proof that God still performs these same miracles.

That passage reads as follows:

"Go into all the world and preach the gospel to every creature. He who believes and is baptized will be saved; but he who does not believe will be condemned. And these signs will follow those who believe: In My name they will cast out demons; they will speak with new tongues; they will take up serpents; and if they drink anything deadly, it will by no means hurt them;

they will lay hands on the sick, and they will recover" (Mark 16:15–18, NKJV).

As I indicated earlier, unfortunately, many leave out the remainder of that passage because either they find it offensive, or they feel that it's not politically correct, but as I also said earlier, I was through playing church, and I wasn't concerned about pleasing anybody but the Lord.

As I began to speak that morning, long before I got into any teaching as to the meanings of those verses, a hush fell over the sanctuary just as what had happened so many times before. A sense of awe and, I suspect, a little fear were present. I'm not some wild-eyed screaming preacher, but as was true, so many times when I spoke, the Holy Spirit's presence was felt, and it was tangible. And when that presence is felt—or manifest, if you will—things begin to happen because the Holy Spirit leaves no one neutral. Either you're drawn to him, or you resist and try to get away, just as they sensed the Holy Spirit in Jesus when he approached from afar, shouting, *"Who are you, the Christ? Come to torment us before our time?"* It wasn't much different that morning.

I soon sensed that there was a great deal of agitation with some of the men in the sanctuary, and before long there were three men who were coughing, writhing, and convulsing on the floor as demons began to manifest. I asked the congregation to pray because I sensed God was preparing to do something and also to pray because many in the congregation that morning were scared out of their wits. It was obvious these men were in torment, and everyone present sensed fear and awe—it was unmistakable. I quietly stepped down and walked over to them and prayed a simple prayer that they be set free and delivered from this torment, and within the next few minutes these men were wonderfully and dramatically set free—completely free. Many others surrendered their lives to the Lord that morning.

Next I noticed the pastor over in the far corner, kneeling and weeping loudly. When I approached him, he finally said to me, *"I've been preaching here all these years, and these men were comfortable during all that time. Nothing I had ever said or done had ever made any difference—I feel like I've failed."*

I comforted him and assured him that things would be different from here on and that he should follow the Lord boldly from this day forward.

Another of the invitations to speak was one of the most memorable. I had been speaking at the local ministerial association as I was often asked to do, and I had been so taken by the fact that some of the local ministers came to me like dry sponges, thirsting for more. I frequently heard comments like, *"I don't know what you've got, but I want it"* and *"I've been a pastor for thiryt years, and I feel like I need to come to you to be taught."* I had felt so inadequate, and yet here were these other ministers coming to me for help, for guidance, and for teaching.

One Catholic priest practically begged me to teach him how to receive the baptism of the Holy Spirit. Within weeks there were many Catholic priests who were seeking a closer walk with the Lord and seeking this baptism in the Spirit. A few other young priests came to my home for teaching. They were so eager to learn. There was nothing religious about what was happening.

the Holy Spirit falls on a group of teenagers...

As a result of my speaking at the ministerial association, I was invited to speak to a small group of Presbyterian teenagers who had been meeting in a cottage south of Lakeland. Their leader was a tall young man in his late twenties whose name was Ronnie Boutwell. This was supposed to be a prayer group, but it was soon evident that it was more of a social gathering that had little to do with prayer and more to do with young people simply getting together for fun and relaxation. There's absolutely nothing wrong with that, and that in itself was a good thing, but it soon became evident that many of these kids, most of them high school students, had no idea about a personal relationship with Jesus Christ.

And yet as it happened so often, when we gathered together and I began to speak, everyone there could sense a very real presence of the Holy Spirit. Again it was happening—*the sense of the very presence of God.* The first time was when I spoke to a group of young adults from Rev. Schuller's church in Garden Grove, and it was as if there were a pattern developing. As I said earlier, I never considered myself a great preacher, but when I spoke, people often sensed the presence of the Holy Spirit in a very tangible way. This was only a matter of weeks after this same presence was felt when the men were set free from demonic oppression in the Baptist church, and now it was happening again at this cottage in the south of Lakeland. It seemed, every time this feeling—this manifest presence, if you will—was sensed—*look out*—something unusual and very special was about to happen.

I told the group of teenagers, *"This is no coincidence that you're all here tonight. God saved me, and he has filled me with his Spirit… for this moment in your lives. To let you know that he is here, and he loves you. Many of you have never sensed his presence before, but you sense it now, and he is here to touch you… to touch you and to bathe you in his love."*

I didn't get much further before one of the young ladies began to weep. At first it was a wailing, loud, and pitiful weeping, and you could tell it was the Holy Spirit who was convicting her and bringing her to repentance.

I went over to her and told her this was nothing to fear and that it was actually something beautiful. I gently placed my hand on her head and began to pray with her, showing her how to ask Jesus to come into her life, and then her weeping began to gradually change from pitiful sorrow to that of overwhelming joy. Soon she was feeling real joy possibly for the first time in her life, and the tears ran down her cheeks. She was *receiving Christ in a real and personal way.*

Soon, others in the group began to weep and surrender to Christ, asking him to save them. Several times I noticed that some of these teenagers went over to a friend to ask them to forgive them for something they'd done, and then they would pray together. It was wonderful, and it was God. I simply stepped back and watched it happen. The Holy Spirit was in control, and it was beautiful. Next, *they were leading one another to the Lord!* Several times I witnessed as one of them would go to one of their friends and say something like, *"Let's get saved together,"* then they'd pray with each other to receive Jesus.

The next thing I knew, completely without any orchestration on my part, these young people began praising God—virtually every one of them had an experience with Jesus that night, and without any instruction from me, they were lifting their hands and praising God. This was not a typical sight in this Presbyterian group. It was spontaneous and completely natural and beautiful, and it was an amazing sight to see them with hands raised, tears pouring down, praising God. It was wonderful beyond description—all unscripted, by me or anyone else.

Soon another extraordinary thing happened. Many of these teenagers were being filled with the Holy Spirit, and they began speaking in tongues, raising their hands to God in praise while speaking in a heavenly language. I hadn't even *mentioned* anything about the gifts of the Spirit or speaking in tongues—it was just happening. Just when I thought I'd seen everything, they began *singing in the Spirit*—singing in a beautiful unrehearsed melody, praising God, and singing in an unknown tongue, and it was like the choirs of heaven had opened up. They were singing in their newfound heavenly language. As I said, I had not mentioned the baptism in the Holy Spirit, speaking in tongues, or anything like that to them. It was God doing this—I was merely a spectator at that point. I couldn't hold back the joy. I didn't want to even try.

Occasionally, I would glance over at young Ronnie Boutwell, hoping to gauge his reaction to all this, and it was obvious he was not receiving it well… *not at all!*

I could tell he didn't think this was how Presbyterian young people were expected to act, and I could sense he was also very uncomfortable with all this praising God, raising hands in worship, and "speaking in tongues" stuff. I sensed his uneasiness about all this, so I went over to a corner and simply prayed a very simple prayer, *"Lord, show him this is real."* That's all—just a simple prayer: *"Lord, show him this is real."*

Meanwhile, the Spirit was continuing to move in all these young people. Again, several times I noticed that someone would go over to one of their friends, often with both of them weeping, kneeling down, and asking for forgiveness for some unknown past transgression. I heard *"I'm so sorry"* several times that night—all this while the praising God and the singing in the Spirit continued.

Again, I looked over at Ronnie Boutwell to see if anything had changed, and I caught a glimpse of a most unusual, and what I thought at first comical, sight. This young man, who was well over six feet tall, had his hands outstretched—and *straight up.* Imagine, if you will, it was as though he had a couple of 2×4 boards for arms, awkwardly reaching straight for the ceiling. I gave him a puzzled look, not sure if he was making fun of what was going on or what… but one thing was for certain: his arms were stiff and straight up in the air, and he had a strange, embarrassed look on his face.

Just then I was distracted for several minutes by another young person needing prayer or counseling, and probably ten minutes went by before I looked over at Ronnie again. I was amazed—he was still standing there in the middle of the room with his arms stiff as boards and reaching straight up. I finally walked over to him, not quite certain what to make of all this. I still wondered if he was mocking what was going on with his Sunday school young people. I held back a chuckle, resisting the temptation to say, *"You are joking, aren't you?"* when I saw he had tears in his eyes. He was embarrassed and frightened. He said, *"My hands are stuck. I can't get them down."*

It was then that I received a word of knowledge, which is God's way of giving you supernatural understanding about things you otherwise have no way of knowing. Suddenly, I knew that he *had been inwardly mocking* his young people for carrying on, with all that "raising of their hands and praising God" business, and I told him just that.

Next I knelt down in front of him, and looking up at him, I said, *"God wants you to get on your knees."*

With his arms still stiff, reaching for the ceiling, he looked at me with a puzzled look, and then he dropped to his knees. The second his knees touched down, his arms fell to the floor with a thud, and it was as if a dam had broken. This quiet, reserved, and unemotional Presbyterian Sunday schoolteacher began to weep loudly and then shout out in a loud voice, *"Thank you, Jesus! Thank you, Jesus! Thank you, Jesus!"* while the tears streamed down his face.

He wept, he laughed, he shouted, and he kept crying out, *"Thank you, Jesus, thank you, Jesus!"* Within seconds the Holy Spirit fell on him, and he began to worship in the Spirit, speaking in tongues and praising God. His joy could not be contained. The next thing I knew, he got up to his feet, and he began jumping up and down, shouting, and stomping... *"Thank you, Jesus! Thank you, Jesus!"* He looked like a kid on Christmas morning, only this time his present was from the Holy Spirit, and it was life in Jesus!

Now, I've been to a real Holy Roller church before, but this was a Presbyterian group, and I witnessed something I'd never seen and probably will never see again. Ronnie then burst out the screen door, *breaking it off its hinges as it fell flat on the porch,* and he began to run around this cottage as fast as he could run, shouting and praising God and speaking in tongues! When I left, as I was driving away, I chanced a look backward and saw Ronnie—he was still running around this little cottage, shouting, and praising God.

Ronnie Boutwell later became a vital member of our Youth Challenge team, serving on our board of directors as our bookkeeper and treasurer, and now, decades later, he is still serving the Lord, and he tells me that most of the young people who were touched by Jesus that night are continuing in the faith today. Ronnie still lives outside Lakeland where he is raising his family.

the definition of a fanatic...

I'd once heard that the definition of a *fanatic* was... *"anyone who loves Jesus more than you."*

I know this next bit is really dating me *(hey, Ken, this is your autobiography, and everyone who reads it will know how old you are, dummy)*, but the Miami Dolphins went 17-0 in 1972. It was the first and only time any team had gone an entire season undefeated, and during that year I became a true Dolphins fan.

Bob Griese, Earl Morrall, Jim Kiick, Larry Csonka, Mercury Morris, and Paul Warfield made up the team that went on to reach legendary status, and they captured the hearts of football fans everywhere. We were all glued to our TV sets, and when Paul Warfield would make one of his spectacular acrobatic catches in the end zone, we'd all leap to our feet, shouting, *"All right... go, team!"* or some other intelligent and articulate football technobabble. Or Larry Czonka would take a trap play up the middle, knocking tacklers over like bowling pins, and someone would inevitably knock over the bowl of popcorn, shouting, *"Go, Czonk!"* I often hollered so much on game day that my voice was hoarse come Monday because of all the shouting over the Sunday games. A few decades later when Dan Marino was the Dolphins' number one gunslinger, setting all the passing records (some of which still stand), I was an even more rabid Dolphin fan.

The word *fanatic*, of course, is a derivative of the word *fan*, and I saw nothing wrong with being a football fan (still don't). But it's a strange and paradoxical world in which we live, isn't it? The world thinks nothing of jumping up and down and losing your voice over a football game, but let's not get too fanatical over this business about Jesus, the Son of the living God, who took the rap for us so we would never have to stand before God and hear the word, "Guilty."

If we, as Christians, *really believe* that Jesus Christ saved us from a world of sin and the fate of death and if we *really believe* that he's God in the flesh and that *"in the beginning was the Word, and the Word was with God, and the Word was God"* (John 1:12) and that Word *"became flesh and walked among us"* and that our praises are an incense to God, then why is it that we have so much difficulty with the concept of praising him?

Why is it so easy to get into all the craziness and the shouting and throwing confetti at a football game, but the idea of the man who was healed by Jesus who was seen *"walking, and leaping, and praising God"* seems so foreign and alien to us? *Don't get too excited about this Jesus business—they'll think you're a fanatic.*

If a football game is cause for excitement, then true Christians shouldn't have a problem with being thrilled and excited about being *touched by God* and being filled with the Holy Spirit.

The apostle Paul said, *"For the preaching of the cross is to them that perish foolishness; but unto us which are saved it is the power of God. For it is written, I will destroy the wisdom of the wise, and will bring to nothing the understanding of the prudent. Where is the wise? Where is the scribe? Where is the disputer of this world? For after that in the wisdom of God the world, by wisdom knew not God, it pleased God by the foolishness of preaching to save them that believe"* (1 Cor. 4:18, KJV).

"And I, brethren, when I came to you, came not with excellency of speech or of wisdom, declaring unto you the testimony of God. For I determined not to know anything among you, save Jesus Christ' and him crucified. And I was with you in weakness, and in fear; and in much trembling. And my speech and my preaching was not with enticing words of man's wisdom, but in demonstration of the Spirit and power that your faith should not stand in the wisdom of men, but in the power of God" (1 Cor. 2:1, KJV).

The world, in all its wisdom, considers the things of God to be foolishness because the world, by wisdom, *"knew not God."* Think about it. The secular world certainly doesn't ridicule and, in some ways, even reveres some holy man who believes that the spirit of an eagle was turned into a mountain or that the thunder we hear is the voice of the Father Bear, and never do you hear the secular world ridicule the shaman or an Eastern guru. They speak with a reverence when they talk of some primitive tribe's belief that their ancient forefather was a *shark who became a man* or when a *buffalo took on the spirit of a man and became the grandfather of the human race* or legends to that effect. The secular world gets all warm and fuzzy over such religious proclamations.

In films and on television, you never see a Buddhist monk or a tribal spiritual leader or a Hindu holy man from the East mocked or depicted as a religious fanatic. It's always the Christian. In the movies it's the Christian who's the wild-eyed fanatic who approaches the alien monster, only to be eaten or zapped by mysterious rays (always good for a laugh from the audience). It's the bungling, foolish-looking Christian who messes up everything, and the good guy has to come in and save the day. And it's the religious right, the fanatical Christian, who is always the butt of off-color humor in today's sitcoms or secular talk shows.

In the Million Man March, which was held by the Nation of Islam, you never heard from the National Organization for Women about the fact that in some areas in the world, in the Muslim faith, a woman is merely chattel, just property, and has virtually no rights. Women can be subjected to sexual mutilation, sometimes called female castration, because some radical Muslim men believe a woman has no right to enjoy sex, and if a young woman is found to be no longer a virgin, she can be stoned to death, but when the Promise Keepers held their sacred assembly, the NOW Group was up in arms and all over the news media about how the Promise Keepers simply wanted to subjugate women and keep them under the men's thumbs. Wow, no hypocrisy there, right? What about a Muslim woman who's been raped, but she needs a minimum of four men as witnesses, but under sharia law the man only needs one witness in his defense—naw, no hypocrisy.

Some years back I had a dream in which I saw multitudes, millions, of people heading for a cliff. As I looked closer, I saw that all the people were blind and completely oblivious to the fact that they were headed for a horrible death. And yet, they came. They came by the tens of thousands. And they continued to plunge to their deaths at the edge of the cliff. And in the dream, I saw a few men and women who were, against all odds, standing at the edge of those cliffs, shouting, trying to warn the people that if they didn't stop and turn around, they'd fall to their death.

That dream was immediately followed by another in which I was driving down a dark and winding road during a terrible storm. The road was in the middle of a forest, and just as I rounded a bend, I immediately came upon a bridge that had been washed out, and I just missed a headlong plunge into a gorge hundreds of feet below. In the dream I turned my car around and headed back up the road a ways, parking my car as best I could to block the road. I then set off flares in the road up ahead because I knew that if the oncoming traffic were not warned, they would certainly plunge to a horrible death. The dreams continued.

Next, I was in a laboratory, and somehow I had been given the cure for cancer, a formula that would cure one of the most damnable diseases mankind has ever faced. I actually had the cure—a formula, if you will—and it was all neatly written down on a sheet of paper. I folded the piece of paper and put it in my back pocket. As I left the laboratory, I was suddenly surrounded by people, people everywhere, who had cancer and needed the cure—*the cure that I had in my back pocket.* Would I be too *embarrassed* to share that cure with them? Would I be too worried they might think me a *fanatic* if I told them about the cure?

What man or woman, even an atheist, would not willingly share the cure with a cancer-riddled world? What kind of a human being would hide that cure, keep it in their back pocket, and selfishly deny it to those in need?

What man or woman, even an atheist, would not attempt to block the road and warn the oncoming traffic that the bridge was out and that to continue would mean certain death?

What man or woman, even an atheist, would not be willing to stand at the edge of the cliff and warn the multitudes that if they continued in their blind walk, they would fall to their death on the rocks below?

Who's a fanatic? Is it fanatical to tell a lonely, frightened, and dying world that the Son of the living God came down to earth and took our punishment on himself for our sins? He took the pain, the shame, and for that brief moment, the separation from his fellowship with the Father, and it was then and there that he became sin itself so that we could escape our deserved death sentence. Is it fanatical to tell a lonely, frightened, and dying world that we have the cure… the cure for that which is far worse than falling off a cliff or plunging off a bridge… far worse than cancer… and that cure will save us from death and hell itself? Who's a fanatic? Who, indeed, is the fanatic? Aw, don't get me started!

Chapter 11

There were many healings that occurred in the meetings, and aside from the boy who was healed in front of a group of mocking teenage boys and Bill Davis's miraculous healing from the bleeding ulcers, most were unspectacular. No one was raised from the dead, there were no blind eyes healed, but there were people whose vision was healed and who immediately found that their eyeglasses were useless to them, and sometimes unusual and chronic pains would go away.

One woman, although not totally without sight, had been legally blind, and when I prayed for her, I wasn't praying specifically for her eyes to be healed, but after I prayed, she couldn't use her glasses any longer because God healed her eyes. One lady was able to throw off her back brace after months of constant pain. And one man, in his midsixties, who'd been a minister for nearly forty years, was instantly healed of a two-pack-a-day cigarette habit, and he'd been smoking that way for about thirty-five years. Some were quite unusual, maybe even extraordinary, but others were of a different variety.

Although I'd first encountered this phenomenon back at the home meeting in Garden Grove with the young man who howled like a wolf, I was taken aback by the fact that when the Holy Spirit was present and there was a powerful anointing, there were so many occasions when otherworldly spirits manifested themselves, many times in very ugly ways, and they had to be dealt with.

I soon discovered that when you are filled with the Holy Spirit and you have the anointing of God, there are demons of varying rank, power, and propensity, and they can sense the presence of the Holy

Spirit in you, and they manifest themselves, sometimes very angrily. This happened to me many, many times.

The daughter of one of our close friends, whose name I will omit so as not to embarrass anyone, had some severe problems. I'd been called to the home in which she was a guest, and when I walked into her room, I could hardly believe my eyes. Shortly before I had arrived, this sixteen-year-old girl had picked up an entire bed, frame and all, and she had thrown it up against the wall. She'd torn off much of her clothing, and she'd ripped up the living room carpet, and when I entered, she was rolled up in the carpet she had pulled from the floor, rolling violently back and forth on the floor, spewing green vomit across the room and laughing and speaking in a deep guttural voice such things as, *"I'm not coming out"* and *"You can't have her... she's mine,"* along with a great deal of swearing and vile comments. Hers was one case where help did not come immediately, but gradually over time. Usually, though, those being tormented were set free immediately, and their joy was understandably overwhelming.

Over the next few years scenes like this were repeated many times, usually with similar demonic manifestations.

On another occasion Rev. Karl Strader, pastor of the First Assembly of God church in Lakeland, called me to ask for help with a twelve-year-old boy who had caused quite a stir. When I got there, this young fellow had picked up entire rows of six or eight metal chairs that had been fastened together, and he was swinging them about like a baseball bat. His deliverance came a little more easily than the girl's.

One evening at the Dove coffeehouse as we were all standing around, singing, a hellish voice cried out of one young lady, and I knew it was demonic. She began screaming a bloodcurdling scream, and I could tell she was terrified. All the while, during her screams another voice manifested from her, and it was a deep, hellish, and demonic male voice laughing and spewing out vile words. When I commanded this evil, unclean spirit to come out of her, she collapsed to the floor, and instantly the spirit went out of her and went into another young woman, and it manifested itself in the exact same voice, saying exactly the same words, and with the same hellish laugh, almost like instant replay. This wasn't the first time I'd heard two voices coming out of the same person—the first voice being their own frightened screams and the other, evil and demonic.

The second girl, whom the spirit had now entered, burst out the door and ran down the middle of the street in traffic, terrified, screaming and tearing her hair out and ripping at her clothing. I ran out into the street with traffic streaming by in both directions, and when I caught up with her, I picked her up and set her down at the side of the busy street, and amid all the traffic, I cast this demon spirit out of her. She was terrified by that experience, but when she was set free, she was overcome with joy. These were always very, very ugly experiences until, that is, they were set free. Then the ugly turned to glorious.

Soon the word was out, and people were coming to me for help from all over, even one who came for help from across the country—for *deliverance*. This was never anything that I had ever wanted or would have chosen, but it was a manifestation of a great spiritual need.

A certain man who lived in Michigan heard that there was a man in Florida (me) who had power over demons. He had a neighbor whom he later said was demon possessed, and nobody was able to help him. I'm not sure how he managed to persuade this man to make the trip, but the two of them drove straight through from Michigan to Florida, stopping only for food and gasoline until they arrived at my little coffeehouse during a meeting that was underway.

The Christian neighbor came through the door first, followed by his friend who was tormented by demons. This man, who appeared to be in his midforties, stepped through the doorway and took one look at me, and it was as if pure hatred and evil emanated from him as he gazed at me with a look that can't be described. *He was only a few feet from the door when our eyes met, and it was as if an irresistible force slammed head-on against an immovable object* as though he were trying to confront me with hell itself.

Without saying a word, I looked at him from across the room, and the instant our eyes met, the *power of God hit him, knocking him back against the wall next to the door.* He shook violently for a few seconds and then collapsed on the floor, and then deliverance came. Within minutes this man was completely set free. Oh, that more people took such matters this seriously. This Christian neighbor went to considerable trouble and great expense, giving up his time and money and driving for some twenty hours each way just to help a friend, and he did it out of love because he believed that Jesus could set his friend free.

an angel appears?...

On one Friday night at the coffeehouse a young woman was struggling with demonic influences, and we began to pray, asking for her to be set free from this terrible oppression she'd been experiencing. We brought her out of the main room and into my little office so we could have some privacy as we interceded on her behalf, and just as we entered the room, she suddenly fell to the floor and began screaming, followed by a series of dramatic and very violent convulsions. And as so often was the case, demonic voices began to speak through her—deep, growling, and angry voices that were spouting out some rather vile things. Several of us knelt down and began to pray fervently over her, demanding that these devilish forces leave her alone.

The coffeehouse was particularly crowded that night with people coming and going, but no one was milling about when we started to deal with this evil thing that had taken over her.

Then without warning, an elderly man appeared inside the coffeehouse, and without uttering a word, he lay down directly in front of my office, blocking the entrance. I soon realized this was an attempt to keep anyone out who might interfere with this spiritual warfare that was going on. I'd never seen this man before, but anyone who tried to enter my office at that time was blocked by his body, which was barricading the entrance. When I glanced in his direction, he was lying on his back, with arms raised, and he appeared to be praying very intently. This must have lasted some ten or fifteen minutes until we finally had victory over these evil forces, and once the young woman was set free, I looked up, and in the time it takes to blink, the man simply disappeared in front of us. I am convinced to this day that God had sent an angel to make certain nothing interfered with helping to free this woman.

I can't overstate it. Deliverance is not pretty, but when it comes, when they are set free, it is the most wonderful and amazing experience imaginable.

For each time someone was led to Christ or there was a healing or a deliverance or someone was filled with the Holy Spirit and there was rejoicing for those occasions, there were also the times when people rejected Christ, or there was no healing, and we were unable to effect a deliverance, or someone was seeking to be filled with the Holy Spirit, but they went away still seeking. And those are the ones that haunt me and sometimes awaken me in the middle of the night.

Deliverance—now there's a word. It also means *"set free!"* The religious world calls it *exorcism*. Unfortunately, exorcism is a religious ritual, and all it does is make the demons angrier. In fact, if you want to really make the devil mad, attempt an exorcism. *It pisses him off!* (Sorry if my crude colloquialism offends you, but I can't come up with any better way to describe just how angry religious exorcism makes the devils.) So if you seek a religious cure, try exorcism, but if you want the person to be *set free*, use deliverance through the power of the Holy Spirit. But remember Jesus's admonition when his disciples were unable to help someone who was tormented by demons. In certain situations he said, *"However, this kind does not go out except by prayer and fasting"* (Matt. 17:21, NKJV).

Late one afternoon I had been getting caught up on some of the work in preparation for our next newsletter when I looked through the large bay window of the coffeehouse and saw a man walking across the street… in what was possibly the most pathetic sight I'd ever seen. *This man was shaking and convulsing, and his entire body was in uncontrol-*

lable spasms. When he saw me looking at him, he turned and walked toward me from across the street to the front door of the coffeehouse. His legs were in such spasms that walking was nearly impossible for him. I greeted him and asked him if there was some way I might be able to help him.

His spasms made his speech completely incoherent, particularly since his tongue was violently wagging in and out of his mouth, and he was drooling saliva everywhere. In fact, everything about him was in spasms. His eyes rolled around in his head, jerking rapidly in every direction, and he tried in vain to wipe the spittle from his mouth, but his hand shook so badly he couldn't make it touch his mouth to wipe away the drool. And if that weren't enough, he was perspiring, seemingly from every pore in his body, with sweat dripping from his eyebrows and from his chin. His body odor was foul, and it was almost unbearable. His thin legs were in such violent spasms that he could barely stand, and I was so touched with this man's pain and torment that I could hardly hold back my emotions. It was then that I suddenly understood that had he been the world's only lost soul, Jesus would have gone to the cross and died to set him free.

"Do you mind if I pray for you?" I asked.

Since he was shaking so much, I couldn't tell if he nodded, and if he did nod, I wasn't able to tell if it was a yes or a no or just more spasms. I gently laid my hand on his shoulder, and quietly, in little more than a whisper, I began to pray in the name of Jesus for this thing to come out of him.

Instantly the man's shaking stopped, and it stopped completely. It was as if a terrible storm, suddenly and without warning, was completely calmed. The look on his face was one of surprise, even *shock*. His eyes were still and clear, and his tongue and his lips and his entire body had completely stopped their spasms. I knew I was dealing with demonic forces. I talked with him, and he calmly spoke to me in what was a completely normal and lucid conversation. From his speech I suspected this was an educated man.

I then explained to him that he needed to *give his life to Jesus* in order for this healing to continue. I briefly explained the story in the Bible in which when the unclean spirit had gone out of a man, it went about looking for a home, and having found none, it came back into the person, and the result was much worse than the beginning (see Matthew 12:43; Luke 11:24). He hesitated briefly, and without showing any emotion, he calmly looked me in the eye and, in a clear and unwavering voice, responded, *"No, I don't want to do that—I don't want Jesus,"* and he walked away, out the door and across the street.

By the time he reached the far side of the street, this demonic thing went back into him, and he began to spasm and convulse as badly as before. He turned and looked back at me, and his appearance seemed frightened and confused. It was as though he expected me to help in some way, but when I stepped to the doorway and looked at him, he paused for a moment, then as though he was resolved to accept his fate and live out his life in this tortured condition, he turned and began to walk away, still in spasms so that he could hardly walk. I went back to my desk and wept. I could not be consoled.

Another young man, Owen, whom I had just recently led to the Lord and I'd baptized in Lake Morton in Lakeland and who'd gone back home, joyfully proclaiming his newfound faith in Jesus, only to be harangued and ridiculed by his family for getting involved with "those Jesus fanatics," went out and hanged himself. When I heard the news, I wept. Again, I could not be consoled.

sadistic murders…

There were other failures too. A tall, lanky young man, whom the local youths called Lurch because of his resemblance to the character on *The Addams Family* television series, used to hang around the periphery of our meetings, never quite joining in. Many times we attempted to reach out to him, but he always walked away anytime I or any of our other team members approached and tried to come near to him. This went on for months—he'd come around our meetings, and he'd look on from a distance, but if anyone tried to come near, he'd walk away. It was not until later that I learned the extent of the demonic influences in his life.

Within a year or so there were news reports of a rash of brutal and sadistic murders in the Lakeland area in what was turning out to be a string of serial killings. One young lad who had been to many of our meetings, a young boy I'd personally led to the Lord and baptized in Lake Morton, suddenly disappeared. Weeks later he was finally found. An anonymous tip to police led them to drag the bottom of one of the lakes out at Christina Park where they found his body. The police discovered he'd been tied to cement blocks and tossed into the lake. The autopsy revealed he'd been brutally attacked anally with a broom handle and then bound and thrown into the lake alive, tortured, and left to drown.

Meanwhile, there was one young man who had been found burned alive in the trunk of a car.

It was not long before I heard the news of Lurch's arrest, and soon the stories began to unravel. The newspaper reports said he'd been frequenting local gay bars with an accomplice. One of these incidents occurred after they picked up a homosexual young man at a well-known gay bar known as the Green Parrot. He was then forced into the trunk of a car, then struck with a tire iron. Then they drenched the car with gasoline and set it on fire while he was still alive in the trunk, screaming for mercy. The victim could only be identified by his dental records since there was nothing else left but charred ashes.

Finally, he came to distrust his accomplice, so he murdered him as well, stabbing him repeatedly, but when his buddy refused to die, he held him underwater until he drowned. Who knows what might have happened or what might have been prevented from happening had we been able to reach this young man before he went on his murderous rampage? Even though society has a right to impose just punishment, I cannot forget the scripture that says, *"For God is longsuffering toward us, not willing that any should perish, but that all should come to repentance"* (2 Peter 3:9, KJV).

What would have happened had we persisted in reaching out to him? I'll never know. The young man we knew as Lurch was Dennis Wayne Smith, who was convicted of first-degree murder in a Florida court in 1976. It was never clear as to how many of these other murders could be linked to Smith since there was more than one case of a homosexual man being burned alive in his car.

I want to make it very clear that there was nothing inherently good in me that would cause such manifestations as demons reacting to my presence. It was simply because I was willing. The failures weighed heavily upon me then, and they still do today. I knew the successes were the work of God, so I knew not to even try to take credit for them. In fact, when something really significant or miraculous happened, I usually found it to be a very humbling experience. I couldn't heal anyone or save a soul or cast out an unclean spirit—not in my own power. On my own merits I couldn't even light a candle in the house of the Lord. So when these things happened, I knew it was not of my doing, but God's… so after something miraculous happened, it always humbled me so that I would often find a corner to weep and pray.

The film *The Exorcist,* in spite of the Hollywood sensationalism surrounding it, was not unlike some of the things I witnessed over and over, and often God used situations such as these to convince the unbelievers. If you're not sure there's a real God, after witnessing a few scenes like these, you're soon convinced of a very real Satan, and many times I've seen those who were uncommitted to the Lord, after witnessing terrifying demonic manifestation, followed by a demonstration of the Holy Spirit and power to effect a deliverance, drop to their knees and surrender to Jesus.

I always knew that I was a very flawed man, who led a very imperfect life, and if left to my own devices, I would be back to groveling in the mud were it not for God. But these were hard lessons to learn because there were struggles going on at home that could easily be my undoing…

Chapter 12

During those years in Florida I met a man named Al West who was a writer and editor for a Tampa magazine, which was where he lived. Al and I became as close as brothers, and many times he and I ministered together at a church in Tampa, where he served as one of the elders. I often spoke there, and each time there were many people who were touched by the Holy Spirit. This was a small congregation of about one hundred fifty to two hundred. It was also during those years that Al had begun to write my life story. He usually carried with him a tape recorder and a notepad, and each time we were together, he would take notes and make additions to the book. At some point, he received word that he'd been hired as the editor-in-chief at Logos International, which was one of the largest and most influential publishers of Christian books in the world at that time. This appointment would require him to move from Florida to New York.

    Al and several others often asked me when I would begin a church, because with my following, he felt I would likely be able to have a very successful church ministry. I must admit, the suggestions were tempting, not so much because I felt I was pastor material, but without a church foundation, we often found ourselves struggling just to pay the bills, and a church foundation seemed a possible source of steady support. The financial struggles, whether in our personal finances at home or in the ministry at the coffeehouse or the Jesus House, were ever present, but we always managed to pull through. The bills always seemed to get paid although God often seemed to be testing our faith by waiting until the eleventh hour before funds came in. I never had what one would call a successful ministry if you rank success by the world's standards, but although it was small, many said it had great and lasting impact. In later years I would discover how that *ripple effect* would reach out and become worldwide.

As I said, it was never my intention to build a church, and I never deluded myself that I was cut out to be a pastor. Even though I had discipled many of the young people, it wasn't quite the same as the calling to be a pastor. My gifting, if you will, was more as an evangelist and teacher.

I had led many, many to Christ*, and there were many more who had found a deeper walk with him through the infilling of the Holy Spirit. But there needed to be a covering, nurturing, and sheltering environment for these young people, and we had neither the ability nor the facilities to care for so many young and hungry Christians. Yes, there were the meetings at the coffeehouse and at the Jesus House. And at times God had given me wonderful insight and spiritual wisdom in helping to train and prepare these young people for life.

And in many respects it was the ability to teach that was the most rewarding. The response from so many hungry young Christians certainly made it all worth it. Many times it was the *teaching* that brought the young people to flock to the meetings at the Jesus House, and it was the *teaching* that had them sitting on the staircases, in the window sills, and on the porch and out on the lawns, straining to hear as I spoke. And as was the case so often, it was during the *teaching* of the Word that some miraculous things happened during many of the meetings, completely unplanned and unscripted. Often it was during the teaching that someone would be set free, or someone would be healed.

Meanwhile, the speaking invitations kept coming in to the point where I had to enlist someone to handle my busy schedule. The invitations seemed to come in from everywhere—from the churches, the schools, the service clubs, and the jails. At one of these meetings at which I spoke, which, as I recall, was with the Lions Club, there were many politicians and influential businessmen in attendance, and one congressman, a Democratic US congressman, said to me, *"I sure hope you never go into politics. We wouldn't stand a chance against you."*

One night a young African man from Kenya was visiting in Florida, and he had heard about my work.

*Someone once introduced me, saying I had led thousands to Christ. My response was, "I don't know about that, but I do know it was never enough."

He approached me before the meeting started at the Jesus House, and he asked permission to set up a big rally—possibly, a series of them—in Nairobi City Stadium in Kenya, Africa. He said he'd done this before, and he thought it would be a great blessing if I could come and speak to the large crowds that would gather. He indicated to me that he would arrange for all the promotion and for radio and television coverage—all I had to do was show up and speak. A blessing for them? I was convinced it would also be a great blessing for me.

A month or so later I received a call from him, and he said everything was set up and that we could expect around one hundred thousand people in a series of rallies at the stadium. As I recall, the rally had been scheduled to take place in about six weeks. I'd spoken to large crowds before, but nothing like this. But at that time I was operating on holy boldness, and I had no problem with the thought of preaching to that many people. I felt it would be a terrific opportunity.

So I announced it in my monthly newsletter, and soon afterward I got a call from one of our supporters, a middle-aged woman, who, as I recall, was a widow. She informed me that God had told her to provide me the money for the trip, and she said, "Don't worry about it. I'll take care of it." So a few days before I was scheduled to make the flight to Africa, I began to wonder if God was going to once again wait until the last minute before the funds would come in—still no word.

The day of departure came and went, and still I heard nothing from the woman. I tried calling her, but I didn't get an answer, and in those days most people didn't have answering machines. I called my friend in Africa and explained that the money that had been promised didn't arrive, and he said they were going to go ahead with the plans for the rally at Nairobi City Stadium, and they'd have to arrange for another speaker. He expressed his regret that I'd not be there, and I, in turn, expressed my deepest regrets that I wouldn't be able to live up to what I felt was a commitment I'd made.

A month later the same woman finally walked up to me after one of the meetings at the Jesus House and said sheepishly that she'd spent the money—no explanation, simply that she'd spent it and that she was sorry. Yes, about one hundred thousand people did attend the series of rallies in Nairobi City Stadium, but I was not the speaker.

Another disappointment was when then Senator Lawton Chiles said he had submitted my name to be considered as the speaker at the National Prayer Breakfast.

I didn't know a great deal about the National Prayer Breakfast or the history surrounding the event, but I later learned just how significant this prayer breakfast was and the role it played in Washington. Every US president since Dwight Eisenhower has participated in this breakfast event, with the list of speakers that included Mother Teresa, Dr. Ben Carson (twice, in 1997 and 2013), Max Lucado, Tony Blair, Mark Burnett, and Roma Downey.

Although I was not the one selected to speak, just to be considered for the event was quite an honor. As I indicated earlier, Lawton Chiles and I had become friends, and he'd had me over for dinner at his Lakeland home, and both he and his lovely wife, Rhea, were gracious hosts. I also met with him twice at his invitation in his Washington senate office. I mentioned that it was a disappointment because Chiles later called me and said that although he had campaigned for me to speak at the prayer breakfast, in the end someone else had been selected.

The late Lawton Chiles, US senator from
Florida, and Florida governor

Lawton Chiles died in December 1998 at the age of sixty-eight during his eighth year in his term as governor of Florida. He was found next to his cycling machine in the gymnasium at the governor's mansion in Tallahassee, dead of an apparent heart attack. When I visited him in Washington, he had a pair of bronzed walking boots next to his desk as he had been known as Walkin' Lawton, having walked more than one thousand miles throughout the state of Florida, campaigning to win his seat in the US Senate in 1970, a seat that he held for eighteen years. When mourners came to pay tribute, one woman left a poignant reminder of Sen. Chiles's campaign, a pair of her walking shoes.

Since we weren't trying to build a church, we usually directed most of the people we'd led to the Lord into the First Assembly of God church, where the pastor was Rev. Karl Strader. I knew him to be a sincere man of God, and I knew of no better place for these young people to be nurtured in the faith.

Besides, I had learned long ago that Church was not something you could attend. Jesus said, *"I will build my church, and the gates of hell shall not prevail against it"* (Matt. 16:18, KJV). And yet we all have heard of cases where church buildings were destroyed by some calamity or another, such as wars and natural disasters. Racial hatred has been the cause of many churches being burned or bombed, and certain dictators have made it their personal mission that churches be destroyed.

The Church is made up of "living stones" (believers), and he is the "chief cornerstone." That's the church. It's not a building, and I'm not sure how that building over at the corner of Tenth and Whatever ever came to be called a church. These elaborate edifices are simply glorified "sheep sheds," places to get the Christians in out of the rain or the wind and sun while they come in to be nurtured in the faith. And these living stones, we the believers, are the building materials he used for his church, and that's what he referred to when he said, *"The gates of hell shall not prevail against it."*

So when I taught these principles, it was the young people who saw and understood these revelations. Often it was the older Christians who looked at you with a glazed look in their eyes when you spoke of such things as a divine order in the Church, but the younger ones got it. I knew I needed "divine order" in my home, which included a covering, if for no other reason other than spiritual protection. I knew my own home was out of order, and I was headed for deep and troubled waters.

Chapter 13

One day Al West told me that doctors had discovered he had leukemia, which was cancer of the blood and bone marrow, and that he didn't think he would be able to finish my book. He had already moved to New York to join *Logos* magazine as editor, but on one of his return visits he and I drove to Melbourne, Florida, to meet with Jamie Buckingham. Buckingham was considered the foremost Christian author of the day, having written forty books with sales of more than twenty million. Some of the books he wrote for many prominent Christian ministries included that of Kathryn Kuhlman and Nicky Cruz.

Jamie Buckingham was a quiet, unassuming man who was very gracious, and Al presented him what he had written to that point regarding my life story. Jamie indicated he needed to finish some of his previous writing commitments, but once they were completed, he would begin work on my biography.

As I've said, Karen and I had been having difficulties for quite some time. Even though our love early on was very deep and I know we adored each other in the early years, there was trouble brewing, and I didn't know how to cope with it. And I want to make it clear from the outset that I didn't know how to cope with it. I place no blame with Karen.

At the risk of sounding preachy, I've written the next few paragraphs to explain how and why I failed. It's one thing to know the truth, but still another to live it, and I'd been so involved in the ministry God had given me I'd neglected my wife and family. The scriptures advise us, *"Wives, submit yourselves unto your own husbands, as unto the Lord, for the husband is the head of the wife, even as Christ is the head of the church..."* and then it goes on to say, *"Husbands, love your wives, even as Christ also loved the church, and gave himself for it"* (Eph. 5:22–25).

There are times I have actually wished there were separate versions of the Bible, one for husbands and one for wives, because in some ways it would be better if husbands never read the verses that spell out the wives' responsibilities to their husbands (verses 22, 23, and 24) if they're going to try to become God's enforcers. Husbands should *only* concern themselves with verse 25 where we are instructed how to do our part. Our part is not to enforce wives into obeying verses 22–24. That's between them and God, and that, my friend, is none of our (men's) business. Our only concern should be how we could learn to love our wives as Christ loved the Church and gave himself for it (Eph. 5:25).

Because if we men would do that, concentrate on loving our wives and giving ourselves to them as Christ gave himself to the Church, then the Holy Spirit would be free to supernaturally intervene and take care of our families and our family problems. It's because we (men) want to handle things ourselves and take matters in our own hands that things get so messed up.

Let's say John's wife, Susie, flatly refuses to be in any way submissive or even respectful to her husband. He decides it's up to him to be *the enforcer*. He sticks out his chest (it seems manlier that way) and shouts, *"Susie, the Bible says you're to submit to me and that you're to obey me—you got that?"*

This approach simply reinforces Susie's belief that John's really a jerk, and she resolves that she's never going to give in—not with that *"I'm the boss"* attitude.

But if John left the matter in God's hands and he concentrated on being the best husband—*the best man of God he could be by loving Susie as Jesus Christ loved the church and gave himself for it*—wow. That will sooner or later break down Susie's resistance by melting her heart and making her *want* to submit to him. If John simply used the "coals of fire" approach mentioned in the Bible (see Proverbs 25:22)—by doing so this melts her heart and *allows the Holy Spirit to work in her.*

On the flip side, here's another way to look at the matter. If a man says to his wife, *"You have to obey me—it says so in the Bible,"* then it's as if we're telling God, *"OK, God, I'll handle this. I'm trying to straighten my wife out. Can you help me out here a little?"*

God doesn't need our help. He's quite capable of handling things if we'll just get out of the way and do our part. But because we try to be the man and make things happen, we only get in the way. That's right. We get in the way of the Holy Spirit.

It's the same dilemma many Christian wives face, especially if they have an unbelieving husband. I've seen this happen many times. A wife's got a husband who's not a Christian, and after a while his habits begin to get on her nerves. Many nonbelieving husbands have some rather bad habits, and all too often the wife begins to nag her husband. She chides him with, *"If you'd only go to church with me,"* or worse, bitterness creeps in, and she says, *"I've had it with your beer cans and cigarette butts. Clean it up yourself—I'm going to church."*

Wow, that approach is going to make him get down on his knees, repent, and become a new man, right? *(Not!)* Instead he's probably thinking to himself, *If that's what Christianity is all about, forget it.*

But if Susie decides that her only real responsibility is to be the best wife she can be, then here's how things will begin to work. Susie's decided to become loving and kind and do everything for John as though she were doing it for the Lord. She brings him his coffee and says, *"Here, honey. I've discovered that Jesus wants me to be the best wife I can be, so you're going to begin to see a real change in me—compliments of Jesus."*

Do you see where I'm going with this?

Karen had felt a growing resentment toward me because I was gone so much of the time, and although I was doing God's work and reaching out and helping so many young people, I should have spread that love around by spending more time with her and the children and by doing more to show her I was loving her and giving myself to her even as Christ gave himself to the Church. I'm convinced that many of the problems we would soon face could have been overcome had I remembered these simple truths and put them into practice. I've shared these things with you so that you might begin to understand what was coming next.

Whew! Now that that's over, you probably know by now that I'd been preaching to myself—guilty as charged.

I struggled greatly over this next part of my story. I told you at the beginning that I would tell my story—that is, *the good, the bad, and the ugly*. If I followed my own advice and it still ended up with the same (sad) results, at least I would have a clear conscience.

How do I explain what happened without sounding as though I'm laying the blame on Karen? Should I just skip that part of my life and leave these chapters blank? I want you to understand what happened, but when I talk about the troubles Karen was going through, I hope you can understand that I'm not blaming her. In fact, I'm the one who failed her. If she was ill, then I needed to be there for her as the spiritual protector of her and the family as a conduit for the Holy Spirit to affect healing. I loved Karen, but I was simply unable to help her, and she repeatedly rejected any attempts to get at the root of the problem.

There were times when she was so troubled in her spirit that she would go for months actually hating me and hating everything about me. She wanted nothing to do with me, and everything I did was a source of resentment for her. I don't want to belabor the point, but at times it was quite hellish—hellish in that she sometimes got violent.

Once, while clearing the table after dinner, I spilled the pepper shaker, leaving a sizable mound of black pepper on the table. It was one of those large aluminum pepper shakers you might see in a chef's kitchen, and while I was washing the pepper off my hands over the kitchen sink, I unexpectedly got a wet sponge filled with of a heap of black pepper right in my eyes. The pain was unbelievable, and I cried out in agony. I kept splashing water on my face over and over, and eventually, I managed to get nearly all the pepper washed out of my eyes when I was hit with another sponge full of even more black pepper, again right in the eyes.

There was another time I was at the receiving end of a frying pan when she hit me over the head with it, actually denting it (the frying pan, not my head).

One night Pastor Karl Strader asked me to speak at the First Assembly of God church, and just before I walked out the front door, I was confronted with a barrage of slaps to my face, one after another after another. Resisting the temptation to hit her back, I stood there and simply said, *"Are you about finished?"* and then walked out to the car. Imagine trying to speak to a congregation of three or four hundred people with that hanging over your head.

I never quite knew how to handle these situations. I did, however, know my own strength, and I always feared what might happen if I struck back in anger, and I had never believed any man was justified in hitting a woman for any reason.

Often these scenes were in front of the children, and because of that I would sometimes pick her up, carry her to our bedroom, and plop her on the bed, saying, *"You're not going to do this in front of the children."* As I said, I'd never felt a man was justified in hitting a woman. I'd always believed that any man who struck a woman was a spineless weakling, so I managed to resist the temptation to hit her back. But there was one time after she repeatedly slapped me that, in a reflex action, I instinctively hit her with my back hand, knocking her over the bed and onto the floor on the other side. I felt terrible about it. I'd failed, and I'd failed on a matter I had felt so strongly about. I felt so very weak.

Here I was supposed to be the *man of God* and, at times, being used by God in miraculous and wonderful ways, but I was unable to bring healing into my own home to my wife who so desperately needed help. I clearly recall one time after more than a year of wanting to have nothing to do with me and hating me and everything about me, she came to me, weeping and saying, *"Ken, I don't know how you've put up with me, and I don't know why I've treated you the way I have. I am so sorry,"* and we held each other and wept. For a while things were wonderful as though we had begun a second honeymoon. Unfortunately, that only lasted for a few months.

Then without warning one day I woke up, and the hatred and resentment were there once again. I never knew from day to day which Karen I would face that day. Was it the loving, kind Christian woman I fell so deeply in love with, or was it the one filled with hatred and spewing vile curses at me? I always believed these problems had spiritual origins, but she continually resisted when anyone suggested intercession and a way for her to be free of the hate and bitterness.

I loved her, and I loved God, but at times I was sure I would lose my mind. My ministry was sure to suffer, and at times I worried that the anointing of God would slip away. But it didn't. This was all happening during the times some of the greatest moves of God were happening in my ministry. The miracles at the rock festival, at the schools, and at the prisons, when people were set free from terrifying demonic activity, and wonderful things were happening all around me, but I was failing where it meant the most—at home. Once I confessed to a close friend that it was as though World War III had begun, starting with my marriage. I hated fighting, and I had always refused to get into an argument with her, and when she seemed intent on getting me to fight with her and I refused, this made her even angrier.

And these were not fleeting incidents, but circumstances that continued for years… a seemingly endless time of spiritual victory and joy and blessing in the ministry and *trench warfare at home*. And I knew that if I failed at home, I would ultimately fail.

During another of those periods that lasted several months, during which Karen wanted nothing to do with me, at times refusing to speak to me for weeks on end or going to the other extreme striking out with pure hatred and violence, I was fighting another battle… over temptation. I had not given into this temptation, but the temptation was there nevertheless.

I can recall one temptation in particular. I had been invited to spend a weekend of relaxation at a small cottage on Little Gasparilla Island on the gulf coast of Florida. The home was owned by a retired minister who had become a close friend. He was a very active man in his midsixties, and he was also very appreciative of the work we had done in the community. He not only made frequent contributions to my work, but he also often had us over for dinner. On one particular occasion he offered to take me fishing and to spend the weekend at his cottage, which was on Little Gasparilla Island. The only way to get to the island was by boat, and so we made the crossing in his small aluminum boat with an outboard motor.

We spent the day fishing, then later that evening his daughter arrived by boat at his bayside dock—with a friend. His daughter's friend was a young woman about twenty-six or twenty-seven years old, and she was a stunningly beautiful young blonde who'd been on the cover of *Seventeen* magazine several years earlier. All of us had dinner that evening, and since I was very tired and also suffering from a bit of sunburn, I decided to retire for the evening on a small sofa bed in the living room. Later that evening after everyone was asleep, I was awakened by this young lady who at first seemed to just want to talk for a while. So I sat up and began to chat with her, and after a few minutes of pleasant conversation, I was stunned when she simply stood up, unzipped her jeans, and made her intentions known to me.

In cases like this, I had a defensive tactic… and it seemed to work well in these situations. I simply began to witness to her about the Lord, and I told her that Jesus loved her and so on. She didn't give in to the Lord, but at least I had managed to overcome the temptation and not give in to her, and she was a very difficult temptation to overcome.

There were a number of young people, mostly young adults, who worked as volunteers in the ministry. There was Sally Walker, who tirelessly volunteered to help in what I'm sure amounted to thousands of hours, and Ben Stone and Paul, Willie, and Wayne and Charlie. I had led a neighbor family, who lived next door to us, to the Lord. It was Mike Barrington and his brother Steve and their younger sister Beverly. Steve was always there and could be counted on for help. There were also many from Rev. Strader's church who volunteered their time and efforts.

Ben Stone had become my assistant, and not only was he like my right hand, but he was also like a brother. Ben was a big man, who dwarfed me in physical size, and he was always so affable and cheerful. He also had a way with the young people, and I felt that anytime I could not be there, my group was in good hands.

Meanwhile, I had gotten a call from my mother, who was still living in Garden Grove, California, and she told me Dad was dying. We had known he had been battling cancer for some time, and he had actually convinced the doctors to sever his spinal cord, paralyzing him in order to manage the pain. I had never heard of such a case, before or since. He didn't want to spend his remaining months in an anesthetized drug stupor, but wanted to be lucid and able to communicate his love to his family. He was only fifty-two then, and he had shriveled down to a weight of about eighty-five or ninety pounds.

Money was always tight, but a Christian friend and supporter, W. H. Stuart Sr., who was a wealthy cattleman from Barstow, had always been there for us when there was a need, and he provided me round-trip airfare to California so that I could go to my father's side. When I arrived at the little home on Harbor Boulevard, my dad looked like a skeleton. He still had a little movement in his arms, but he was otherwise completely paralyzed, and he had now been bedridden and paralyzed for more than a year. I had always felt guilty about leaving my mother and father and heading off to Florida even though it was for God's work, but now the guilt was overwhelming.

Dad and I visited over the next two or three days before I had to return, and I knew that he had accepted Christ as his Savior. I also knew that when I left, I would never see my father alive again, and he and I wept as I held his head next to mine and we hugged each other. I'd never seen Dad weep before. Mom had said that Dad was always in good spirits, and never once did she hear him complain about the fact he was dying… never once did she hear him say, *"Why me?"* My father's character and courage will always be remembered because he had such a profound influence on my life.

After returning to Florida, it was only a matter of weeks before I received another call from Mom saying that my dad had died, just two weeks after his fifty-third birthday, which was in May 1971. He had withered to a mere 78 lb. before his death, still never complaining about his fate.

My friend and benefactor, Bill Stuart, once again provided me money for the plane tickets, and I returned for the funeral. People from all over the country came to see him and pay their last respects. Dad had never achieved much in his life if you're measuring by the world's standards. He'd simply been a hard worker, usually with owning and operating service station dealerships, and he'd never had much in the way of material things, but his kindness and his character had affected people all his life, and he was bid farewell by hundreds of loving friends. They asked me to speak at his funeral, and God used this opportunity to touch many peoples' lives.

On a side note, during one of my flights to California to see my father, we were flying toward the mountains that were nestled up against Palm Springs when the pilot announced we should expect some turbulence ahead. Since I'd flown that route before, a route that took you over the ten-thousand-foot peak of Mount San Jacinto, the updraft of warm desert air from Palm Springs below often caused turbulence, so I didn't think this was a cause for concern. We had a couple of good jolts, but most of the passengers just took it in stride. Fortunately, the captain had been warned of a possible severe downdraft, and he instructed the passengers to strap in for a bumpy ride.

Then suddenly it felt as if the airplane hit a brick wall. They'd just served champagne to many of the passengers, and I'd been eating an apple when suddenly we fell so fast the negative G forces slammed my apple up against the storage bin above me, and everyone's champagne glasses smashed against the ceiling as well. At the same time the yellow oxygen masks fell from the bins, and there were pillows flying about the cabin. Just prior to this happening, the flight attendants had sat down and strapped themselves in, bracing for the turbulence ahead. It's a good thing because otherwise they could have been killed by slamming against the ceiling. People were screaming, and the cabin quickly turned to bedlam. I stood up and spoke to some of the people around me and said, *"There's nothing to worry about. God's not going to let anything happen to me or to you today."*

When we arrived at LAX, the pilot didn't bother to make the usual approach into the airport—he just flew straight in. On the return flight about a week later, I noticed I'd gotten the same pilot, and so I managed to speak to him about the incident. He confirmed that he didn't make the usual approach because he'd declared an emergency. The plane had been grounded because they wanted to X-ray the entire aircraft to determine if there'd been any structural damage. He said that we'd fallen nearly three thousand feet in just a matter of seconds.

After Dad's funeral, when I returned to Florida, I had to face another heartbreak. I found my ministry split down the middle. While I was gone, Ben Stone had formed another group across town, and some of our young people had gone with him. This, in itself, would have been a blessing because it was never a case of "yours and mine." There was always more work to be done than any one man could accomplish. After all, we served the same Lord, and this was simply dividing up the work we had before us.

But the heartbreak came when I began to hear rumors… rumors that his young people were forbidden to come around the Jesus House or the Dove coffeehouse at all… and they were not to have anything to do with me. One of the boys, who had left to join Ben's ministry while I was gone, disobeyed that directive and came by to see me anyway. When I pressed him for an answer as to why we were all being shunned, he said, *"Ben told us that God had shown him that you were a homosexual and that we were to have nothing to do with you."*

I was stunned. I thanked him for being frank with me, and I assured him that Ben was wrong. I was not, nor had I ever been, a homosexual, nor had I ever been tempted in that manner. I had never had any effeminate traits, so I was dumbfounded as to any reason Ben might say or think such things. I tried numerous times to speak to Ben over these accusations, but he refused. My heart was greatly saddened over this, and I recall spending a great deal of time in prayer over the matter. But Ben continued to refuse to speak with me, and to this day we have not spoken since. I still don't know why he would say such things. God had used me in the past to lead a few homosexuals to the Lord and to find healing and restoration for them, and I sometimes wondered if Ben had somehow misinterpreted that.

During that time of emphasis on restoring divine order in the Church, there is a scriptural method for dealing with a problem such as this. The scripture clearly instructs us:

"Brethren, if a man be overtaken in a fault, ye which are spiritual, restore such an one in the spirit of meekness; considering thyself, lest thou also be tempted" (Gal. 6:1, KJV).

If Ben had been concerned about me and suspected me of being in sin (homosexuality), he should have come to me, along with some other mature Christian brothers and, in the spirit of meekness, confronted me on the issue.

Had it been true… if he had followed those scriptural instructions, he could have, as the apostle Paul instructed, ministered to me about this problem and possibly brought about healing in my life… had it been true.

Or had he come to me and learned this was untrue, he would have been able to correct the problem and put an end to the rumors. Instead, it was handled in an unscriptural manner, certainly not one under God's divine order, and there was a rift in the body of Christ… one that was never healed.

This is one example Apostle Paul used when he said we could bring damnation onto ourselves by not *"discerning the Lord's body"* (1 Cor. 11:29). Ben is my brother, and I am his, and we both are part of the body of Christ. And I'm not "casting stones" at Ben, for I too live in a glass house. I give these examples in the hope that others in the body of Christ can learn from these mistakes and that one day he and I can be restored in the fellowship. I know Ben loves Jesus. But if someone is rumored to be in sin, it needs to be handled scripturally.

There were also a number of Christian ministers who had been so helpful during these years. I spoke many times to Pastor Strader's congregation at First Assembly of God, and for several years that church took offerings on behalf of our work, support without which we would not have been able to continue. There was never much money to go around, but the needs always seemed to be met. Many times bags of groceries would be anonymously left on my front porch, and it usually came at a time when we were simply out of food.

During the early seventies we arranged for Max Rapoport, along with Charles Hardin, who was the president of the United Evangelical Churches, to come to First Assembly of God for a week of services. Charlie was a powerful speaker with an entertaining demeanor and a terrific sense of humor. He and Max alternated speaking during that week, and the services went well. Harden had been kicked out of his denomination after he received the baptism in the Holy Spirit.

I also arranged for Nicky Cruz to come to Lakeland, and we had a rally at the local stadium, followed by a series of meetings at First Assembly. Nicky Cruz's life story was played out in the movie *The Cross and the Switchblade* released in 1970, based on the best-selling book of the same name, by David Wilkerson, who was portrayed by Pat Boone. Nicky's role was handled by Erik Estrada.

The stadium rally was preceded by a parade through town that finished at Joker Marchant Stadium. The city had given me great cooperation, and it was quite a sight to see several of the main streets of downtown Lakeland shut down for this parade, which was made up of dozens of young Christians, many of them former addicts and dope pushers, all eager to share the good news. And the number one rock 'n' roll radio station, which was owned by baseball great Joe Garagiola Sr., gave us free airtime to promote the Nicky Cruz rally, and they frequently played excerpts from his testimony that had been recorded a few years earlier.

A close friend during those years was Wayne Johnson, who was the pastor at Youman's Baptist church in Plant City, was always there for us as well, and his congregation frequently asked me to come there and speak to his gathering. I had spoken in that church so many times I lost count, and the people there were always warm and receptive—so much so that once, during a period of an incredibly busy schedule, I had forgotten about being asked to preach at their church one night.

Exhausted from burning the candle at both ends, I was sound asleep a little after eight o'clock one Sunday evening when the phone rang. It was Wayne Johnson… and where was Ken? The people had been waiting for me to come and speak for nearly an hour. By the time I got dressed and drove the five or six miles to the church building, it had been almost an hour and a half, and everybody was still there—nobody had left. We had one of the best services ever that night even after I had basically *forgotten* I was supposed to be there. Wow—wonderful people!

Chapter 14

Speaking of burning the candle at both ends, we hadn't had a vacation since heading to Florida several years earlier to begin a ministry. I had a Christian friend, Carlos, who lived in Tampa, who told me we could head down to Galveston, Texas, and use his vacation home out on the beach. Carlos had been on the Cuban Olympic wrestling team, and when the Summer Olympics was held in Mexico City in 1968, Carlos had defected to the United States. Following that time, Carlos had given his life to Christ, and when he managed to make his way to Florida, he and his wife had started a successful hair salon business in Tampa that they now owned. The more we thought about such a trip, the more it appealed to us. This would mean some much-needed quality time for both Karen and me. He also said that if we wanted to take the vacation even farther, he had some Christian friends in Veracruz, Mexico, and if we drove there, he was sure we'd be welcomed. We decided to go.

At that time, Tammy and Jeff were staying with their mom in California, so we headed out for Galveston, and after spending the night at his beach home, the plan was for us to then head on to Mexico. It was Karen, Scotty, Kimmy, and me. I had a two-door '67 Ford sedan, but it was comfortable and roomy, and the air conditioner worked great, which was a real plus.

Picture, if you will, the contours of America around the Gulf of Mexico, because the plan meant we'd be driving *around the entire Gulf of Mexico,* which would include stopping at Galveston, where we met Carlos and his wife and then followed them out to their beach home. I'd heard Carlos describe how their vacation home was on the beach, but I never imagined it several hundred yards *out on the beach* and standing on stilts a good eight or ten feet off the sand. I wondered if high tide would come in and if we'd end up being high and dry (actually, that'd be *high and wet*, wouldn't it?). In later years I also wondered how it fared during hurricane season. Anyway, it was a nice stay, but the next morning we got up, and we headed off to Laredo, Texas, then across the border to Nuevo Laredo, Mexico. The trip from Lakeland, Florida, to Veracruz, Mexico, was considerably more than two thousand miles and would require at least thirty-six hours of driving.

The first problem we encountered was when we entered Mexico at Nuevo Laredo. Two of their customs agents frisked me, then they searched our car from end to end. I did, however, learn that the men they selected for this job must have been true diplomats because they spoke perfect English, and they had no problem articulating their sincere desire to keep up US-Mexican relations by soliciting some undocumented compensation—a $20 bribe for each. I was irate.

I marched into the office and demanded to speak with a senior official—a head honcho, if you will. When I explained to him how his employees had tried to shake me down for a $20 bribe, I said, *"I'm an American citizen, and I demand an apology."*

It turned out that this senior official at the border crossing was just as articulate as his employees, and with the same diplomatic smile as the others had shown me, he explained that he shared their same keen interest in US-Mexican relations, and he seemed to take great pleasure in explaining that it was my civic duty to kick in another $20 for him as well. So my "permit" to travel through Mexico cost me $60 in bribes, and nowhere in my budget had I made any provision for bribes.

no toilet seats...

One thing I had noticed while traveling through Mexico—there seemed to be no toilet seats anywhere. And occasionally, when we stopped at a gas station, we'd find no toilet—just a hole in the floor (sorry about that, Mexico)... *"If you fix it, they will come."*

We had loaded the trunk of the car with as much used clothing as possible since we'd heard that we would likely encounter some very poor people during our travels in Mexico. We'd decided to take a little side trip to some caverns near Monterrey, called Las Grutas de García (the Garcia Caverns—amazing). Access to the entrance of the caves was by means of something that resembled a San Francisco cable car, which ascended the steep mountain to the entrance of the caverns. When we were seated in the cable car, we were headed nearly straight up, and our backs were pressed hard against the seats. Inside the caverns was an amazing array of stalactites and stalagmites, rather like the caverns at Carlsbad, New Mexico, except on a somewhat smaller scale.

After leaving the caverns, we drove to an area outside Monterrey where we noticed what appeared to be ten or twelve abandoned railroad freight cars on some railroad tracks that seemed to go nowhere.

real poverty...

We were about to get our first look at real poverty because we learned there were possibly as many as ten families living in those railroad cars. When we looked inside one of the "homes," we saw they had managed to build a makeshift stove inside the boxcar, and we also learned that the women and children slept inside, and the men slept outside between the tracks underneath the boxcars.

We saw several of the older children carrying buckets of water, using a large stick, with the stick being carried balanced on their head, and a bucket of water on each side. We learned that it was some ten kilometers' (about six miles) round trip for these teenagers just to fill the buckets for their families. When we began handing out some of the clothing to them, they gathered around as though we were handing out bags of gold and silver. Although I'd seen some people living in sharecropper shacks in the American South, I'd never seen poverty like that. But the people were so friendly and very grateful.

From there we made our way southward on to Saltillo and then on to Querétaro, followed by the three-and-a-half-hour drive on to Mexico City.

The "no toilet seat" trend continued even on into Mexico City, where we stayed at a nice hotel overlooking the famous Angel de la Independencia plaza, where the famous gold statue stands—nice hotel, but you guessed it: no toilet seat.

During our stay in Mexico City we traveled out to the Teotihuacan Pyramids, and during our climb to the top, I began to have some serious chest pains, so after lying there on the steps for about half an hour, some twenty or thirty steps up the pyramid, we headed back to the hotel. Since I had a strong heart, and I knew instinctively there was nothing wrong with my ticker, I later learned I'd picked up a bad case of amoebic dysentery the Mexicans not-so-affectionately refer to as Montezuma's revenge, which gave me a serious case of heartburn. After only one night at that hotel we headed to an even higher elevation into the mountains before going down to Veracruz. I'd been warned about Montezuma's revenge, and people had told me to always ask about the water, "*Es potable, o es purificado?*" which translates, "Is it just drinkable, or is it purified?" I learned, that was the question you should always ask concerning the water.

Unfortunately, everybody always said it was purified water, but that "purified water" nearly killed me. Since my Spanish was limited to asking directions or to asking how much something cost, and it was certainly not conversational, I learned something else the hard way while traveling in Mexico—no one will admit to you that they don't know where something is; they will give you directions even if they haven't a clue as to how to get there, *so be careful!*

Even though Mexico City is about seven thousand three hundred feet in elevation, we climbed still higher, and just as we entered a heavily wooded mountain area, when I rounded a corner, there was a boulder on the road, and when my car struck the boulder, my steering wheel *fell off into my lap!* Here I was, unable to steer, so I slammed on the brakes and came to a stop. Next I managed to push the steering wheel back on, but all I could do was tighten the nut on the steering wheel with my fingers since I had no tools with me. That was on my to-do list when we got to a city and located a mechanic—to make it so I didn't have to push down on my steering wheel every minute I was behind the wheel just to hold it in place. Oh, and the jolt also damaged my driveshaft, so I also added that to the to-do list for when we got to Veracruz.

My to-do checklist—let's see: (1) find mechanic; (2) put steering wheel back on the car and install new U-joint on the driveshaft; and (3) get some medicine before this dysentery *kills me!*

We came to a tiny Mexican village in the mountains, and when we saw a hotel sign, we pulled into what appeared to be an interior plaza for parking surrounded by the motel rooms. By that time I was quite sick and needed to find a place to rest, so when I saw all the chickens scatter as we drove into the plaza in the hotel, I said, *"Whatever,"* and we went in to register.

When they showed us to our room, they had to *shoo* six or eight more chickens from the room. Again, I mumbled, *"Whatever"* to myself. I needed a bed and a good night's sleep. So while we checked in, they mopped up the chicken poop from the floor in our room, because apparently, those chickens thought it was their home, and so the rest of the night we had to keep scattering the chickens away because they wanted back in their room. It was a good-sized room with two double beds, a few old blankets, and a bathroom. And you guessed it—no toilet seat.

By the time we drove the steep mountain road down to Veracruz, I was quite sick. I couldn't manage to stay away from a toilet for any length of time. I had the address of the friends in Veracruz whom Carlos had told us about, so I drove through the narrow streets, finally locating the address and the family. I truly wish I could recall that family's name, but they were wonderful people. But they spoke no English, and my Spanish was very (very) limited. In fact, because I speak a little Spanish with no discernable gringo accent, most of the people thought I was fluent in Spanish *(not)*. So they'd hear me say something in Spanish, and they'd begin to rattle off for several minutes before I could interrupt them with, *"Despacio, por favor—no entiendo"* ("Slowly, please—I don't understand").

Meanwhile we'd managed to locate a mechanic who made the repairs on our car. This man was amazing. His name was Eduardo, and when he spoke English, it was clear, crisp, and almost perfect. When I asked him where he'd learn to speak English so fluently, he simply told me, *"Oh, I learned to speak English when I spent three weeks in the States a few years ago."* Wow! That'd take me three years, not three weeks.

The family we stayed with had two children—a boy who was not yet ten and a girl who was only slightly older. The mother appeared to be in her late thirties, and there was no husband around. I never did learn if she had been widowed or if there'd been a divorce, because my limited Spanish language skills made that too big a hurdle to overcome. But they were terrific people. They were quite taken with Kimmy, who also wasn't yet ten, and I remember they called her *Keemy*.

By this time, I was in serious shape, and I spent the next seven or eight days between their couch, which had been turned into my bed, and the bathroom. I'd lost quite a bit of weight, and I hadn't felt well enough to get up and shave, so I looked quite a sight. Their bathroom (actually, a toilet room) was across an open courtyard and in another building, and since it'd been raining almost the entire time we stayed with them, I had to get up and walk through the courtyard in the rain to use their facilities, and this happened several times every night. Also, during this extended and unexpected stay, during which we had to pay for a mechanic and for a new U-joint for the car, we had also given them all our remaining money to buy food. Except for gasoline credit cards, we were out of money. At the time, I hadn't noticed that there were no Shell, Texaco, or Chevron stations—only Pemex.

I do recall, however, one Wednesday night I had been feeling well enough to drive to a nearby prayer meeting, and so the seven of us piled into my car and drove to a section near downtown Veracruz.

The church building was actually just an empty space between two buildings. Someone had put up some boards so they could cover it with plywood and corrugated aluminum, and with a bunch of wooden boxes and broken chairs for pews, these wonderful people had church. The only musical instruments they had for worship were a couple of tambourines. *Wow.* What great people, and what a great time I had, sick and all. I was amazed to learn that regardless of what corner of the world you find yourself in, Spirit-filled believers are one. If there were any doctrinal differences, you'd never know it, and the language barrier didn't seem to matter. I'll never forget those people crowded between two buildings, dancing and praising God—another *wow.*

In addition to the $60 in bribe money that we hadn't counted on, the car repairs, and our stay being extended by nearly two weeks due to my illness, we found ourselves low on money. I asked our gracious hostess about the gas situation, showing her our Shell and Texaco credit cards, and she said, *"No, Pemex es la única estación de servicio de gas en México."*

I couldn't translate what she said exactly, but I figured out that the gist of what she was saying was, it was Pemex or nothing. Our gas credit cards were useless to us.

So when it came time to leave our friends and their wonderful hospitality in Veracruz, we were out of money. These poor people, who had to buy milk and cheese from a local vendor with the few pennies they had for their meals, were now going throughout the neighborhood, taking up a collection so that we could get back to the United States, where our credit cards would be honored. Because of our time in Veracruz, that's a time in my life I will never forget.

finally, a toilet seat...

On our journey back north to the United States, we went through some barren desert country on Highway 101, south of Matamoros, and we hit one stretch of road going through a barren desert valley where the pavement suddenly ended. Incidentally, many of the paved roads in that part of the country were excellent—that is, until you came across the potholes. It was a bit unsettling because you'd be moving along on a very good, smooth paved highway at 100 kph (the speed limit was 100 kph, which translated to 62 mph), and then suddenly you had to swerve to miss potholes, three or four of them at a time, some of them as large as Volkswagens. I imagined it as being something of a war zone with the roads being pockmarked from bomb blasts.

So when the pavement ended, there was a valley ahead, and we could see a small town nestled –four to five miles ahead in the middle of the valley. We were low on gas (remember, we couldn't use the credit cards), so when I saw a Pemex sign ahead, I pulled up into the driveway and looked around for a gas pump. Here we were in a Pemex station, and there were no gas pumps. Soon a man walked up to my car, and I inquired, "*¿Tienes alguna gasolina?*" ("Do you have any gasoline?").

Quickly he walked inside, and just as quickly he came out rolling a big thirty-five-gallon barrel on wheels. Then he cranked on a hand pump that was atop the barrel and filled up a can, much like the cans you use to water your plants, except the sprayer end had been knocked off. So he was able to fill the can, lift it up, and pour the gas into my gas tank and then repeat the process, which took five to six times before he filled my tank. The problem was, there was no electricity—*in the entire town.*

Inside the building next to the gas station there was a small store, and canned goods were on the shelves, along with a few packages of tortillas and a loaf of bread or two. Apparently, when the supply truck came in with more groceries, the food quickly disappeared off the shelves. As I recall, we bought some bread to munch on as there was nothing else in the store for us to eat, and when they rang it up, they had an old manual cash register because there was no electricity.

I had to use the facilities (I hadn't completely recovered from my bout with Ol' Montezuma), so I asked, "*¿Dónde están los baños?*" ("Where are the bathrooms?").

The man pointed to the back, and so I walked around the building, and I wasn't the least bit surprised when I saw an old outhouse, and this one looked like it belonged to the three little pigs because the big bad wolf could have blown this one over with a big huff and a puff. You could see through it because some of the boards were falling off. I opened the door, and to my utter amazement, not only was there a toilet seat, but it was also attached to a brand-new aqua-colored toilet, which was sitting on a newly poured concrete slab. This was too much. My business could wait. I walked back out to the car, grabbed my camera, and took a picture—of the first toilet seat we'd seen in all of Mexico.

By the time we reached the US border, I hadn't shaved in nearly two weeks, my hair was long and scraggly, and the US Customs inspectors must have thought I was a doper or, worse, a drug smuggler because they stripped our car down to the floorboards. They took the wheels off and checked inside the tires and pulled the seats out and checked inside the springs. Of course, they put it all back together for us—somewhat. But we were back in the United States, where our credit cards could get us home.

more real poverty...

Hit the Fast-forward button for a minute, please.

The next time I was to see poverty, anything like what I'd seen when we visited the families living in the abandoned railroad cars near Monterrey, Mexico, was some twenty years later in Saint Vincent and the Grenadines (SVG) in the Caribbean. I'd traveled to Grenada on banking business. I had a friend who was close friends with some of the directors of the First International Bank of Grenada, and their corporate offices were set up in the nearby island of Saint Vincent and the Grenadines, which was less than a thirty-minute flight.

While there I stayed with a friend, Jim, whom I'd met in the States and who was living in a two-story old Colonial-style home in SVG. While there I learned he had a houseguest—a green gecko, and it had the run of the place. Jim had given the little fella a name, which I can't recall, and said he was his house pet. He'd made breakfast the following morning, so I decided it was the least I could do to wash the dishes. Standing before the sink, I looked up at the little green gecko, which was standing atop the chrome faucet over the kitchen sink about eighteen inches from me. He was a cute little guy—he just looked at me, completely unafraid, and occasionally tilting his head from side to side as if to say, *"Did you know you could save 15 percent on car insurance by switching to GEICO?"* (Sorry about that—I couldn't resist. A hundred years from now someone will pick up this weathered old book and wonder, *What on earth is this guy talking about? GEICO? Gecko? Huh?* The gecko was real, but I couldn't get him to say a word. I don't think he worked for GEICO.)

I knew the home was probably quite elegant in its day, but that day was long ago. It wasn't air-conditioned, and the humidity in the Southern Caribbean was stifling, to say the least. Having lived with the humids in Florida, I knew that one of the ways to cool off was to take a cold shower for as long as you could stand it—until you wrinkled up like a prune—and it drove the core body temperature down. So I tried the cold shower remedy and then tried to lie down on some cool, dry sheets for what I thought might be a comfortable night's sleep. It was too hot to wear anything to bed, so here I was, trying to stay cool by sleeping *au naturel* when I was awakened by something crawling on me—hundreds of *somethings* crawling on me. I jolted up in bed, only to see that my body was covered in ants—on my face, in my hair, on my ears, and on otherwise private parts where ants simply didn't belong—*ugh!* I tried the cold shower again, washing off all the ants, but within a couple of hours I was once again awakened by the creepy-crawlies.

Since I was grateful for Jim putting me up for the night, I didn't have courage to ask him how he was able to stand living there.

That day, I was scheduled to catch the plane back to Grenada so I could return home when I heard a knock on the door. Jim wasn't there because he'd gone down to the office in downtown Kingstown on business, so when I answered the door, I was surprised to see three very thin black children, the oldest of whom was about ten or eleven, and the youngest, about six, standing by the door, completely naked. They told me in their broken English that they lived in a little shack nearby, and then they pointed to their home over at the edge of the jungle. Their home wasn't much more than a few boards and some corrugated aluminum. They said they hadn't eaten in a couple of days, and they had no food at the house. Since I already had my tickets for the flight and since there wasn't anything else I needed money for, I gave them all the money I had with me.

That was poverty—real poverty. Unfortunately, so much of what we call poverty in America simply means people are struggling to get by. If you have a roof over your head, clothes on your back, and food to eat, you're richer than much of the rest of the people in the world. In America it seems that poverty often means your children can't wear Nikes, or you can't afford insurance for your car, or you can't afford to get your color TV fixed. After Grenada and Saint Vincent, I knew what real poverty was like.

A few years later I learned that the bank had all its assets seized, and the directors of the bank had been charged with bank fraud, causing investors to lose millions. I never knew the details, but I was saddened and also felt lucky that I only lost a few thousand dollars at the bank in Grenada. I had become friends with the founder of the bank, who later died of a heart attack before going to trial, and another one of the men who ended up in prison over the whole affair. They had assured me what they were doing was entirely legal and ethical, but later I had begun to question some of the things I'd seen, so I never quite knew who or what to believe. I'm just glad I don't have to deal with it now.

Okay, now you can hit Rewind and go back to where we were in Mexico.

After surviving the search at the border between Mexico and the United States, we put the wheels back on the car, returned the front and backseats to their places, and repacked all our belongings. They were gracious enough to mount the tires back on the wheels, but it was up to me then to mount the wheels on the car. As I said earlier, after being sick for so long in Mexico, I'm sure I looked quite seedy when we finally got to the border, so when the US Customs agents stripped our car and didn't find anything, I actually thought they were surprised and a little disappointed.

We were broke, disheveled, and hungry when we reentered the United States. There were several times along the way up the east coast of Mexico that we'd stopped to pick some bananas growing in the jungles alongside the road. That helped to sustain us and keep us going. Now we had to once again make the trip all the way around the Gulf of Mexico, but this time with only our gas credit cards, which meant we had to stop at gas stations that had little grocery stores inside in order for us to buy something to eat. I wasn't sure why, but the trip from Florida to Mexico didn't seem nearly as long as that endless trip back—around the Gulf, first through Texas, then Louisiana, on to Mobile, Alabama, and then finally to Pensacola in the Florida panhandle, followed by about eight hours more back to Lakeland. When we finally made it back home, we needed to take a vacation to recover from our vacation.

Chapter 15

Telling this next story, this next chapter, is one of the most difficult and painful things I've ever had to do.

There was also a beautiful young Christian woman who had been a volunteer in the ministry. So as not to embarrass her, I will call her Ann (not her real name).

Ann was a devoted helper and a devout Christian. Along with several others, we worked together closely for well over a year when I realized I was developing strong feelings for her although I never let on for a moment that I felt that way. I later learned she felt the same way too, but we both restrained ourselves, never giving any indication of our feelings, and neither of us behaved in any way that was inappropriate. I saw to it that we were never alone together, and that seemed to help. But it didn't help matters that things were going so badly at home with Karen, and as I said earlier, for long periods, sometimes more than a year, she wanted nothing to do with me unless it was to vent her bitterness and anger. Sometimes Karen would turn violent. I was a strong, healthy young man, and I feared if I ever did strike her, I could hurt her badly. As I indicated earlier, I'd always felt that a man was never, ever justified in striking a woman. I'd seen too many cases where men beat their wives or girlfriends, and there was never any reason to excuse something like that.

At times I was convinced Karen truly hated me. I often thought, *Poor Karen*. She needed my help so desperately, and I just wasn't able to give it to her. I often thought, *How is this possible? I know she loves the Lord, and yet for months at a time nothing but hatred came from her.* I wondered how a Christian could have so much hatred, and I often referred to the scripture that speaks about a fountain having both good, clean water and bitter, foul water, indicating that this wasn't supposed to be (see James 3:11).

Yes, she was definitely crying out, and I was helpless to do anything about it. I knew the devil was actively involved in trying to destroy our marriage because there was spiritual warfare going on over her soul just as there had been over mine—it's just that hers was manifested in a different way. But when I tried to help her, to minister to her, or to take her to others I knew she respected in order for her to get help, she always backed away.

To this day I believe that Karen loves the Lord. Years later she expressed regret—said she was sorry that those things came in and destroyed our marriage. I've chosen to remember the good times, so for me to recall these ugly times for the purposes of this book are quite painful for me. I much prefer to remember loving her deeply. I hold no bitterness toward her, and I've told you all this in my feeble attempt to explain what I was going through and how I got to this point.

Often people would ask, *"Can Christians be influenced by demons?"* My personal experiences said, *"Yes, a Christian can have pretty much whatever they want."* Sometimes hanging on to resentment toward someone feels good for a while, especially if they feel it's justified and they have good cause to feel that way, but over the years it grows like a cancer. It's something of a procession: first, resentment, then bitterness and anger, and then eventually, hatred finds its way in, and along with it dark spiritual forces take over.

During all this, which was at the height of my work that I'd been sent there to do, with the miraculous happening, the work continued. I was getting invitations to speak, seemingly from everywhere—churches, civic groups, and the schools—and the invitations continued seemingly without end. More schools wanted us to come and speak, followed by calls to speak at jails and youth prisons. We frequently drove seven or eight hours north to the Florida panhandle to visit the Marianna Boys School (prison), and we had great results.

During this time we had a series of Jesus Rallies in Lakeland, and we had billboards located all over Central Florida for the Christ-in-a-Park (Christina Park) rallies held during 1972. We had billboards like this advertising the rallies throughout the area.

Christ-in-a-Park Jesus Rallies

And the calls kept coming in from ministerial associations, from the Rotary, Kiwanis, the Lions Club, and the Sertoma Club. Deliverances continued, and occasionally, people were healed—during what was, at the same time, hell at home.

One year the Sertoma Club called me for a special gathering, and when I arrived, I was surprised when they honored me with their Service to Mankind Award, and the local newspaper headlined the story with "Man of the Year." Yeah, man of the year, all right—I felt like such a hypocrite with all the strife and tension at home.

And during this time Ann was there along with the others when we went to the prisons, to the rock festivals, and to the schools, and it wasn't long before I noticed my heart would begin to race each time I was near her. I was certain she'd find out about my feelings, and I did my best to conceal them. The fact was, I was falling in love with her, and fight it as I might, I couldn't help myself. I, of all people, knew how wrong this would be, along with the devastation it would cause on my life and marriage, but my emotions seemed to overwhelm me at times.

Although God was using me in mighty ways, and many were coming to Jesus, and many were being set free from demonic oppression, and God was sometimes miraculously healing the sick, my home continued to be a battleground. I knew God was trying to teach me some valuable lessons, but I was simply overwhelmed and unable to cope with the problems at home.

I wept before the Lord, confessing my feelings and asking for God to deliver me from this… because I knew that if I gave in—if we gave in—the results could destroy us both.

Then one day I was determined to tell her. Part of me hoped she'd leave, and another part of me feared she would leave, but I just knew we couldn't give in to the temptation. Still another part of me hoped we could find a way to be together although I knew deep inside that was just wishful thinking. I knew just how wrong that would be. We'd just finished the Jesus Rally at Christina Park, just south of Lakeland, and so I asked her if she would go for a drive with me.

We drove to the park, which was full of oak trees with hanging Spanish moss and next to a series of small lakes. We'd just had a series of rallies at Christina Park, and many had come to the Lord. In fact, Walter Cronkite had been doing a story about the Jesus Movement in America, and he mentioned our Jesus Rally at Christina Park on the evening news. There were many rock festivals during that time, and the Woodstock festival was fresh on everyone's minds, and often some of those events got out of hand, and Cronkite expressed concern that this one would end up like Woodstock.

I told Ann of my feelings for her and that I had been holding it back for more than a year. But I also told her we couldn't give in to this. She too confessed she had the same feelings for me and that she couldn't bear to see me hurt and that she couldn't give in either because she felt it could destroy our relationship with the Lord. Determined to be strong, we decided that we would come up with a plan in the next day or so… either she would leave, or I would leave… something.

The next few days were miserable, and we both felt the ache inside. There was a Christian album out at that time, and it had meant a lot to all of us at Youth Challenge. It was called *Truth of Truths,* and in it, on the one side devoted to the Old Testament, there was a song David sang to Bathsheba, in which he sang, *"I feared of the Lord, for what he would do… Oh, my sorrow… for loving you."* David had given in to temptation and had taken Bathsheba while they were both still married. Even though this was nearly the undoing of David, costing him much of his kingdom, the result of their marriage after David arranged for Bathsheba's husband to be killed in battle was the birth of Solomon, who would later be the wisest king ever to rule in Israel. The only thing that saved David was that he wept before the Lord and repented of his sin.

Ann and I couldn't stand it any longer, and so one day we gave in to the temptation. I had never been unfaithful to Karen, and although our marriage had begun with the two of us being deeply in love, the increasing hostility I'd been feeling from Karen had eroded that love to the point it seemed hopeless. What started out with Ann was an innocent friendship between two Christians; when we surrendered to the temptations, what soon became a passionate and beautiful romance turned into a blueprint for disaster. She was such a kind and loving person that I soon realized that for so long I'd been yearning for love and affection, characteristics that had become so sadly lacking in my marriage with Karen. There was nothing sordid about it—we were in love, and yet we knew it was wrong; it was sin in the eyes of God, and it was separating us from our intimate fellowship with the Lord and destroying our walk with him. For months we met secretly, hoping to savor the few precious hours we had together. But the secrecy was also eating away at both of us.

Years later I wrote a poem that seemed to underscore how something that felt so right could be so wrong. I hadn't written it specifically about Ann, but I'd written it for someone elusive, almost an unknown someone as my love. So without reciting the entire poem to you ad nauseam *(yuck)*, it ends with the following:

> *And where have the flowers gone?*
>   *Flowers that I gave you a lifetime ago*
> *Flowers that would have gladly given their lives to wilt*
>   *Pressed between the pages of our Great Expectations*
> *But who cry out in silence to have given so much*
>   *To die forgotten*
>
> *Ah, but some say poetry should rhyme*
>   *Keep in time, each alternate line*
> *So I shall close, with a departure from prose*
>   *This indecent exposure of my mind*
>
> *But, if Fate should decide this is only deceit*
>   *Then Life Itself is deception*
> *For if love this true could be so wrong*
>   *Then I curse my day of conception*
>
> *Why are you hiding, my Love?*
>   *For I wait in hope and sorrow*
> *Please come back, my Love*
>   *Return on the wings of tomorrow*

If I can resist the temptation for clichés, this was a great mystery to me. How could something so good, something that felt so right, and something that I longed for and that filled a love void in my life at the same time be so wrong?

Soon after we gave in to our passions, the anointing—*the Lord's presence* that I had felt for so many years—simply left me. *It was gone, and there was nothing I could do to conjure it up.* I was guilty. We continued seeing each other for nearly a year, but one day we knew it had to end. It was destroying the both of us, and it was destroying the work that God had started with me.

Painfully, tearfully, the two of us spoke of this for hours, and then we decided to part, and we have not seen each other since that day. A few months later the pain, the guilt, and the confusion got the better of her, and she tried to take her life. When the family she was living with called me, I rushed to the house where she was staying, in Leesburg, Florida, and I spoke to her through the bathroom door, but the people with whom she was staying wouldn't permit me to see her and rightfully so. She told me, talking to me through the bathroom door, that she should have bled to death because she had repeatedly slashed her wrists, but the wounds wouldn't bleed, and apparently, God was not going to let her kill herself. That was the last time I was near Ann.

If ever I do see her again, I will beg her forgiveness, for I feel I wronged her and caused her great suffering for which I could never repay. I was supposed to be the mature one, the man of God. She was young and vulnerable. It is my prayer that nothing ever again comes between her and her walk with Christ again. If it's any comfort to her, the love I felt for her was deep, and it was real.

Chapter 16

"Humpty Dumpty sat on a wall. Humpty Dumpty had a great fall. All the king's horses and all the king's men couldn't put Humpty together again."

Most of us can usually remember our first nursery rhyme. I certainly did. I must have been four at the time, but I can remember feeling so sorry for Humpty Dumpty and wondering why no one could put him back together again. Now, I was broken—shattered—and no one seemed to be able to help me pick up the broken pieces of my life. I distinctly remember once preaching, *"Even if the whole world backslides, I'm going on for Jesus."*

I resigned as the director of Youth Challenge. I had been the founder and its only director, but I could not continue if continuing meant living in hypocrisy. I knew I had to somehow bring my life back into order. I knew I had to repent and get right with God once again. It was also at this time I traveled to Melbourne, Florida, and met with Jamie Buckingham and asked him to discontinue the writing of my story. I didn't want anything to be published that would be a bad testimony and bring reproach to Christianity. A short while later I learned that my dear friend Al West, who had originally started writing the book, had died of leukemia.

I didn't know how many people knew about my love affair with Ann. That was the least of my concerns. I wanted to find some peace and to find some restoration with God. But not knowing how much of this affair had become known, I wasn't sure how many people would be willing to help me in this time of need. Unfortunately, I soon found out. I discovered it were as though I had leprosy… and it must have shown. Everywhere doors were closed to me, and people with whom

I had once been close avoided me as if I had some terrible contagious disease. The flood of requests for me to speak all stopped overnight.

Those who *would* see me were more interested in rebuking me than in helping. I had fallen. I was like the sinking ship… everyone wanted out and wanted to get as far away from it as possible. This is not to be critical. The fault was mine, and I brought it on myself. That fault was also to have a devastating effect on my marriage.

After a few months of trying, of fasting, and of seeking God, it seemed as though the heavens were shut, and I couldn't get through. My prayers seemed to bounce off the ceiling… and I began to gradually give up. It didn't happen overnight. The weeks turned into months, and the months turned into years.

I had been so accustomed to living with the presence of God and walking with an anointing on my life… it were as though I was completely dried up. There was nothing. *I was, of all men, most miserable.* For to have tasted of the living waters, to have walked in his light, and then to no longer have his presence and his touch was agonizing.

The distractions of life, of family, and of simply trying to make a living and put food on the table seemed to become a way of life more and more so over the years, and although I never turned my back on him and denied him, I was definitely not serving him according to my calling. I was in the midst of a spiritual battle, and I was no longer fighting. I had resigned myself to defeat and would soon begin to see the consequences of that acquiescence that would last for more than fifteen years.

Meanwhile, the problems Karen and I had continued to get worse. She didn't know about my relationship with Ann, and after Ann and I had left each other, I was determined to make things right at home and restore my marriage, but I also knew that if she knew about Ann, the marriage would be over, and I'd already seen the devastation that divorce wreaked on the children once before.

And to complicate matters, Karen's resentment toward me often was vented toward Tammy and Jeff, who were from my marriage with

Carolyn. Frequently, if I did anything to give her cause to be angrier at me, Tammy and Jeff suffered her wrath for it. Karen was very troubled and confused, and in her frustration she often took it out on the two of them. Yes, she was troubled, but I firmly believe I failed her. If anyone is to blame, it's me because I was the man of God, and I failed to protect her.

Before leaving Youth Challenge, I had decided to get back into radio to supplement my income, and for a short while I handled both. Now, after resigning from Youth Challenge, I was without a ministry too. I had been working at WVFM radio station in Lakeland, which was an "easy-listening format" station with a large audience in Central Florida. Months went by, and I was settling in to the new job. A few months later I was promoted to news director.

the lost years...

I was, however, completely unable to come to grips with my spiritual life (or absence of it). I was beginning to settle in to this new situation, and as I said, after all the months of fasting and praying and trying to get counseling for us, I realized I was gradually giving up. I gave up too soon. My prayer is that you don't make the same mistake. It took me many years to recover from *giving up too soon*.

And this is the saddest story of all. My heart aches when I think back on all those years, for I was beginning to forget who I was... you see, I had been seated with Christ *"far above all principality and power and might."* I had forgotten that he'd *"raised us up together; and made us sit together in heavenly places in Christ Jesus"* (see Ephesians chapter 2).

I had forgotten that he had *chosen* me to be his messenger... that he'd filled me with the Holy Spirit. I'd forgotten that I had the power of God in my life and that there were times I came into a place, being full of the Holy Spirit—even the demons were in fear and trembling—and that in my presence often the demons scattered and ran.

I'd forgotten that once, God called lightning from heaven... that he'd healed the sick... that he'd opened the doors of the prisons and the schools. I'd forgotten that I had led many to the Lord and that every time a soul is won to Christ, the Bible says, *"The angels in heaven are rejoicing."*

I'd forgotten his sweet presence in my life. I'd simply forgotten who I was. I had never known a greater shame, and unless you've experienced shame of this magnitude, you could never understand it. It was years later that I learned that maybe God allowed this into my life so that I might have compassion on other Christians who had been wounded and felt abandoned.

For years I had complicated this matter. I was bitter over having failed with Karen and having been unable and powerless to help her when she needed it most. I was bitter about having to give up Ann, because I loved her deeply, but after having given her up in an attempt to restore my marriage, the marriage continued to fall apart and actually got worse.

But most of all, I was angry with God. I finally came to a place where I said it—*I was mad at God!* I was mad at God because his presence was no longer with me. What arrogance! I was mad at God. Imagine walking with his intimate presence in my life, being in the midst of his power, and walking a daily walk that was miraculous by most anyone's standards and then having it all gone... *all of it*—*gone.*

Yes, I knew the scriptures. I knew that he had never left me—I had left him. I had become bitter and angry.

I screamed out at God, *"You ask too much of me! I gave up Ann. I came back to Karen. I fasted, I prayed, I wept. And instead of it getting better, it got worse. What more do you want?"*

In the final analysis it all came down to not being able to feel his presence in my life anymore. I knew he hadn't left me, but his manifest presence was no longer there.

Through those years, seemingly everywhere I turned, someone was being set free, someone was being healed, and he was answering my prayers with signs and wonders, *and it was all gone!* I was hurt and bitter over losing that presence. My temper tantrum was to last many years, years of learning that he was testing me to see if I would continue to love him and serve him *without the miracles and without the manifestations*—without *feeling* his presence.

Do you recall when I met the man with the spirit of palsy, who came into my office and had such pitiful spasms his whole body convulsed and shook, and when I prayed for him, the violent spasms immediately and miraculously stopped? Do you remember when I told him that he needed to *"give his life to Jesus in order for this healing to continue"*? This man walked away, and there in the middle of the street the demonic spirits reentered him, and he reverted back to his earlier condition.

I was not much different than this poor soul. I realized I had not been willing to pay the price God was requiring, because...

"I wanted to be able to save my marriage," and when that failed,

"I wanted to be with Ann...

I wanted to be able to keep my ministry,

and most of all,

I wanted his continued presence in my life" as it had been.

"I, I, I."... It wasn't a very pretty picture.

I know this sounds preachy, but I'm really preaching to myself. What I really needed was to *give my life to Jesus*—let me repeat that: I needed to *give my life to Jesus*—I needed to surrender all over again, not because this was what God unmercifully demanded, but because in order for me to truly *be a Christian,* to *live the life of a Christian,* I had to recognize that the old Ken was already dead and the only life I could now live was for Jesus to live in me.

In *The Normal Christian Life,* written by Watchman Nee, a Christian friend of his had been traveling by train somewhere in China, and during that journey he was invited by some strangers on the train to join in their gambling games, and his reply was simply, *"I cannot, for I did not bring my hands with me."*

Our hands, our feet, our eyes, our voice, our mind, and our entire being were crucified with Christ long ago, and the hands and feet, eyes, voice, and mind we now use do not belong to us, but belong to Jesus Christ. *Whoa*, these are hard sayings. What about, "Give your life to Jesus, and life will be full of lollipops and roses"?

Chapter 17

As I mentioned earlier, since I'd had a background in radio during the sixties, I decided to see if I could get back in the field. I drove out to WVFM radio station south of Lakeland, well out into the country, and I spoke with Bud Kurtz and Duane McConnell, the station's manager and owner respectively, and after cutting an audition tape, I was hired as an announcer. McConnell had pulled off some wire copy for me to read for the audition, and as I recall, one of the prominent Soviet officials in the Kremlin, Konstantin Chernenko, was mentioned in the article, and when I pronounced Chernenko's name perfectly, he was impressed, so when the news director position opened up, I was selected. Meanwhile, McConnell had learned of my writing and typing skills.

the radio years...

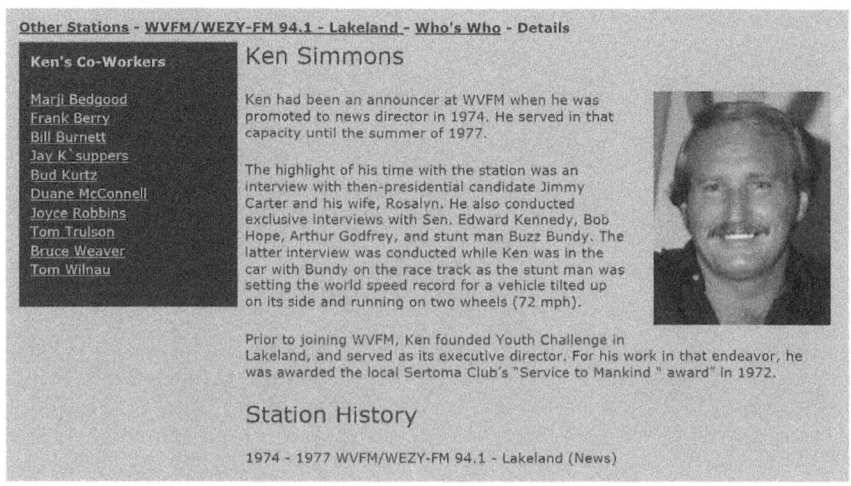

http://radioyears.com/other/details.cfm?lid=8&id=678

I was unaware of this Web site, but in 2010 I discovered it, and I learned it'd been there for many years. During my time at WVFM, I met and interviewed many celebrities and dignitaries. I was covering a speech at the Lakeland Civic Center, and the speaker that day was Georgia Governor Jimmy Carter, who was seeking the Democratic Party's nomination as their candidate for president in 1976, and he'd just recently won the New Hampshire primary. I was sitting in the front row because I'd gotten there a little late, and I needed to get my microphone set up. Just at the last minute I got things ready when Governor Carter was introduced.

The meeting was attended by about a hundred and fifty, maybe two hundred people, and after the speech, Governor Carter went to the front row and sat down next to me. I didn't quite know what to make of it when he put his arm around me and asked me if I would join him for lunch.

We met at the restaurant at the Holiday Inn, and I found him to be a warm and sincere person, but when he asked me if he could count on me for my support and for my vote, I informed him I treated all candidates equally and that I would give him a fair shake. About my vote, with a warm friendly smile, I told him, *"Governor, you're a bit too liberal for me, but don't worry—I'll treat you fairly."*

A few weeks later I got a call from the Carter campaign asking if I could meet with Rosalynn Carter for an interview. The interview was set for a Saturday, my usual day off, but I agreed, and about one o'clock on that Saturday afternoon the First Lady of Georgia arrived, and she had her daughter Amy with her. Except for the weekend announcer we had on air during that time, we had the station to ourselves, and I spent the next ninety minutes in my newsroom, interviewing her.

I found Rosalynn Carter to be a lovely and gracious woman with a good grasp of the issues of the day, and for the next hour and a half we had an excellent interview. Her daughter, who was about nine, had the run of the station that day, and she had a great time. She was well-behaved, but her curiosity took her all over the radio station, investigating everything and looking at the archival photographs and checking out all the equipment.

About a year earlier they'd moved the studios from out in the country (actually in the middle of a large orange grove) to a downtown location on E. Lime Street in Lakeland, which was just across from the FBI's second-floor offices. The station looked good—very professional, which was a far cry from the small offices and studios we'd used out in the orange grove south of the city. About the only time little Amy interrupted us was when she wanted to know why all the walls were covered with lime green-and-yellow shag carpeting. I explained to her that the carpeting helped deaden the sound, and it eliminated any echoes.

Earlier that same year I was covering a big meeting of prominent politicians at Walt Disney World Hotel, in one of their conference rooms. This was prior to the time that Carter locked up his party's nomination. I particularly wanted to get an interview with Senator Ted Kennedy because press reports indicated he'd not made up his mind about running for president, and the rumors were that his mother, Rose Kennedy, didn't want him to run. I had a reputation for being able to secure private interviews when others seemed unable to get them, so I was finally able to get a one-on-one with Ted Kennedy in an anteroom next to the larger conference room. There were only three of us in the room—Senator Kennedy, myself, and another man I assumed to be his aide. The interview started off well, and I also found Senator Kennedy to be quite articulate, having an excellent grasp of the issues.

However, the world press still had lingering questions about the events at Chappaquiddick and the death of Mary Jo Kopechne at Martha's Vineyard some six years earlier.

Ms. Kopechne had drowned, and her body was found in the backseat of the senator's mother's car at the bottom of a tidal channel on Chappaquiddick Island in Massachusetts on July 19, 1969, following a party the night before.

There were many questions regarding that night, but one of the main concerns was why the senator had waited until the following morning to go to the police and report what had happened. At that time he told police investigators he had informed the party the night before that he wanted to leave, after which Ms. Kopechne asked if he would give her a ride to her hotel. Kennedy then claimed he made a wrong turn and ended up going over a small bridge and into the water with Ms. Kopechne in the rear seat, where she drowned. Many of the facts didn't seem to add up even after all the years since the tragic death of the young woman, and many, both in the United States and world press, still had the uneasy feeling that Senator Kennedy had not been entirely forthcoming about the events leading up to the young lady's death.

Because of the controversy, I wanted to get his take on what happened that night and give him an opportunity to put the issue to rest. But not wanting to bluntly jump right into the subject, I began asking him questions about his decision about whether or not to run and what factors might be involved in his decision if he did decide to run for president. Kennedy assumed I was looking for some scoop about the rumors that his mother, Rose Kennedy, didn't want him to run, so he very quickly stated that although two of his brothers had been assassinated, the elder Mrs. Kennedy's concerns would not be a factor in his final decision to run for the presidency. When I asked him if Mrs. Kennedy would play any role in his decision-making process, he replied, *"I'm looking into many factors before making my decision, but I can assure you that whatever I decide, it will be my decision alone. I am my own man."* My questions next were the following:

"Senator Kennedy, if you do decide to run, are you prepared to deal with the inevitable questions from the world press about the events at Chappaquiddick, especially since the media has lingering questions and seems unwilling to let this issue go?"

Immediately Kennedy's face turned red, and I could see he didn't like my question. In fact, he was *livid over my question*. He glanced at his associate in the room, whom I soon discovered was his bodyguard, and I quickly found myself being lifted to my feet and manhandled out of the room by this very large man. I tried to interrupt the shoving with, *"Senator, you know the press is going to be asking these questions, and if you're not prepared to answer them now, how will you ever handle them if you become president?"*

I quickly saw I was going to lose the battle over being muscled out of the room, so I lashed out with, *"Senator, you put your pants on one leg at a time, and you don't intimidate me. If you've got any hopes of being president, you can't be so thin-skinned."*

In retrospect I wasn't proud of the way that I'd handled that matter—not exactly in the manner of a professional journalist.

Kennedy entered the race shortly afterward and was one of the challengers to Governor Carter during the primaries, but he was unable to gain any real traction with the voters, with many claiming it was an issue of trust, and he was simply never able to overcome the groundswell that Carter was riding. He withdrew early in the primary races, leaving the field open for Carter. The events at Chappaquiddick seemed to dog him throughout the campaign, and many political pundits claimed, the nagging questions surrounding that event were finally his undoing.

Anyway, that was a rapid end to my first and only interview with Senator Edward Kennedy. I was somewhat uneasy about writing my encounter with Senator Kennedy because he died of cancer in August of 2009, and I didn't want this to seem as though I were attacking a man who was unable to come to his own defense, so I just laid it out for you because that was simply the way it happened.

six handguns pointed directly at me…

My workday at WVFM started at 6:30 a.m. when I would begin writing stories for the news broadcasts, the first of which was at seven. I would scour the UPI and AP wire copy that reeled off their machines, looking for any local and national stories that were important enough to be included in the news, and I would also look through the Lakeland and Tampa newspapers. As was my practice, during my drive to work, which would typically start out at about 6:00 a.m., I'd stop by a local convenience store to pick up the newspapers, but this particular morning proved to be very different. As I walked out of the little country convenience store with newspapers in hand, three Polk County sheriff's cars pulled into the dirt-and-gravel parking lot, skidding to a halt, and as the dust cleared, I could see six deputies crouching behind the patrol car doors with their weapons drawn, yelling out, *"Freeze!"*

"Whoa, fellas... I'm frozen!" I shouted back.

It turned out that someone had been robbing convenience stores in the early morning hours in that area, and their car matched my big blue Chevy station wagon to a tee. When the officers discovered who I was, they offered their apologies, and later that day the Polk County sheriff called me at the radio station and invited me out to lunch to further the apology.

Part of my responsibilities as news director of this radio station was investigative reporting. I suppose I'd have left this next news story alone had it not been for the fact that about once a month, almost like clockwork, the local police in Lakeland would raid a floating crap game, which was run by a local black man in town, called Muley. And it seemed so hypocritical for the local officials to bust this guy for his penny-ante gambling games when most of these same officials had been at a Christmas Eve party that featured big-time gambling and where a close friend told me he'd personally seen $30,000 change hands over one roll of the dice at the table.

During the midseventies, one local businessman, who had sold a patent (reportedly for $6 million) for a new fast-freezing process for freezing vegetables to a major food company, had apparently decided to impress his wealthy friends. He'd completed some major expansions and renovations on his beautiful lakeside home, and he invited hundreds of important people over for a Christmas party. This was a *large* party by most anyone's standards because I'd heard he had more than a hundred guests for a sit-down dinner.

The party also featured high-stakes Vegas-style gambling, including roulette wheels, crap tables, and slot machines. And they had imported some Vegas shills (prostitutes) who would help keep the gambling going and the stakes high and who were also available for upstairs entertainment for the guests later that evening.

Present at this party were city and county government officials and politicians, and there was even a federal judge at the party. Many of Central Florida's wealthiest and influential people were present, including the head of a major grocery store chain. I knew most of these people, including all the local government officials.

A friend of mine was the director of one of Lakeland's finest museums where I'd displayed some of my photographic artwork, and this young man was also a well-known classical pianist. He'd been asked to perform at a big pre-Christmas get-together at someone's home, and that was where he'd witnessed what appeared to be a major gambling operation.

After a few weeks of investigating, I took what evidence I had and went to the district attorney's office in Bartow, the county seat for Polk County. When I gave him the information, also telling him about some of the high-ranking people who were involved, he turned pale then simply got up and walked out of his office, leaving me there. Assuming he'd probably gotten up to use the restroom, I waited for about twenty minutes, but when he didn't return, I went out to ask his secretary if she thought he'd be coming back, and she simply told me he'd left for the day. The man was truly frightened.

After a similar response at the local district attorney's office in Lakeland, I then decided to try to break this story to my friend, John R. Harrison, who was publisher of the *Lakeland Ledger* newspaper as well as a vice president of the *New York Times*. Jack and I had become friends over the years, and he respected my opinions. Frequently, during my ministry, I would simply call up the newspaper and indicate I wanted to hold a news conference about some upcoming event, and I would soon have reporters and photographers on the scene, and sometimes television camera crews would show up, simply because I'd asked for a press conference. As I mentioned earlier, it was his reporters covering my street ministry and later the coffeehouse and Jesus House work, which opened so many doors to us with the favorable publicity.

So on the occasions when I asked for a press conference, I always got full cooperation. This happened several times, and once, television reporters showed up for my little press conference. I announced that I had arranged to bring Nicky Cruz to Lakeland and that we would be holding a rally at Joker Marchant Stadium where the Detroit Tigers held their spring training. It was then that the city of Lakeland agreed to shut down much of downtown Lakeland for our Youth Challenge parade leading up to the Nicky Cruz rally.

With that as a background, I anticipated being well received by my friend Jack Harrison at the *Lakeland Ledger*.

After being seated in his office, I explained that I had information that had the potential to topple much of Central Florida government. Jack immediately got on the phone, and within minutes the room was full with at least twelve to fifteen people taking notes, including their editor, the "City" editor, their "Lifestyles" editor, and several of their best reporters—reporters with whom I was familiar and who had covered much of my work.

About ten minutes into my story, I was surprised when Jack suddenly stood up and excused everyone else from the room. I didn't know what to make of it, but I soon discovered that, much to his embarrassment and mine, he revealed he was at that party as well. He explained that he was unaware that there was going to be any gambling and that he'd not been involved in it, and he said that it put him in a very awkward position. But he explained, there were too many of his friends there that night for him to allow the story to be printed.

He said that even though the *Ledger* had gotten a reputation for being a tough newspaper, willing to tackle anything and anybody, with a "let the chips fall where they may" attitude, he simply couldn't print this. I told him I understood how this put him in an awkward situation, and we parted on good terms.

Meanwhile, I had been contacted by the FBI, who had gotten word that I was investigating this gambling party, and they pumped me for information. They indicated that much of the gambling equipment—that is, the roulette wheel, crap tables, and slot machines—had been provided by a major gambling ring. They tried to persuade me to allow them to put a wire on me (for sound) so I could go in to this man's house on the pretext of interviewing him about his newfound wealth he'd acquired from the sale of his patent. I never went through with it, sensing I might be getting in over my head. And it wasn't long before word got around, and someone from the Central Intelligence Agency in Miami called me at the radio station and attempted to recruit me. This guy kept referring to "the company," so when I asked him flat out, *"Are you talking about the CIA, and you're saying the CIA wants me to come to work for them?"* He said, *"Yes, your investigative work has come to our attention, and the CIA has expressed an interest in bringing you into the company."*

The money he talked about was good, at least a lot better than I was currently making at the radio station, but I got a definite check in my spirit and turned him down.

My next option was to take this matter to my friend, the chief of police, whose name I will leave out for obvious reasons. He was always very friendly to me, and he and I had been on a first-name basis for several years.

"Hi, Ken, what can I do for you today?" he said with a smile, but his tone quickly changed when I explained the nature of my call. I not only gave him the information about this major gambling operation, but I also explained how I'd gotten nowhere with the local and county district attorneys and that I'd had no success with the *Lakeland Ledger*. Without mentioning any specific names, I also began to tell him that many of the major politicians, including federal judges and power players in Central Florida, along with numerous wealthy busi-

nessmen, had been at the party. About that time, his face took on an ashen appearance, and he walked over to me and took the tape recorder out of my hand, set it on his desk, and made certain it was turned off. He then turned to me and said, *"Ken, since you're my friend, I'm going to give you two choices. If you'll promise me—give me your word that you will forget all about this—I'll give you my word, nothing will happen to you. But if you don't, I can tell you that before the day is over, you'll end up in the bottom of one of our lakes, wearing a pair of cement boots! And if that's your decision, I'll give you a chance to make one phone call home (pointing to the phone on his desk). Call your wife, and tell her not to pack—just put the kids in the car and drive, and keep on driving. Tell her, 'Don't look back,' and tell her to get as far away from Florida as she can get."*

I am not fearful of many things, but when my family is threatened, I tend to take it very seriously. I agreed to drop the subject right then and there. To this day I still don't know if the threats were coming directly from him or if he was simply warning me and giving me a message for others because he knew what the people involved were capable of doing. In any case, I took it seriously.

To accent the seriousness of all this, the next day at the radio station I received two anonymous telephone death threats. The word was out that I was investigating this big gambling party, with so many of Central Florida's government officials and wealthy and powerful people in attendance and some who were actually involved in the gambling and the prostitution, and I was stirring up a hornet's nest with my snooping around. And since many of the radio station manager's friends had attended the gambling party, I was told by both the station's bigwigs that if I aired that story, they'd see to it I would never work at another radio station again.

Chapter 18

A neighbor of mine had recently started trucking, driving a big rig up and down the East Coast. I personally had never been inside, let alone driven, an eighteen-wheeler big rig truck before, but after all the death threats I'd received, I made a major decision. The following day I took what savings I had and made a down payment on a tractor-trailer rig. I was now in the trucking business. Most of it (the savings) came from the insurance payoff when Kevin, the boy we'd taken into our home since he'd been abandoned by his mother, set our home on fire (actually, he set our house on fire twice), and since I'd done the work myself, I had some money left over. At that time we were living out on Jim Johnson Road in Plant City, about ten miles west of Lakeland, and if it hadn't been for a courageous neighbor who crawled on his hands and knees through the smoke and flames and used our garden hose to put out the blaze, our home would have burned to the ground.

Anyway, I withdrew the money from the bank and put several thousand dollars down on a Cabover Peterbilt and a forty-foot Great Dane refrigerator trailer, and I drove up to the radio station and walked in and quit. No more politics to deal with, no more investigations of gambling operations, and no more death threats—*I quit.*

Two days later I was headed for Boston with a full load of frozen orange juice concentrate, and it took me at least five hundred miles before I could figure out how to shift the darn thing. *I'd certainly never driven a thirteen-speed before!* The shifter had a splitter (I had no idea what a splitter was or what it was for), and I learned later that although it was called a thirteen-speed, it actually had fifteen forward gears except that two of the gears were almost never used.

On my first trip to Boston, hauling frozen orange juice concentrate, my trailer slipped on the ice at the unloading dock at the warehouse in a suburb of Boston, and it broke a rear axle on my Great Dane trailer. I had to chain up the right front axle on the trailer and return to Florida empty (which is called *deadheading*) to get the axle repaired. I spent the next year or so hauling frozen orange juice from Florida to the various corners of the United States, usually either to some place in New England or to Portland or Seattle, and coming back with everything from a truckload of pillows from Boston or lightbulbs from New Jersey or ketchup from Pittsburgh or lobster tails from Maine.

The time away from home, sometimes for as much as two to three weeks at a stretch, seemed to do Karen and me some good for a while because when I returned, she really did seem to miss me. However, spiritually, I felt completely out of my element. *What on earth was I doing, hauling orange juice around the country?* I just didn't belong anywhere—certainly not in this Peterbilt, driving all over the United States.

And I sometimes found myself in some dangerous situations—so much so that I began to carry a handgun under the mattress in my sleeper. I also know that there was a time I would have simply prayed for God to keep me safe, and I would have rested in that assurance.

During one trip to Boston, in which I delivered forty thousand pounds of frozen orange juice concentrate to a warehouse just outside the city, I made a stop at a motel in Foxborough, which was located about a block from the stadium where the New England Patriots played football. I'd used this location before since I'd made several previous trips hauling the OJ concentrate to the same location, but this time I was intrigued by a sight I saw after dropping off my trailer at a nearby truck stop, and that was people skating on a small lake near North Attleboro just a few miles south of Foxborough. I'd never seen anyone skating on a lake before, and since I'd been living the past several years in Florida, it was something of a novel sight to me.

I dropped off my trailer at a nearby truck stop and drove my big Cabover Peterbilt up next to the lake and got out to watch this beautiful winter scene. It was a stunningly beautiful night, and before walking any farther, I stood just for a moment to take it all in. It was exhilarating, with nearby lights surrounding the lake, all highlighting a light snowfall that was coming down; for a moment I was able to forget about the troubles at home. My boots crunched on the snow and ice as I approached closer to the little lake, and I had to admit being a bit giddy with excitement. So when a Massachusetts state trooper walked over to me and began with what I, at first, thought was a bit of chit-chat, it didn't break my mood. I loved the feeling of the brisk air on my face and the sight of my breath in the night air. So when the officer commented on how unusual my huge Peterbilt looked sitting there next to this peaceful winter scene, I was still taking in the moment when I explained to him that I'd just brought in a load of frozen orange juice from Florida, and I wanted to witness people skating on the lake. I took a deep breath, basking in the beauty of it all, when the trooper interrupted my "wonder of it all" moment with, *"Yeah, but what's the big rig doing parked here?"*

I politely explained that I didn't have a car with me, and since I'd parked my refrigerated trailer at the truck stop, it was the only transportation I had and the only way I could get there to take in the sights that night. Then my momentary bliss was again rudely interrupted with, *"I know you guys carry a lot of contraband with you, and I think I'm gonna get up there and search your truck."*

I suddenly realized I might be in serious trouble——not because I was carrying any drugs or what he referred to as contraband, but because I knew I had my Western-style revolver under the mattress in my sleeper. When I'd checked into the motel in Foxborough earlier that afternoon, several times I heard messages on the television about the new Bartley-Fox law, and the message suddenly rang in my ears, *"Carry a gun—go to jail."*

I'd also heard that the law carried with it a mandatory jail sentence of one year—with no appeal, no plea bargaining, and no commutation of sentences. You're caught carrying a weapon without a permit—either on your person or in your vehicle—and you go to jail, period.

Still trying to hide my fear of what this man could do to me and to my future, I tried really hard not to let my fear show. Then mustering up every ounce of courage I had within and in a very calm and deliberate manner, I took a step closer to him, and face-to-face I looked him in the eye and quietly responded with, *"Officer, you don't have my permission to get in my truck. But if you do get in my truck and you find anything, anything at all that causes me one minute of concern, you'd better make damn sure you have probable cause, because if you don't, I'll hang you out to dry for illegal search and seizure."*

A bit dumbstruck over my boldness, the officer stared right back at me for what seemed an eternity, then he simply walked off without saying another word. *Whew!* (Double *whew!*)

Little did I know that very soon, having that handgun with me would save my life more than once, starting with my very next trip up the East Coast. But before I could haul another load of OJ to the East Coast again, I needed another load because the last thing I wanted to do was deadhead back to Florida. Deadheading meant hauling a load of sailboat fuel—nothing. Deadheading meant no money.

The broker I'd been using to secure loads for me (for a percentage of the fees) had arranged for me to pick up a load in Niagara Falls, Canada, and when I got to Niagara Falls, I was thrilled to see them—*completely frozen!* What a sight. During the night I discovered they lit the falls with pink and blue and green lights—in a display I'd never forget.

Picking up a load in Niagara Falls had required some unusual procedures. It meant that someone had to unhook your trailer while another company hitched it to one of their trucks, and they drove on to a nearby destination where they loaded it with products, so when

I finally got my load, I got lucky because this load was destined for Florida.

armed robbers...

On my return trip back up the East Coast, I remember so vividly the night I pulled into Hunts Point Cooperative Market in the Bronx in New York City. This was a huge warehouse and shipping complex in which most of the Big Apple's produce arrived each day, and it's a *very seedy* area of New York. All the roads near the market seemed to converge at one point, somewhat like a river delta coming to a point, and you needed to be signed in at the front gate the night before, or you wouldn't be unloaded the next morning.

There must have been at least one hundred trucks waiting in line to get in, and there were dozens of prostitutes going from truck to truck, hoping to make enough money—maybe for their next fix or maybe just to feed their children; who knows? I just remember feeling how desperately lost these people seemed and how in times past I would have gotten out of my truck and told them of the love of Jesus. Instead, I just drove through the gate and pulled up to one of the unloading docks, waiting for my turn to be unloaded. The offloading of goods and materials would begin at about 7:00 a.m. the next day, but I didn't mind because I had a comfortable sleeper berth in the truck, and I was looking forward to a good night's rest.

At about 2:30 a.m. I was abruptly awakened as my truck began to shake from side to side. It was completely dark inside my sleeper, so I quietly unzipped the leather curtain that divided the sleeper from the cab, and I could see that someone had climbed up onto the footstep on the outside of the truck, and I saw that a black fellow had his hand through the wind vent and was rolling down the window. For a brief moment I was intrigued at the strange sight of him cranking open my driver's-side window with a gun in the same hand he was using on the window crank. In the dark the occasional reflection of the gun made it look as though the gun were moving in circles all by itself.

On the other side of the truck another black man was also attempting to open the passenger-side window. I slowly reached under the mattress and quietly withdrew my .357 Magnum, and then I slowly pointed it directly at his face within just inches of his nose. I then used my other hand to switch on the overhead light.

When the truck's cabin suddenly went from near total darkness to bright light, you couldn't even imagine the fear that came over this guy's face as he stared down the barrel of my hand cannon. He screamed out and fell over backward onto the pavement below, and when he hit the ground, he accidentally dropped his gun. When it hit the asphalt, it went off with a bang, loudly echoing through the surrounding buildings. He scrambled back a few feet to pick up his gun, and then he took off running. I fired a couple of shots into the ground for good measure as he and his buddy ran off into the darkness. I didn't want him returning, and I wanted to make sure he knew I meant business. Apparently, the sound of gunfire in that neighborhood was somewhat of a common occurrence because no one responded to the shots fired.

To this day I believe they would have killed me over the few hundred dollars I was carrying had I not been able to scare them off with my gun and send them running for their lives. I was one of many truckers who didn't use credit cards for their gas purchases in those days.

And that was not the only time I came close to being killed. Truckers usually carry several hundred dollars cash in order to fill those two-hundred-gallon fuel tanks, and there's always a certain element of thieves willing to take a chance for that money or to hijack you for your truck and your cargo.

There's an old trick many long haulers use in order to get out of paying the fees at truck scales and border points of entry, and that's *running the scales*, which meant taking another route in order to avoid having to go through the checkpoints and onto the scales. I'd learned that by driving down Highway 301/121 near the Okefenokee Swamp in Georgia, and by avoiding Interstate 95 as I entered Florida, I could usually save $20 or $30 in fees by going around the truck scales. There wasn't anything illegal about it, but it often meant having to get by the scales at odd hours of the night.

more armed robbers...

So one night I headed down that same route I'd traveled before, taking me close to the Okefenokee Swamp and avoiding the scales in the hopes of getting by them one more time and avoiding those nasty fees. It was a very dark night, almost pitch-black, and there was no traffic on what was otherwise a lonely back country road near the Okefenokee. The scales on Interstate 95 usually caught most of the truckers, and only a few drivers knew about this detour, but as I drove on, I came across an old set of truck scales, scales I thought that'd been abandoned. My previous time heading down this route I'd gone by those same scales, which were always closed and looked abandoned. It was 2:00 a.m., and the grounds around the scale house were almost completely obscured by weeds and tall grass, and it looked as if they'd not been used in at least a year. When I got near the scales, I was approached by two uniformed Georgia state troopers signaling me with flashlights to enter the scales.

Oh no, all that trouble for nothing, I thought. *Guess I'll have to pay the fees after all.* When I pulled up next to them, one of the officers said to me, *"I know a lot of the drivers avoid the scales on I-95 by going this way, and we'd like to check your paperwork and logbooks and weigh your rig."*

But something didn't look right. For one thing although they were in uniform, only one of them was wearing a badge. Something seemed out of place. Their uniforms were a bit wrinkled and were not at all the snappy uniforms you'd expect from state troopers.

Then as I put the truck in gear to follow them over to the scales, I noticed when they were walking away from me and toward the scale house, one of them was wearing *tennis shoes.* That looked mighty suspicious to me. I slowed down and surveyed the situation, but they kept waving me to pull over to the scales. I could tell they were getting impatient, and I almost decided to comply, but then I caught a glimpse behind the scale house, and it wasn't the back of a Georgia state trooper vehicle I saw, but the back of an old pickup truck… there was no patrol car in sight, and I suddenly knew this was a setup for a robbery or a hijacking. I couldn't tell if these were rogue cops or phony Georgia state troopers masquerading in stolen uniforms, but I wasn't waiting around to find out.

I slammed the truck into gear and floored it, and I managed to get about a quarter mile down the road before I saw their pickup in my rearview mirror, and they were gaining on me. The next thing I knew, they were shooting at me… and that's a pretty scary sight, looking into both my rearview mirrors and seeing flashes of gunfire from both sides of their pickup. I'm certain now they would have overtaken me and probably killed me either for the money or for my rig and the valuable load I was carrying in it, but I'm sure that what I did next came as a huge surprise to them.

I hit the brakes and jackknifed my rig just enough to enable me to get a clear shot behind me, and my truck skidded to an abrupt stop. I then opened my driver's-side door, stood out on the side step, and—*bang, bang, bang, bang*—I began firing off shots in the air, not actually trying to hit them. I'm sure that the last thing they'd expected was to see the flash of my handgun, lighting up the night sky because the next thing I saw was when they slammed on their brakes, skidding off onto the grassy shoulder of the road. They then burned a quick *brody* and spun around, kicking up a lot of dirt and gravel, and headed off in the other direction. I'm sure they saw the flashes and decided, *This one isn't going to be an easy mark* as they sped away.

When I got back to Florida, I told this story to my broker, who arranged for most of my loads, and he said he'd been hearing reports of fake Georgia state troopers pulling off hijackings in south Georgia, and he said he'd heard of another such incident in Maryland in which a driver was shot and killed.

Hauling products up and down the country's highways was a tough business. There were always the breakdowns, and everything on a truck that broke down was *expensive!* And then there were the long hours.

all without sleep...

Once, I drove, stopping only to fuel my truck and to eat (no sleep) from Hamilton, Canada, to Boston, then from Boston to Atlanta, from Atlanta to Gainesville, Georgia, then on to Miami—*all without any sleep!* I was carrying a load of frozen chickens that had to be on the boat in Key Biscayne in four days. So you find yourself driving until you can't drive any longer and hope that when you do stop, you won't oversleep. I can remember driving down Interstate 95, and I was hallucinating. I was swerving to miss cars *that weren't even there!* Even then I was more than four hours late getting the load to the docks at Key Biscayne. Luckily, the cargo ship was delayed, or I would have been left with a load of frozen chickens that were to be delivered to Jamaica.

Next, I thought hiring a driver might enable me to spend some time at home and also possibly give me time to find some much-needed work to supplement our anemic finances. The man I hired was a man named Josh, and after taking a trip together so that I could determine if he was a competent driver, I set him loose to handle loads for me. I should have checked out his character references as well. I know you're not supposed to mention someone's name in a book without their permission, but maybe this scoundrel will come forward and try to sue me—*I can hope, can't I?*

Anyway, this arrangement went well for about a month before Josh suddenly disappeared with my truck. Just before he went silent on me, he'd informed me that he drove through a picket line in Gloucester, Massachusetts, and that a striker on the picket line had shot out my truck's radiator, costing me $880 to repair, so after sending him the repair money, when I didn't hear from him, I at first feared something had happened to him. But after several weeks with no news, I began calling law enforcement, hoping to learn something of his whereabouts.

One police official suggested I contact the FBI to report that my vehicle had been stolen and that it was being used to transport goods across state lines, but the FBI informed me that since I'd given him permission to drive it in the first place, it would be months before they could begin any investigation.

I finally got a call from Josh, and he told me he'd been hanging out in Gloucester, Massachusetts, with some party girls, and he was bragging about *"getting laid and getting stoned every day."* He said he was having a *"great time,"* and I could tell he was enjoying reveling in the fun he was having—he was rubbing it in, and he told me he had no intention of returning my truck.

Again, I tried to enlist the help of local law enforcement, but they said there was nothing they could do.

Several weeks later I got a phone call from a truck stop in Maryland. It seemed my truck had been abandoned, and when the truck stop manager looked through the glove box, he located the registration, and so that's how he managed to locate me. I had to fly to Dulles International Airport in Washington DC, and, from there, hire a cab to take me to my truck. I later learned he had drained the transmission case—just for spite. Incidentally, no repairs had been made on my radiator because it had not been shot crossing the picket lines. He'd just scammed me for $880.

Staying ahead of the repair bills and the costs of fuel, oil, tires, and insurance meant I had to keep on driving and driving. After locating the truck, since I had no load for the trailer, which, luckily, was also left there at the truck stop in Maryland, I had to deadhead back to Florida, carrying that proverbial load of sailboat fuel, which didn't pay well at all.

After finally managing to get another load of orange juice concentrate, I headed for Portland, but before I could get there, I crossed over the Oklahoma panhandle into Colorado, and my truck broke down.

The thirteen-speed transmission went out on me in a tiny town called Eads, Colorado. It was then that I learned that Josh had drained my transmission, and that was the reason the gear had cracked and broken. When I finally located my truck in Maryland, I'd been so desperate to get back on the road and start bringing in some money but soon endless repair bills would spell the end of my trucking business.

Often I described driving a big rig up and down the highways of America as unimaginable boredom occasionally punctuated with intense excitement and occasional terror (such as the times when I could have been killed by robbers and hijackers). Sometimes you invent ways to break up the boredom.

Through all this, though, the empty void in me continued to grow. What on earth was I doing? Why was I running up and down the roads and freeways of America, hauling who knows what—and for what? For money? I used to live by faith, and God always provided my needs. I felt like I was back in that quicksand in the Los Angeles River—up to my neck—and there seemed no way out.

I once picked up a young woman hitchhiker in Pennsylvania. Normally, I never picked up hitchhikers, but when I drove by, the young woman was frantically trying to get someone to stop. Even though I had not been serving God for quite some time now, I immediately sensed that when she got up into my truck, there was a great deal of demonic activity going on with her. She had demons—lots of them. I had no idea why she was out on the side of the highway, but now here she was inside my truck, and her eyes were nervously flashing around.

Every time I tried to talk to her, she would scream, and I could tell she was in torment. I tried witnessing to her and talking to her about the Lord, but it had been so long since I'd felt the Holy Spirit in my life it seemed I had nothing to give her. When I asked her if I could pray for her, she screamed, "*Stop the truck, stop the truck,*" so I let her out. I felt miserable. I couldn't help myself, nor could I help anyone else.

Still not fully recovered from that episode with the hitchhiker from hell, when I crossed into West Virginia, I noticed three frantic teenage girls trying to flag down a ride. I slowed down, but when I continued on and I didn't stop, I noticed they were running after me down the side of the road. *What on earth is going on?* I thought. I reluctantly pulled over to the side of the road about fifty yards ahead of them, and I was just planning to ask them why they were out there on the highway, running, but they just opened the passenger-side door and climbed up into the truck, one of them in the front seat and the other two back in the sleeper. I said, *"Girls, will you tell me what's goin' on, why you got in my truck, and why you're out here hitchhiking in the freezing cold?"*

The three of them all tried to talk at once, and I couldn't make sense of it. It was a cacophony of high-pitched voices—all nonsense—three teenage girls all babbling at once, and it didn't help that they were all shivering from the cold at the same time. I've got one of those booming voices you can hear on the back side of the moon, so when I finally shouted out, *"Stop! Stop! Stop, and shut up!"* the girls stopped, and suddenly there was dead silence.

I shouted, *"OK—one at a time. You—you look like you're the oldest. You tell me what's goin' on and why you girls are out here in the cold, running down the highway, trying to hitch a ride."*

It turned out one of the girls, one who was 15, claimed she'd been raped and was now pregnant from the rape, and she said her rapist was someone in her family. But as if that weren't enough, one of the girls opened her purse and showed me a handgun they were carrying. She said they were afraid of that family member, the girl's incestuous attacker, and that's why she had the gun for protection.

We were less than thirty miles from the state line. Here I was with three underage teenage girls—one of them, fifteen, and the other two, sixteen, and one of them, a pregnant rape victim who was carrying a loaded handgun—and we were about to cross into North Carolina. If I crossed a state line with these girls in my truck under these outrageous circumstances, I could end up in federal prison for violating the Mann Act (illegally taking minors across state lines). I told them, *"You've got a lot of troubles—more than I can solve. You need to pray and ask for God's help because my help ends five miles up the road at the next truck stop. I'll give you some money for the pay phone if you need it, but I'm leaving you there, and you need to call the police for help."*

I pulled in at the truck stop, and I walked with them to the pay phone where they used the change I'd given them, and they called the police. I left there, thinking, *What was that all about? I could have ended up in prison over that little incident.*

Due to my truck being stolen a few months earlier, along with all the endless repair bills, I had fallen behind on my truck payments. I'd been driving night and day all over the United States, trying to dig myself out of the hole, but the harder I tried, the more helpless the situation became.

Finally, after one trip up north, I managed to come home for Christmas. There wasn't much money to go around for presents for the kids, but at least I was home for Christmas. Just as we sat down at the table to have our Christmas dinner, I noticed a tow truck outside on our driveway. On Christmas Day my truck was repossessed.

I'd heard about a local company that was hiring drivers to haul chemicals in that area of Florida, so I signed on, driving for them for a few months. That didn't last long, though, because once I was delivering a load of liquid sulfur when the connecting hose broke and hot yellow sulfur spilled out, covering me and my clothing from the top button of my denim shirt down to my pant legs. I only ended up with minor burns, but strangely enough, I was fired (they insisted I didn't connect the hoses correctly) -- fired although nearly being killed by liquid sulfur.

Chapter 19

Over the next ten or fifteen years the list of failures in my life was endless and unremitting. I had left my ministry in disgrace. I'd had to quit my radio job because of the death threats over the gambling operation. Then there was the house fire, followed by the truck repossession. Next, I tried selling new and used cars for about a year, but my conscience gave me fits over that one. *I couldn't believe the lies we were expected to tell in order to sell a car.* So I managed to fail at that as well.

Davey Power Gas, in Lakeland, a major builder of hydroelectric dam projects around the world, hired me to be their writer and public relations man. I was supposed to report to work on a Monday, but the Friday before that I dropped by the office to pick up some information to help me prepare for starting work, but it was then they advised me I wouldn't be coming to work on Monday after all. A major contract to build a hydroelectric plant in a South American country had been lost, and they were cutting back—another failure.

I began to fall on desperate times, and I remember searching through garbage cans to locate soda pop bottles for the refund money, just to be able to make phone calls to try to find some work, some way to pay the bills.

Sometimes I even had to look to churches to help us out with food so I could feed my family. Living outside of the Lord's will is tough life at best and a living nightmare at its worst.

Meanwhile, Karen and I were struggling to make things work in the marriage. There were periods, sometimes months, in which it looked as though things might work out, and Karen would be very loving and sweet for a while, then without warning she would wake up one day hating me all over again. As I said earlier, I never knew which Karen I would wake up with the next morning—the beautiful and loving young woman I'd fallen in love with and married or the woman who hated me to my very core. This tore at my heart because when we'd started out, we were both very much in love, and when we both came to the Lord at just about the same time, I thought this must be a match made in heaven, so when things continued to get worse, I could tell Karen was in torment, but there was nothing I could do to help her. She didn't want my help—she didn't seem to want anyone's help.

Out of desperation, both financial and marital, I called my mother and asked if we could come back to California to live with her for a while until we got back on our feet. Mom wired us the money, and we were all soon headed back to California.

A few weeks later I landed a job as an area manager, then later as regional manager, for the American National Volleyball Association (ANVA), which groomed young female athletes for our future Olympics effort in volleyball. They had charge of the Junior National Women's Team, and had placed most of the women on the US Olympic team. Within a month they transferred me to start up an office in Denver. Eventually, I had more than twenty offices nationwide under my supervision. Often I would have to travel to a city, locate a suitable office, and then hire managers and train sales crews who would sell tickets to volleyball events that were held, pitting our Women's Junior National Volleyball Team against one of their best local men's teams, and the girls never lost.

There were also times an office was failing, and I had to travel there to find out why, sometimes having to fire the manager I'd hired, because he wasn't performing. That was a tough one because I'd always been a bit of a softy when it came to that sort of thing. But I had a rule that if someone was worth saving and holding on to, I'd chew them out and let them know they needed to shape up, or they'd soon be shipping out. On the other hand, if I knew someone's job simply was not salvageable, if I knew they weren't cutting it, and I was going to have to let them go, I was always gentle and soft-spoken with them. It was bad enough for them to lose their job—they didn't need to be beaten down and kicked by me in the process.

With an office in Denver that needed to be established, I had to leave Karen and the children at my mother's back in California while I headed for Denver and opened up the new office. Within two weeks I received a call that Karen was in the hospital in serious condition with a tubal pregnancy and was going to have to undergo surgery. She had been admitted at the same hospital in Orange County where our daughter Kimberly was born. I rushed back to California, driving non-stop except for gasoline, for some sixteen hours straight and much of it at 80 and 90 mph, not even stopping to eat. When I arrived, she didn't even greet me. She simply acknowledged my presence. I was like a stranger to her, almost an enemy.

We all moved to Denver, but within less than a year the situation with Karen deteriorated even further. During that time, for a while I was living in my office. It was a bit awkward, but I couldn't pay the rent on our house in Lakewood, on the west side of Denver, and buy groceries for her and the children and also keep up a household myself, so I stayed in my office, which was a six-story building comprised of converted condominiums and apartments, so even though it served as my office, it also had a full kitchen, a bedroom, which served as my office, and a living room, which served as a meeting and training room. After a short time Tammy and Jeff came to live with me, and a few weeks later Kimmy ran away from home, and she also came to live with me at the office. During this time Karen had been contacted by Tina, Kevin's birth mother, and she allowed Tina to take him with her to Arizona. Soon she filed for divorce and left to return to Florida.

I'd never believed in divorce. I'd always thought this was a covenant that shouldn't be broken, and yet once again my wife—first Carolyn and now Karen—was divorcing me. Scott returned with her to Florida, and the four children who'd grown up together for twelve years were now split up. Now I had Tammy, Jeff, Kimmy, and Kevin living with me. The devastation this divorce would wreak on the children would be felt for many years to come.

I will never forget the day when Scott and I parted. He explained that his mother would need him, and therefore, he felt he should go to Florida with her. It was many years later that I learned that Scott had to face some of the people in Florida, people who had looked up to me, but people whom also I had let down, and the shame I had caused devastated him. What had started out with Karen and me and our little family, with such great hopes and expectations… as our journey into *"Happily Ever After"*… had unceremoniously ended.

And so the failures continued.

Although I soon had more than twenty offices nationwide under my supervision, stretching from Chicago to Atlanta, we all know what happened to the 1980 Olympics. The Soviet Union invaded Afghanistan, and my old friend Jimmy Carter had declared the United States would boycott the Olympics. The 1980 Olympics went on without the United States, and the American National Volleyball Association never recovered because people were no longer willing to donate money for the Olympics when America wasn't participating in it. When I returned to California, ANVA's huge new gymnasium had been boarded up, and they were in foreclosure.

I returned to California with my children, Tammy, Jeff, and Kimberly and Kevin. By that time Tina had brought Kevin back to me because she was out of money, so she abandoned any claim to him—then. Since years earlier I had been awarded custody of Tammy and Jeff by a Florida court, and then I had also been awarded custody of Kimberly by a Colorado court, it was comforting to know that at least someone, if only some judges in Florida and Colorado, thought I was doing a good job. We moved in with my mother, who had recently moved into a large older home in Upland, a home owned by my cousin Karen.

As a single parent now and having just relocated to California, I began driving a truck hauling cattle feed, which was not exactly my calling in life, but it was putting groceries on the table. After working for O.H. Kruse Grain & Milling in Ontario, I sometimes had to haul 40,000 lb. of chicken poop (I know you're tempted to call it something else—*I'll bet you're thankful I didn't call it that*). Don't ask me why, but they do use this as a supplement in their cattle feed, along with cottonseed hulls, dried orange pulp, almond shells, and beet pulp. However, after about a year I injured my back on the job and was fired because I was barely able to work, and although I sued and it was settled out of court, this was yet another failure.

After more than a year of being on disability and workman's compensation, along with some painful physical therapy, I went to work as the investments director for Cornerstone Development, a real estate holding company in San Bernardino, and I also did numerous television commercials for them to promote their real estate investments, but within a year the company filed for bankruptcy and folded. And the beat goes on.

It was during that time I had a bad accident on my Harley-Davidson motorcycle while coming down the mountain from Running Springs on Highway 330. I had been looking for a location for an office in the mountain resort areas when I rounded a curve, and my motorcycle slipped on a rock that was on the road. It'd rained a few days earlier, and just seconds before I rounded the curve, one of the rocks, about the size of a loaf of bread, came loose, and it rolled in front of me and struck my front wheel, and since I was leaning into the curve, I didn't have much room to maneuver, and I crashed head-on into a granite cliff. My left knee was severely broken. The bumpy ride in the ambulance down the mountain to the hospital was almost unbearable. I had been doing television commercials for the real estate company, so when I was wheeled into the emergency room, the doctor on call in the ER that afternoon called out to me from across the room, *"Hey, I know you… you're the guy in those TV commercials!"*

The doctor made his way over to me while I was still on the gurney. He asked me what was the problem, and I'd told him my left leg was broken. He put one hand on my knee, and with the other hand, he grabbed my ankle. Lifting my knee up so that my leg was bent at a 90° angle, he suddenly began violent jerking motions banging my knee around, back and forth, up and down, several times, and it was severe. He said, *"Yep, you were right. It's broken for sure."*

I yelled out in pain, and then I sat up enough so that I could take a big swing at him. He flinched back just enough so I only clipped him on the chin, but it was hard enough to get his attention. If he hadn't flinched, I'm sure I would have coldcocked him right then and there. He yelled out, *"What'd you do that for?"*

I screamed out, *"You idiot. I told you my leg was broken when I came in here—what do you think they make X-ray machines for, you moron? Do you have any idea how much that rough jerking my leg around hurt?"*

I don't remember him giving me any more compliments on my television commercials after that.

Soon I found myself in surgery (yep, same doctor) to repair what they called a tibial plateau fracture. The surgeon had to put a flat piece of stainless steel next to my knee and down along the tibia. They then drilled through the bone and then fastened this contraption with large screws securing the bone to the steel rod. When I saw the X-rays, it was really strange seeing the large screws, threads and all, protruding through the bone and coming out the bone on the other side. That plate remained in my leg for the next twenty years. That was the first in my series of injuries.

A *jack-of-all-trades* (and master of none), I then took courses to get my state contractor's license, and I began building custom homes in the mountain resort communities of Lake Arrowhead, Running Springs, and Crestline, which is in the San Bernardino Mountains, about a ninety-minute drive from Los Angeles. The real estate company I'd been working for as investments director had wanted me to open up a branch office for them in the mountains, and they wanted me to set it up and run it for them—at my expense. So I decided to strike out on my own, and that was why I made that fateful trip up the mountain that day, scouting out a location for a new office.

I ended up building many fine homes in Lake Arrowhead, Crestline, and Running Springs and in Lytle Creek, and I got great satisfaction in building something that would still be there one hundred years from now. But one of the obstacles we soon faced became evident when we made it clear we wouldn't "play the game" with the local Building and Safety officials.

I'd hired my younger brother, Les, as my construction superintendent since he'd had several years' experience building homes for another contractor. During that time there was one particular building inspector who made life quite difficult for us. More than once he gave us instructions about a procedure he insisted we had to follow, often at considerable expense, only to be told later that he "never said that." These unexpected adjustments to the plans were always after our plans had been approved, so that meant, whatever it was he was requiring hadn't been budgeted and ended up coming out of my pocket

On one particular site, I drew the line. I had just completed expensive adjustments to the plans that this inspector required, which included having to hire the services of a civil engineer, when he tried the *"I never said that"* routine on me again. At the time, Les was standing near me when the statement was made, and I said to Les, *"Hand me your framing ax, brother, I need it for something."*

I held it for a moment, and then I handed it to the building inspector, who I'm sure was wondering why I'd handed it to him. I then said, *"Les, did you hear what he just said? He threatened me with your framing ax, and I'll bet his fingerprints are all over it,"* I said.

I grabbed the framing ax from him, and I was holding it in a menacing way when that guy's face turned ashen. I went on to say, *"Once again you've lied to us. We did exactly as you said we should do. We completed everything you required right down to the last expensive detail, only to hear you once again say, 'I never said that.' Greg, I don't ever want to see you on one of my construction sites again. In fact, I don't ever want to see your face again, because if I do see you—every time I see you—I'm going to beat the hell out of you. Now get out of here—run!"*

He ran off the jobsite, and from that moment on he avoided me like his life depended on it. I'd never been a violent man, but that day he made my blood boil.

Soon after that I learned why we were getting so much heat from the officials. Another building inspector, an older man who'd been inspecting jobsites in the mountains for many years and who had gained a reputation as a fair and honest inspector, told me that a few months earlier there'd been a meeting at Building and Safety in Twin Peaks, and the instructions were, *"Get Simmons. Run 'em out of business. Run 'em off the mountain."*

When I asked why, the answer was, *"Because you won't play the game."*

It was true—there'd been strong hints from time to time that if we'd just pay off the right people *"like everyone else did,"* our problems would go away, and I wasn't about to join their game… of pay to play.

After a little more than five years building homes on the mountain, one day while we were unloading lumber for a resort home in Lake Arrowhead, I was struck by a forklift, which was carrying 22 ft. long floor joists, and it caught me from behind at the back of my knees. Over the next few weeks I gradually began to be paralyzed in my right arm and down my side. The injuries I sustained required a neurosurgeon to remove a disk in my neck. Thankfully, the surgery relieved the problem. My absence from the business came at a time when we had six or seven homes under construction at once, and I ended up going over budget and being unable to complete some of the homes.

At that time we were also building two homes for a Christian conference center in Lake Arrowhead, and we'd reached a little more than 95 percent completion on the two homes when we had to shut down. During the year that followed, the conference center sued although I didn't know anything about the lawsuit for about a year. Through legal maneuvering, along with their attorney lying to the judge who was overseeing the case, claiming he'd been unable to reach me (they had my address and phone number the entire time), they got a summary judgment against me.

They then waited until one day before the one-year statute of limitations had expired for me to file an appeal. And because they "didn't know where Simmons was or how to reach him" (a lie), they had managed to pierce my corporate veil, and that's how they managed to get a summary judgment against me personally for nearly double the *entire construction contract amount*—as though we'd never built anything or spent a dollar on their project, just the same as if we *"took their money and ran."* Imagine that; they sued me and won a judgment for almost twice the whole contract amount although the two homes were more than 95 percent complete. I know some Christian attorneys—theirs couldn't have been one of them.

The lawsuits that resulted forced me into bankruptcy. I truly loved building homes, and some of them were substantial and quite beautiful, but if you build homes, it's almost a given that you will be sued sooner or later. In one lawsuit the homeowner complained that he could see nailheads on the wooden siding on the outside of his house. This was the outside of the home—not finish carpentry like cabinets on the inside. I built them according to industry standards, and I built them well.

After shutting down my contracting business, I had a short stint doing carpentry for various residential framing contractors. Following that I was hired as a construction superintendent by Lewis Homes. Lewis was a major residential and commercial developer in California and Nevada, but after completing my first tract of twenty-four homes in Desert Hot Springs near Palm Springs, the bottom fell out of the construction market, and they laid off all but their most senior superintendents. The failures continued.

Next, I learned of an advertising business in Orange County that was servicing real estate companies, and there was apparently no one providing that service for the Inland Empire, which is an area of Southern California that encompasses Upland to the North, San Bernardino to the east, Corona and Riverside to the south, and Claremont and San Dimas to the west. So I sold my Harley and used the money to buy a computer that I would need for the business, and I began doing real estate advertising. This went well for a while, but every year more and more real estate offices were closing their doors, and after three years I was forced to sell the business—another failure.

I even tried marketing home and personal security equipment, but that soon proved a bust. As I said, the string of failures continued unbroken and unrelenting. What's the old saying? *"If it weren't for bad luck, I wouldn't have any luck at all."* And yet during all this there was still something that yearned within me for that fellowship I had once had with the Lord. Nothing the world had to offer could ever fill that, for nothing could ever give me the joy and peace I once knew.

In fact, the only success I had at all during that time was in finding Diane.

Chapter 20

(Okay, you can hit the Rewind button—just a little.)

The summer before Diane and I met, we were homeless. Tammy, Jeff, Kimmy, Kevin, and I—all of us had, for all intents and purposes, been homeless and living out of a tent and my mother's seventeen-foot travel trailer in a campground in the mountains at Mount Baldy, which is about thirty-five miles east of Los Angeles. We often fished for our supper, sometimes catching enough trout to make several meals. That's not to suggest that we were going hungry, but money was scarce, and we did anything we could to help scrape by. I'd been saving up money for the deposits to rent a condominium in Upland just off 13th Street. I still had my car, a beautiful 1979 Ford Thunderbird that I'd bought when I was regional manager for ANVA, and the kids loved the trips up and down the mountain with the T-top off and the wind in our hair—we made the best of it.

I'd been seeing a young lady in La Verne, and one night I'd walked over to the outdoor pay phone at the Mount Baldy Lodge across from the campground to give her a call. We'd been chatting for about ten minutes when I noticed something crawling over my bare feet. It was a rattlesnake. I asked her to hang on for a moment, then I reached down and picked it up and then continued my conversation with her. I was still on the phone when this crazy rattlesnake began making quite a racket, and she said, *"What's that noise?"*

"I think it's our supper," I said.

So you guessed it. We had rattlesnake for dinner that night—a little tough, *but tasty as all get out.* The snake was about four feet long, and after cutting off its head so we could cook it, this snake, now without a body, turned its head and looked directly at me as if to say, *"What have you done to me?"* I also cut off its rattles and attached them to a leather necklace I'd been wearing, so when I met Diane a few months later, I was wearing that stupid rattlesnake tail around my neck.

The night we met I had just broken up with the girl who lived in La Verne a few hours earlier. I walked into Reuben's Restaurant on Mountain Avenue in Upland because I'd heard that one of my favorite musical groups, Second Nature, would be playing there that night. They played great oldies, mostly classic rock. But because of the breakup, I was feeling a bit melancholy, and I hesitated for a moment. I started to leave, and I turned around to walk out, but at the last minute something made me decide to stay anyway. *Maybe it would cheer me up,* I thought.

Diane Gerwing was celebrating her upcoming thirtieth birthday, which was just three days away. Earlier she'd told the Lord, *"If I don't find the man I'll marry when I turn thirty, I'm going to go into a convent."* Diane was there with two of her sisters and her brother-in-law when her younger sister nudged her and said, *"There's a cute guy, and he's coming over here."* (Hey, don't blame me—that's what her sister said. Did you want me to say she said, *"There's this ugly guy, and he's coming over here"?* Gimme a break).

The restaurant had a dance floor, and Second Nature was playing some songs I recognized. Since I'd heard them before when they performed at the Buckhorn Lodge in Mount Baldy Village, I was familiar with them and their music. I asked the lead singer to perform some of the Righteous Brothers' music, and so when I walked across the dance floor, they began playing *"You've Lost That Lovin' Feelin'"* when I saw a bright-eyed and happy young woman sitting there along with some friends. Little did I know that song would later become the number one most requested song in the world, and little did I know she would become my wife. Even though it's a bit of a sad song, every time we hear it, we're reminded of the night we met.

Anyway, Diane later said her younger sister was disappointed because she had thought she was the one I was about to ask to dance.

We began to date, and it wasn't long before I knew she would be good for me and for the children. Her gentleness and kindness quickly won my heart and won me over, and in January 1981, we were married at the Assemblies of God church on Grove Avenue in Upland. The well-known gospel singer Sylvester Blue sang at our wedding.

Diane had been a legal secretary with the Federal Bureau of Investigation for several years before we met and continued with them for a total of sixteen years. Following that she joined a major builder-developer firm in Upland also as legal secretary.

Next to the Lord in my life and my children, Diane has been the best thing that has ever happened to me although it took me much too long to realize that. I can't believe all that I put her through, and yet she stood by my side. I loved Diane right from the beginning, but I had been through so much that there didn't seem to be much left for me to give. It was as though my heart had been numbed by all that I had been through. And yet she was so devoted to me and to the children, and she had such patience, especially considering she'd earned a ready-made family, complete with three teenagers and a nine-year-old Kevin.

Diane laughingly recalls how, during those prayers for God to bring someone to her before her thirtieth birthday, or she would resign herself to a convent, she'd also prayed for a family. Now she warns, *"Be careful what you pray for because you just might get it."*

She is also quick to point out that she has absolutely no regrets. I'm continually amazed that she accepted this much responsibility, and she took it in stride. Now Diane and I are wonderfully close, and we look forward to every moment together. Our love goes very deep, and we are committed to spending the rest of our days with each other.

And another thing is, after more than thirty-five years of marriage (as of the date of this writing), we've never had an argument. Sure, we've had disagreements, and we've seen things differently, but we've never, ever gotten into what you could call a fight or an argument.

We respect each other too much to engage in shouting or name-calling, and we have taken seriously the biblical admonition to "never let the sun go down on your wrath," meaning we have never gone to bed angry at each other. That, in itself, is amazing particularly since I put her through a lot of difficulty before I once again surrendered to Christ—so much so it would have sent most other women packing. I don't think she understood it at the time, but I believe God gave her a special batch of mercy and forgiveness, not for herself, *but for her toward me,* to endure the things she would have to endure for her love for me.

She, with her prior Catholic background, has come into a very sweet and personal relationship with Christ, and she has such a precious and warm spirit. Not long ago she was baptized in the Holy Spirit, and this shy and unassuming secretary, my wife, has become a spark plug, on fire for God.

Diane is now my soul mate. My eyes light up when she comes into the room, and my heart beats a little faster each time I see her. Her laughter renews my spirit, and I have found true delight in her. Corny as it sounds, she truly lights up my life, and next to my Lord and my children, she was the brightest spot in my life in the nearly twenty years I wandered "in the wilderness."

Chapter 21

the pains of rebellion...

After years of running from God and being angry with him, I had another injury, this one much more serious than all the others combined, and this injury nearly ended my life. It happened on October 9, 1992.

I was hiding Diane's birthday present in the garage loft when the sixteen-foot ladder I was using slipped out from under me, and I fell to the concrete below, landing on top of the ladder as well. I thought this was the end. I simply could not breathe. My lung had collapsed, and I knew if I couldn't get a breath, I was going to die. The pain was beyond description. Finally, I began to lose consciousness, and as I felt myself slipping away, I sensed I was dying. Then in desperation I gathered up what little strength I had left, and in a huge gasp, I managed to take in a deep breath of life-saving air that filled my collapsed lung, and as the lung filled with air, I felt the crunch of multiple rib fractures all at once. The pain was unimaginable. I had no idea as to the full extent of the injuries. Thank God, a friend found me lying on the garage floor.

For the next three to four hours I was lifted, turned, rolled over, picked up, and rolled over some more, for X-rays, CAT scans, MRI tests, all without anything to kill the pain because they needed to learn the cause of my internal bleeding. The doctors told me I had some eighteen fractures, all on the left side of my body. One of the doctors said they stopped counting at eleven rib fractures, and another one told me he'd counted thirteen. Some of the ribs had broken in two and three places. My left pelvis was broken in two places, including the actual hip socket, and it was later discovered I'd caused a hairline refracture to the bone in my left leg that I'd broken earlier during my motorcycle accident back in 1984. My left elbow was broken in two places.

I also had internal bleeding because the impact had damaged one of my kidneys and injured my bladder, pushing several of my internal organs over to the opposite side of my midsection. For the next three days I received morphine injections every thirty minutes around the clock. I was in traction for nearly a month in the hospital, and then I was moved home where I remained in traction in a hospital bed for another month.

Meanwhile, I'd also discovered I was diabetic. My blood sugar was out of control and sky-high, and my body was a wreck. God had given me a fine body, a strong, and healthy body, but now it was beginning to look more like a bag of broken bones. The entire left side of my body, from under my armpit all the way down to an area below my hip and extending from the middle of my back around to and including much of my torso, was solid black from the bruises. And one of the ribs didn't heal for years. It still ground and popped back and forth, still broken. The hip didn't heal properly either. It snapped sometimes so loudly you could hear it across the room. The elbow ground, sounding like someone walking on gravel, and… well, I was pretty much a mess. But I somehow learned to live with it although I was never free from the pain. Unless unusually tired, though, I was able to walk normally without much of a limp.

I know that God never caused any of this to happen. I had an unbroken string of failures, from personal life failures to those in business and then to physical failures, in which I was beaten up, busted up, and stomped on. It was somewhat like the old Western movie in which the cowboy talked about his horse being *"rode hard and put away wet."* I'd been ridden pretty hard. Earlier in my life I was certain that God, and probably a few of his angels, watched over me and kept me from many calamities. Now, even though God never caused any of this, he also wasn't preventing any of it from happening either. Was it presumptuous of me to think that, like Job, the devil had to get permission from God to do these things to me? I don't know. It is, indeed, painful to be out of the will of God.

In a twist of irony and strange coincidence, exactly one year to the day later, on October 9, 1993, at almost the same hour, my younger brother, Les, was in an accident that nearly killed him. Les had had too much to drink at a Jimmy Buffett concert, and on his way home, his pickup truck flipped end over end three times, leaving him unconscious and near death. A helicopter rushed him to the hospital, and Les had broken his neck and back, he'd suffered broken ribs and a punctured lung, and about half of his face had been torn off, leaving his exposed skull. The doctors spent the next several hours patching him up and also picking the dirt and gravel from beneath his flesh next to his skull. Unlike me, though, Les had a full recovery except for the scarring on his face.

my little miracle...

About ten years later I had what I call my little miracle. One of the ribs on my left side still had not healed, and it would pop and grind during just about any movement. Occasionally, that caused some pain, but mostly, it was just an annoyance. I decided it was time to do something about it, so I called an orthopedic surgeon at Kaiser Permanente in Riverside, California, as I'd recently become a member of Kaiser for their health plan. I don't recall whether it was a CT scan or an MRI, but during the examination, they discovered a large tumor on my thyroid, which had also been causing me difficulty in swallowing and keeping any food down. The decision was made that removing the tumor was a higher priority than repairing the still-broken rib, so they scheduled the surgery.

The surgeon went through my throat in order to remove the fist-sized tumor along with my thyroid, and they immediately took it to the lab for testing to see if it was cancerous. Meanwhile, I had many people praying for me and praying for a positive outcome. The doctor later told me that the tumor looked cancerous to him and that it was filled with ugly nodules, which were often present when it turned out to be cancerous. He said he'd done hundreds of these, and this one *"had cancer written all over it."* But to his surprise, the report came back that it was a benign tumor. To this day I suspect it was probably cancerous—that is, until friends and family prayed, and those prayers killed the cancer cells.

Follow my logic for a moment, if you will. The doctors told me the tumor was life-threatening, and the reason they found this tumor, which (finding it) probably saved my life, was because my rib was still broken and was popping and grinding after nearly ten years. So after they removed the tumor along with my thyroid, the broken rib seemed to say, *"You don't need me anymore. I did my job—they found the tumor, I saved your life,"* and it healed itself within the next two weeks.

more close calls…

In chapter two I made reference to the first of many close calls when I'd been trapped in quicksand in the Los Angeles River near our home in Long Beach. Now let us hit the Rewind button back to the 1970s.

Once, while scuba diving off the coast of Florida near Fort Lauderdale I had a close encounter with a large tiger shark. This was during a shore dive with Bill Davis and Paul Luttrell, and we were amazed at the visibility that day. Typically, shore diving meant poor visibility because of the sand and sediments that had been stirred up by the surf, but this day we had an unheard-of three hundred plus feet of visibility within just a few feet of shore. A few years earlier I'd gone scuba diving at Catalina, then I'd had numerous dives off the Southern California Coast, and years later I enjoyed scuba diving in the South Atlantic in Grenada, Saint Vincent and the Grenadines, and in the Turks & Caicos, but I'd never experienced such water clarity and visibility as that day off the Florida east coast near Fort Lauderdale. Even my dive a few weeks later in the Florida Keys, in which I enjoyed amazing water clarity, didn't quite measure up. Nothing quite matched the clear water on that day.

Just inland there was a yacht harbor, and the yachts had a short cruise out to open ocean, which meant they had to pass through two rock jetties that were one hundred yards apart. At the end of each of the jetties the sea bottom was at a depth of about forty-five to fifty feet, and we knew that we had at least three hundred feet of visibility because while underwater we could see all the way from one jetty to the next.

As we were heading back to shore after about a forty-minute dive, Bill and Paul became preoccupied with a large lobster that was hiding in a group of rocks near the bottom. I was about fifty feet closer to the shore than they were, and using my Mae West life vest, I had established neutral buoyancy at a depth of about thirty to thirty-five feet, which meant that I was neither rising to the surface nor sinking. I began to get impatient, hoping that my friends would either catch the lobster or give up on it as my air gauge was registering I was getting low on air. As I glanced around, something underwater caught my attention about two hundred feet to the north of me. Through the crystal clear water, I could see that it was a large shark. Although I wanted to warn them, I also didn't want to tap on my scuba tank to get their attention, because I knew it would attract the shark. I tried waving at them, but to no avail. They were intent on dislodging and catching that lobster.

It was about that time that I noticed the shark had seen me and was heading my way. It wasn't speeding toward me, but rather cruising in my direction, going from side to side as if to check me out. As it came within about twenty-five feet of me, I noticed the distinctive dark-and-light bands on its side, a clear indication of the stripes of a tiger shark, and this was a big one. I estimated it to be about twelve feet long.

a scared minnow...

With the possible exception of the great white shark, most sharks will approach their prey carefully, often circling them just before bumping. Sharks are wary hunters, and most of them will avoid a fight and thereby avoid injury, so they check by bumping you in an effort to see if you're going to be easy prey or if you're going to put up a fight. This one began to circle me, each time coming in closer, and I suspected he was about to bump me. I knew that if a large shark such as this one bumped me with its rough sandpaper-like skin, it would probably cause considerable bleeding because I wasn't wearing a protective wet suit.

About that time he headed straight for me, coming in for the bump, and I certainly had no intention of being this shark's lunch. Years earlier in California before going back to work as a typesetter, I'd been a meter reader for the Edison Company, and I knew that if you turned and ran from an attacking dog, you were going to get bit, and I didn't want to stir up this big kitty cat's predatory instincts. My instincts told me I should make this tiger shark think I was the biggest and the baddest thing in the sea.

I removed the regulator from my mouth, pointed it at the shark, and hit the air release, sending a stream of air bubbles in his direction, and with my other hand, I grabbed my scuba knife, and I began shouting and growling, aggressively coming at it, attacking it, and blowing bubbles and otherwise making him think I was some kind of mad dog—his worst undersea nightmare. This huge carnivore, which could have easily bitten me in half, turned tail and ran like a scared minnow. *Whew!*

When we got back to shore, I calmly mentioned to Bill and Paul that I'd seen a big shark. Paul was a novice diver, and I didn't want to frighten him.

tap, tap – tap, tap, tap…

A few months later the three of us planned a scuba diving trip, so late in the evening we took off, heading for the Florida Keys, pulling Paul's father's boat behind us. We drove most of the night, and before we got to the Everglades, I began to hear a strange noise coming from outside the car. Bill and Paul heard it too. It was a very distinct *tap, tap*, a brief pause... then *tap, tap, tap*. Then it would stop, then it would start all over again—*tap, tap*—followed by a *tap, tap, tap*. It was a clear loud tapping, but it had a certain rhythm to it, and it was baffling. This strange sound followed us all the way to the town of Homestead, which is the last stop on the mainland before heading out onto the keys.

We stopped in a local café for breakfast, and while we waited for our eggs and bacon, we heard the sound again—this time inside the café. We heard a distinct *tap, tap*—followed by a rhythmic *tap, tap, tap*. The three of us looked at one another, and the hair stood up on the back of our necks. It was a crisp, clear *tap, tap* then *tap, tap, tap*. We turned around and looked, then we saw a long white cane with a red tip. *Tap, tap* then *tap, tap, tap*. *Tap, tap* then *tap, tap, tap*. This was too much. Bill and I began witnessing to the blind man, and before we left that morning, we had led him, along with the cook and a waitress, to the Lord. They prayed with us, and then we had a chance to witness to everyone in the café—what a great time.

When we got back into the car and headed down the road, it began again: *tap, tap... tap, tap, tap*. I got out of the car to check things out. We just had to know what this crazy tapping was all about. It was my seat belt, which had come loose and was hanging partway out the door, and when we were driving, the wind would slap it against the car: *tap, tap* followed by a *tap, tap, tap*. Well, who knows? That crazy seat belt sounded exactly like the blind man's tapping, and in a roundabout way it was responsible for us leading those people to the Lord—crazy, I know, but God does work in mysterious ways.

We hadn't gotten far into the keys, probably only six or eight miles, when we had a blowout on one of the tires on the boat trailer. Since there was a spare for the trailer in the boat, we got out the jack and began to jack up the trailer when the mosquitoes came—*by the millions*. It was about 8:00 or 9:00 a.m., and the swarm of mosquitoes actually darkened the sun, so we quickly jumped back into my little Dodge and waited—and waited.

The mosquitoes weren't leaving. So I volunteered *(what was I thinking?)* to go out and change the tire, mosquitoes and all, and Bill and Paul agreed to stand over me, using the towels to beat away the swarm of bloodsuckers. I can remember a couple of times trying to wipe the mosquitoes off my face, but each swipe of my hand would kill forty or fifty blood-filled mosquitoes. It was maddening. I'd never seen anything like it.

Once the wheel was solidly reattached to the boat trailer, I ran to the nearest water and dove in, clothes and all. The guys said they counted more than a hundred mosquito bites on my back alone, but I remained in the saltwater for probably half an hour, and it seemed to ease the pain and itching. By the time I got out, the mosquitoes had left.

We finally reached the island of Islamorada and checked into our hotel. It was a beautiful room, with windows on one side facing the Gulf of Mexico, and on the other side of the room we had a great view of the Atlantic Ocean. I later recalled seeing the sun set over the Gulf that night and then waking up the next morning to the amazing sight of the sunrise over the Atlantic—amazing.

We'd decided to go diving out at Alligator Reef, which was several miles offshore from Islamorada, and when we got there and anchored, the water was so clear the boat appeared to be floating on air. We dropped anchor about fifty yards away from the lighthouse buoy at Alligator Reef and donned our scuba tanks, masks, and fins, and oh yes, Paul had a little "James Bond" type of speargun that was about two feet long. It wasn't a serious speargun—not much more than a toy.

As we headed for the floating buoy lighthouse (somewhat a lighthouse without the house), we noticed there were dozens, maybe as many as one hundred, king barracuda—six- or seven-foot menacing long-toothed monsters—and I was stunned when Paul took out after one of those huge barracudas. I knew that if he managed to shoot one of them with that little speargun, all he'd do would make it mad, and then it'd turn on him and tear him to pieces, so I lit out after Paul as fast as I could go, trying to catch him, but he was at least fifteen feet ahead of me. The very second Paul got off his shot, I managed to grab one of his diving fins and pulled on it, causing him to miss.

When we surfaced, Paul was really angry at me, but after I explained he'd been going after a fish that was *waaay too big* for that little *James Bond* speargun, I think he finally understood. If he'd managed to actually spear one of them, it would certainly draw blood, and then the giant barracuda would turn on him and draw a whole lot more blood, and we could easily have been in the middle of a feeding frenzy, and we'd have been the main course—another *whew!*

an alligator interrupts a leisurely afternoon swim…

My next close call came while swimming in one of the old phosphate pits northeast of Lakeland. When the mining companies were finished extracting phosphate from the ground, they often left an open pit, and due to environmental concerns, these pits were usually left in neat rows and were engineered to fill up with rainwater and underground seepage. The only thing separating the rows of phosphate pits was usually a small dirt road, which allowed workers to drive out to the various pits and perform some maintenance, or a narrow dirt walkway enabling workers to walk out and do a visual check of the area. This particular phosphate pit had been converted to a swimming lake, complete with lifeguard and sandy beach.

A friend of mine, Walt, with whom I had done some part-time carpentry, had been attacked by a large alligator about a month earlier, and the news story in the *Lakeland Ledger* said he required more than one hundred stitches after the attack. Apparently, he'd been swimming in a phosphate pit that was only a couple hundred yards or so from the lake with the beach and the lifeguard when a big alligator grabbed him, did a death roll, then took him under, and stuffed him under a sunken log. Since gators can't chew their food, they like to let it rot for a while before they come back to enjoy their catch.

Anyway, my friend managed to make it to the surface and take a desperate gasp of air before the gator grabbed him again. Since the reptile had grabbed him around the chest, this time he managed to shove his left hand into its mouth, and in doing so, his fist opened the large flap, called the palatal valve, that keeps the water out and keeps the alligator from drowning, and the big gator coughed and spit him out, and he managed to swim to shore. The news article credited the fact that this large gator was very old, and that's what likely saved his life because the reptile's teeth were worn down due to age (and probably poor dental hygiene practices—I'm sure it never flossed).

It was a hot summer day, and I was enjoying an afternoon swim at the phosphate pit, the pit with the sandy beach and the lifeguard. I'd often swim out to a tiny island in the lake, which was about seventy-five yards from shore, and I'd take a fifteen-minute break to rest and sun myself for a while on the little island before swimming back for shore.

Due to all the newspaper and television publicity I'd had in that area of Florida, it was not unusual for me to find small groups of people who recognized me, often saying, "Are you *the* Ken Simmons?" And so that particular day as I was swimming back to shore, I looked up and saw what I thought was a group of six or eight people waving at me. *Huh?* I thought. *Oh, well.* And I stopped and waved back, then I resumed my swim to the beach.

After a short distance, I again noticed the same small group of people still waving at me, and I wondered, *Who are these people, and why are they waving at me?* Again, I stopped and started to wave back, but this time I noticed they were gesturing about something behind me, and then I heard one of them shouting, *"Alligator, alligator!"*

I looked back, and I was shocked to see a large gator heading right for me. I'd always been a good swimmer, a fast swimmer. That day I made sure I got the maximum out of every stroke—no wasted movements, no splashing around. This wasn't long after Mark Spitz won seven gold medals in swimming at the Olympics, and I thought, *Mark*

Spitz ain't got nothin' on me today. I went from being a good swimmer to a champion swimmer in just the first few strokes. By the time I reached the shore and ran up onto the beach, I saw the gator submerge just a few feet behind me. I'm not certain if this was the same alligator that attacked my friend Walt, but I could see it was a big one, and I wasn't going to wait around to shake hands with it.

Blinky

Without ever thinking, *I'm invincible*, there are times you're convinced that nothing can ever hurt you.

The City of Lakeland had a mascot named Blinky. And Blinky was an alligator—a big alligator… a good ten- or eleven-foot-long alligator. Often you'd see billboards around town, featuring a cartoonist's rendering of Blinky, with a black eye patch over one eye, as though this gator were one of Lakeland's attractions. Most people assumed Blinky was a bull gator, but I later discovered that Blinky was female.

Blinky's usual hangout was on Lake Mirror, which was also the lakeside home of the city's civic center. Once, while my children were wandering around the lake, they took off running and headed down the civic center's large concrete steps, and they almost tripped over him—Blinky, that is. Blinky had been sunning on the civic center stairway. And many local residents reported that a German shepherd was Blinky's lunch one day. There was an underground pipe connecting Lake Mirror with other lakes in town, including Lake Morton (the lake in which I'd baptized dozens of young people), and so sometimes this alligator was found at other lakes. But its favorite hangout was Lake Mirror.

One day while driving by, I noticed that Blinky was in the middle of the lake, resting on a narrow concrete walkway that was only slightly above the surface of the water, and it was surrounded by six or eight small alligators, all of them less than two feet long and all of them just a few feet from Blinky. It was then I knew that Blinky was a female.

I knew because any bull alligator would have eaten the smaller gators even if they were his own offspring.

Anyway, one day a young friend of mine from the ministry was driving with me by the lake, and since I had my camera along, he suggested we stop and get some photographs of the alligator. I know you're not supposed to feed the wildlife, but I had a couple of sandwiches in the car with me, and I used the bread as bait to attract Blinky. After tossing out a few chunks of bread, it was only a few minutes later that Blinky approached and reached the shoreline. Apparently, I wasn't the first one to throw bread out for Blinky. The banks of Lake Mirror are about two and a half feet tall, but they're steep—straight up and down. I decided I was going to get some really, really good pictures of this alligator.

I persuaded my friend to hold my left hand, and keeping my left foot up on the embankment, I stepped down to the edge of the lake with my right foot. I had a strap wrapped around my neck, which held on to the camera. I knew that Blinky was blind in her left eye (that's the reason all the mascot drawings had Blinky wearing a black eye patch), so I positioned myself on her left side—her blind side, if you will—and with my free hand I began to slap her on the nose. Each time I slapped her—*whap*—on the nose, she'd open those huge jaws, and I grabbed the camera, and I got a picture right down her pale pink mouth. *Whap* and I shot another picture, and each time she'd lunge at me, and each time my friend would pull me up onto the embankment. I shot an entire thirty-six-exposure roll of that alligator, most of them looking right down into her gullet.

I later showed those photographs to my younger brother, Les, and he couldn't believe it. Mostly, he couldn't believe that his wiser older brother could be so stupid as to slap an alligator on the nose, not once, but twenty or thirty times just to get some crazy pictures. I have no idea whatever eventually happened to those pictures, but I guess Les is the only one who can prove this wasn't just a big tall tale. Les is quite a fisherman, and he's used to tall tales. He caught his first marlin at thirteen, and once I took a photograph of him with a 156-lb. bigeye tuna that made the front cover of *Western Outdoor News* magazine.

During that time I often did photography on the side, professionally, such as photographing an entire little league and all their teams with baseball Hall of Famer Al Kaline, and sometimes I would do photo shoots of up-and-coming models who wanted me to help produce a photo portfolio for them. I had set up a film lab in the small room next to our swimming pool at our home on Norfolk Circle, and I had all the necessary equipment for processing the film and making the enlargements.

One time I had done a photo shoot of a model, who was, as I recall, the wife of a local attorney, and after I had processed the negatives, I then made a few dozen 5 × 7 prints to show the lady to let her determine what she might use in her portfolio. A few days later I came home to find that Karen had cut up all the negatives and all the prints—she'd trashed it all; such was her jealousy. I had to explain to that lady why I had nothing to show for all my work, and she had paid me about 50 percent of my fee up front so that I could buy the materials. I couldn't reimburse her, but she understood. There was nothing at all in those photographs that was in any way inappropriate and nothing I should have been embarrassed or ashamed about had Jesus been by my side during the whole time.

So I stopped photographing models. Sometimes I resorted to aerial photography, especially when the Sun 'n' Fun Fly-in was held at Lakeland. Once, when the actor Cliff Robertson* was at the air show, I was invited to go up in a chase plane to take pictures as Robertson did maneuvers in an aerobatic biplane. A local doctor had two Stolp Starduster aircraft, which are similar to the Pitts Special, which is probably the most well-known airplane in the field of aerobatics. I was to fly passenger, which was in the front cockpit of one of the Stardusters, with the doctor at the controls, and Cliff Robertson would fly the other airplane solo.

It turned out that Cliff Robertson was an amazing pilot. Prior to the flight I'd interviewed Robertson's wife, actress Dina Merrill (who was heir to the Post Cereal fortune), and she told me the story of her husband's hot-air balloon race (didn't know you could race hot-air balloons) from Santa Catalina Island to the mainland in California, and Robertson had to ditch in the sea. It was because of that incident that she convinced her husband to give up the hot-air balloons because she thought it was too dangerous, but she'd not said anything about stunt flying in high-performance aerobatic aircraft.

Robertson, who had won an Oscar for his compelling performance in *Marty* in 1968 and had played the role of John F. Kennedy in the movie *PT 109*, turned in an equally amazing performance at the controls of the Starduster, demonstrating skills you'd only expect from a seasoned aerobatic performer.

During the flight I took more than three rolls of film while flying wingtip to wingtip during what I was told were *unrehearsed aerobatic maneuvers!* I had no idea and probably would have chickened out had I known it—unrehearsed! That was incredibly dangerous, especially when wingtip to wingtip: loops, with both planes only a few feet apart, and Immelmanns and aileron rolls—wow! Many of the pictures were so close that even without my telephoto lens, you could easily see and recognize Cliff Robertson and his big smile.

flying upside down "open cockpit" and my seatbelt won't fasten...

I'd made prior arrangements with the pilot, the doctor, that I wanted to get some pictures while Robertson's plane was directly behind us, so I told him that I would need to turn around, and to do so I would have to unfasten my seat belt. However, after I turned back around and sat down, I guess the pilot assumed I'd finished fastening my seat, but I hadn't. I was actually reattaching my telephoto lens. It was then that he took us into an Immelmann maneuver, which meant you head straight up as though you're going into a full loop, but while upside down and at the top of the loop, you perform an aileron roll and end up right side up and heading back the opposite direction.

I desperately tried to complete fastening my seat belt, but the high G forces kept me from making that final click. I was holding on for dear life—remember, this was an "open cockpit" biplane. When we finally reached the bottom of the maneuver and were sunny-side up and the wheels were pointing to the ground, I finally heard the sound I'd been waiting for—the click of my safety harness. But much to my dismay, while inverted I saw my favorite 135mm telephoto lens disappear into a swampy area about 1500 feet below.

Afterward I spoke to Robertson and interviewed him for what I hoped would be an article in *Flying* magazine. He gave me his address, and I told him I'd send him 5 × 7 copies of all the prints, told him what the price would be, and then gave him more prices should he want some larger prints. A week or so later I sent more than seventy prints to him, along with a handwritten invoice. The magazine said they wanted to publish the photos and the story I'd written, but I later got word that for some unknown reason someone nixed the idea of the article in the magazine, so it was never published. It was a shame because it was a good article, and there were a number of really great photos showing Robertson's amazing aerobatic skills.

*Robertson died of natural causes in 2011 at the age of eighty-eight.

crop duster kills a friend of mine...

Hit the Rewind button again, and go back even further for just a moment for another flashback.

My first involvement with open-cockpit biplanes was during the summer before my senior year in high school when I got a job working as a flagman for a local crop duster. Brawley is located in the Imperial Valley, and it's one of the most productive farmlands in America. Most of the crops require considerable amounts of spraying or dusting of insecticides. The man I worked for was a large red-haired Swede (whom I'll call Van, not his real name, for reasons that will become apparent), who had three open-cockpit Stearman airplanes in which the front seat (cockpit) was converted to a tank in which to carry such chemicals as malathion. He was also one of the loudest men I'd ever known. Often I'd hear him circling above me and cussing me out. *"No, no, no, it's not that field, you —— idiot, it's that field,"* he'd shout over the big Pratt & Whitney 450 engine, pointing to a field on the other side of the road. Crop dusters rely on flagmen so they can systematically spray or dust a field without wasting any chemicals by making overlapping passes. After each pass I would have to walk eighteen paces over, which happened to be the distance covered by each swath of the crop duster's spray or dusting, and after each pass at eighteen paces, I'd move to the next, waving a bright yellow flag each time.

This guy was an amazing pilot, and he was also an amazingly reckless *idiot!* One day near the desert community of Borrego Springs, he filled the Stearman's fuel tanks with aviation fuel (avgas), then put his thumb over the nozzle, and squirted the bugs off the plane's wings with the same fuel so that the wings were literally dripping with highly flammable avgas, and then he took off with the plane still dripping gas from the wings and the fuselage, pulling it up into a full loop, and then he timed it so that when he came out at the bottom of the loop, he flew the biplane underneath the wires of nearby telephone lines. If that big engine had backfired, the plane would have turned into a huge fireball.

In a scene reminiscent of one from the Hitchcock movie *North by Northwest,* one day after he finished spraying a field, he began to head in a direction that was a bit puzzling. When spraying a field, a crop duster always flies parallel to the rows in the crop, but this time he was flying in a direction that was diagonal to the rows of alfalfa. I'd heard from some of the other flagmen that he occasionally got a kick out of buzzing his workers, and I soon realized he was heading right for me, and there was nowhere for me to run. He got closer and closer, and I could see that the landing gear's wheels were skimming the tops of the alfalfa. I dropped facedown into the dirt, and I could *hear him laughing* over the roar of the nine-cylinder big engine as he flew over, less than two feet over my head. *Whew!*

After getting up and dusting myself off, I noticed he was banking and coming around again for another pass at me. There was a drainage ditch only a few feet away, so this time I ran to the ditch, and when I got there, I saw a bunch of cat-o'-nine-tails (cattails) growing in the ditch. I grabbed my pocketknife, and I quickly cut off five or six of them, and this time when he flew over, I threw them up as hard as I could—you should have seen it. There were fluffs of cattail cotton all over the place when they hit the prop, and when he finally landed, he still had this fluffy white mess all over him and all over his airplane. He began loudly cussing me out, but I quickly countered with, *"The next time you try to buzz me, I'll throw something worse than cattails in your prop—I'll throw something big enough to bring you and your stupid airplane down. In fact, there won't be a next time—I quit!"*

One of my classmates at Brawley High also worked as a flagman for this crop duster, and a couple of weeks after I quit over the buzzing incident, I heard the news that he'd been killed when the landing gear of the big Stearman struck him in the shoulder and broke his neck. In the newspaper interview, Van claimed it was an accident—that my friend didn't duck when he should have. But after my run-in with Van over him buzzing me, I went out to the field where my friend was killed, and I located the spot the airplane struck him.

Van had been buzzing again, and this time a friend of mine was dead because of it. I knew he'd been buzzing him, because the location he was struck in relation to the crop in the field indicated the plane had not been flying parallel to the crop rows—it had been flying diagonally across the rows, heading right for him. I wanted to go to the authorities with this information, but my parents told me that Van would have to live with it, and that'd be punishment enough. The last I heard, Van had started drinking heavily, and eventually, he quit crop dusting.

Chapter 22

the oldest man in the world…

I met several interesting characters over the next few years while News Director with WVFM radio station—not the least of whom was Charlie Smith.

Charles Smith, Civil War Veteran—1842–1979 at age 137.

(http://www.findagrave.com/cgi-bin/fg.cgi?page=gr&GRid=8194153)

I'd been covering a meeting of the county commissioners in Bartow, Florida, which was the county seat for Polk County, and after an uneventful meeting, I decided to walk down the street to pick up a sandwich when I saw about a dozen people gathered in front of a local store. I had walked out of the meeting with one of the county commissioners, so when I noticed the little gathering, I asked him if he knew what was going on. He told me, *"Oh, Charlie Smith's in town today. Everybody knows Charlie—he's the oldest man in the world."*

By this time my curiosity was in high gear. So after standing around the crowd for a while, listening to this very old man spin his yarns, I managed to work my way in closer, and I finally introduced myself. Charlie was a lean black man, who, apparently, always wore a cowboy hat and loved to entertain when a crowd gathered around, and he went on to tell how he'd met every US president since Truman. I asked about his name, Charlie Smith, and he explained that he'd been a slave, and his owner's name was Charles Smith, and like so many slaves on those days, they simply took on the name of their owner. He said, "He gives me his name, he raises me right in the house jus' like his other chillen, but he didn't treat me like no slave—no, sir, he treats me like one o' his own."

He then said something that made my jaw drop. He claimed he was the only living Civil War veteran. I decided I wanted to get more facts about this man, especially to find out if he was given to tall tales, before trying to secure an interview. Everyone that I spoke to around him that day said his stories were true, but I needed to find out for myself. Not having the benefit of the Internet in those days, I was limited in my search for information, but when I checked with the nearby Hall of Records, there was nothing on him. One of the clerks there said they had copies of several newspaper articles about Charlie, and I quickly read a few of them. I learned that Smith was born in Liberia, in Africa, in 1842, and at age twelve he was taken onto a slave ship where he finally ended up as a slave on a Texas plantation.

When I got back to the same storefront where Charlie had been entertaining his friends, I then suspected that Charlie's tall tales maybe hadn't been so tall after all. I later was able to do some more intensive research, and I did learn that... Charlie Smith was, indeed, the oldest man in the world, and he was also the only living veteran of the Civil War. I never did the interview on Charlie although when I met him, he was 134 years old. I heard that Charlie died a few years later at the age of 137.

Another interesting character I met a short while later was…

Kingswood Sprott...

I'd heard that a local attorney, with the unusual name of Kingswood Sprott, was about to make an attempt at the altitude record for a class B hot-air balloon, and I decided I wanted to interview him for the radio station during his attempt.

During that time there was a local businessman with whom I'd somehow found favor. He'd loaned me a beautiful 1967 Ford convertible to use for four or five months, and he often made contributions of $1,000 to my ministry. I'll call him Mr. Jones for reasons that will become clear as you read on. Occasionally, he'd offered to take me up in his twin-engine Lockheed Lodestar airplane, which was a 1930s era aircraft. Earlier I'd been a passenger in his airplane, shooting in-flight pictures of a local pilot's newly restored F4U Corsair WWII fighter plane, and so when he offered me a chance to go up in the Lodestar again—to fly chase, if you will—while Kingswood Sprott attempted to break the high-altitude record, I jumped at the chance.

I'd heard that Sprott needed to reach an altitude of something like 52,000 ft., so when we went out to Lakeland Airport at about 6:00 a.m. on a cold December morning in 1974, I was looking forward to the flight. I learned that the early morning cold air gave the hot-air balloon considerably more lift, and that day the temperature hovered just a little above freezing. I also learned that it made perfect sense that Sprott had donned heavy arctic gear for the flight because at 50,000 feet temperatures can easily drop to 70° below zero.

My friend's airplane wasn't pressurized, so I knew we couldn't follow the balloon up much higher than 10,000 feet. Using the airplane's radio for the interview with Sprott, I recorded much of his attempt at the record. He managed to set another new world altitude record for FAI class's AX-7 and AX-8 balloons (don't ask me what all that means). And a few years later in 1978 Sprott would be the first American to fly a hot-air balloon over the Andes Mountains in South America.

During the attempt that day, I was also taking a number of photographs of Sprott and his beautiful balloon craft, having to move about the empty cargo area of the airplane in order to get photographs out the small windows as we circled the rising balloon. Once, the aircraft banked unexpectedly, and I stumbled to the floor, and I noticed the distinct smell of marijuana. It was then that I noticed a number of pot seeds on the floor of the aircraft, and it was obvious that this Lockheed Lodestar had been used to haul marijuana. The following day, I aired the interview with Sprott on WVFM.

Hot-air balloonist Kingswood Sprott.

A few days later when I called my pilot friend Joe Araldi on the phone, I asked him about our mutual friend, the one who'd loaned me his '67 Ford convertible and who often gave me rides in his Lockheed Lodestar, you know, the one who frequently gave $1,000 donations to my Youth Challenge ministry, and Joe told me, *"Don't you know, Ken, that's guilt money he's been sending you. He's been smuggling marijuana with that plane for years, and because of all your work with dopers and addicts, he's felt guilty about it, and he thought it would somehow make up for some of the things he'd done if he donated money to you and your work."*

It didn't surprise me when, a few days later, I heard that Mr. Jones had crashed at the end of the runway at the Lakeland airport. Federal officials were standing out on the tarmac, waiting for him, and when he touched down and then saw the feds waiting for him, he tried to abort the landing and take off again, but he didn't have enough runway. They recovered a few tons of marijuana from his wrecked airplane. Some even thought I'd turned him in. The last I heard he'd been convicted on drug-smuggling charges.

A month or so later Joe took me up in the company's Learjet, and this small business jet was something of a hot rod in the air. We took off, and it seemed like no time at all we reached an altitude of 10,000 feet. What a ride. Joe told me once he had a demonstration flight in the Learjet, taking off from St. Petersburg airport, which was only a few feet above sea level, and going nearly vertical within fifty-nine seconds, he reached 10,000 feet.

skydiving miracle...

In 1975, on one of the flights in my friend Joe Araldi's Cabin Waco airplane, Joe had another passenger—Arch Deal, who was NBC television anchorman with WFLA-TV in the Tampa-St. Petersburg market. I was in the right front seat at the time because Joe was letting me log some hours at the controls of his classic 1930s biplane, and during the flight Deal and I struck up a conversation. When back on the ground, we continued talking, especially about Deal's love of skydiving. In fact, Deal tried to encourage me to take up skydiving, even trying to talk me into going skydiving with him some time. As I recall, I made some comment about why I didn't have any desire to jump out of a perfectly good airplane. Then Deal told me about an upcoming skydiving event for which he'd be performing, jumping out over the crowds at Cypress Gardens in Winter Haven.

The event was scheduled for July 4, 1975, and when Deal made the jumps at Cypress Gardens, it was during his third exhibition jump, which began at 3,000 ft., his primary chute failed to open, and when he finally deployed his backup parachute, it got tangled in the primary. I later witnessed the video on television as the screaming spectators in the crowd at Cypress Gardens watched him fall. A spectator in the crowd had filmed the entire incident, showing Deal as he violently swung back and forth trying to get his parachute to catch some air and deploy, and he plummeted to the ground at more than 100 ft. per second, landing in loose dirt in a recently plowed orange grove, but Deal survived.

Arch Deal, survivor of a 3,000 ft. plummet.

A few days later I visited Arch in the hospital in Tampa. He was in a body cast, and apparently, he'd broken just about every bone that could be broken. But he was in good spirits, and I was quite surprised when he told me he intended to continue skydiving.

On August 10, which was only a month and six days after his terrible accident, I was in the Atlanta airport, waiting to catch a connecting flight, so I dropped in to the airport's lounge and café to get a bite to eat when someone came up behind me, tapped me on the shoulder, and said, *"Hi, Ken. I told you that little fall I took wouldn't keep me down."*

It was Arch Deal, who had walked into the café with the aid of his daughter and his cane. The man had amazing recuperative abilities. As I understand it, Deal went on to make several hundred more jumps over the years. (Jumping out of a perfectly good airplane—*what a concept!*)

Buzz Bundy...

In addition to my duties as News Director at WVFM I also had some commercial advertising accounts in order to supplement my income. One of those accounts was the Auburndale Speedway, which was a racetrack just a few miles east of Lakeland near Winter Haven. This quarter-mile track often featured stock car racing, and because it was one of my accounts, I was able to come to the various events for free. Several years earlier I'd seen the James Bond movie *Diamonds Are Forever*, and it featured a stunt car speeding through a narrow alleyway up on its side on two wheels. So when I heard that Buzz Bundy, the stunt driver who had performed the feat in the movie would be at the Auburndale Speedway, I thought this might be an excellent chance for a unique interview.

When I arrived at the racetrack that Saturday night, I was prepared with my tape recorder and a notebook, but I was surprised when Bundy said, *"Why don't you come along with me? I'm gonna set the world speed record for a car up on two wheels—you can ride along."*

I was a bit stunned, but I said, "Sure," and the next thing I knew, I was sitting in a little car (a little Ford Pinto), and Bundy headed for a ramp just ahead. The car jumped up on one side, and we were speeding down the racetrack. I was on the low side, and Bundy, up on the high side, was laughing and chatting away with me while I interviewed him for the radio station. I looked tentatively down at the asphalt—*I could have scraped my right elbow with it!* We repeated this several times in front of a cheering crowd before actually trying for the record. We headed for the ramp again, and when we went over it, the car once again lurched up on the two right wheels, and then it wobbled a little before straightening itself out. This time Bundy was a bit quieter because we were moving along at a pretty good clip—I think we made a full lap around the track when, finally, the car slammed back down on all four wheels, and Bundy said, *"We did it—seventy-two miles an hour."*

Stunt driver Buzz Bundy.

That certainly qualified as one of my most unusual interviews.

your "ammy"...

Some of the other advantages of being in radio was having a press pass, which meant that I could often get into events for free. Several times I'd take the family to Circus World, north of Haines City, and because of the press pass, we all got in free. Eventually, I wondered if they would honor my press pass at Disney World in Orlando, and when I called their office, they said, *"Sure, bring your whole family."* We went to Walt Disney World so many times over the next few years that the kids finally got bored with it, saying, *"Daddy, do we have to go to Disney World?"* Who'd a thunk it—children getting bored with going to Disney World?

And for years the kids had heard me talk about Miami when one day they asked, *"Daddy, when are we going to your Ammy?"*

For the longest time I didn't have the heart to tell them it wasn't "my Ammy," but it was *Miami*. But when I finally did try to explain it to them, they still didn't understand, and for the next couple of years, they continued to ask when we were going to "your Ammy." They still chuckle about it all these years later.

Florida Crackers...

After living in rural Florida for a few years, one day I was given a lesson about Florida Crackers—the term for good ol' Southern boys from rural Florida. Although often used as a pejorative or put-down of people considered backward boasters and braggarts, the term *Florida Cracker* actually had its beginnings when Juan Ponce de Leon and the small horseback army with him entered the state in the early sixteenth century and then in 1763 when Spain traded the Florida territory to Great Britain. These original cowboys were called crackers mainly because of the sounds made when they cracked their whips. OK, enough of the history lesson. This isn't in any way putting crackers down; in fact, I'd much rather be surrounded by a group of good-ol'-boy Florida Crackers than a lot of city folk I've met. Come to think of it—I'm kinda fond of Florida Crackers. But I also guess this is my way of saying that not too many JPL rocket scientists have come out of the Crackers. Of course, that spoke volumes about me too because I was living right smack-dab in the middle... of *Cracker Country.*

I was driving west on Highway 92 one day heading from Lakeland to Plant City when I came across a sign advertising new condominiums for sale. The sign was a typical billboard, which was probably some ten feet tall. It was professionally done, which meant this was no homemade amateur job, and it was evident they'd probably paid top dollar for it. The sign also featured an artist's rendering of one of the homes. But the lettering was so large that space on the sign was limited, so they abbreviated. The sign read, "CONDOMS FOR SALE—from $49,000 to $55,000."

I laughed so hard that I had to pull over to the side of the road for a few minutes. It could have been worse, however—just imagine if I'd come by that same location a few years later and they tried to sell some of them as previously owned (used). You can only imagine how that sign might have read. *(Sorry 'bout that one.)*

It was also while living in Plant City that I got a few more lessons from homespun Florida Crackers. A friend of mine came by the house one day, and he had a friend with him. I'd been out working on an oak tree I'd just transplanted in our front yard when his friend asked me, *"Ah just shucked on up to Chipley, so would y'all like a cooter hull o' ford hooks?"*

"A what full o' what?" I said.

When he repeated what he'd said, I told him, *"I have no clue what you just said."* He went on to explain, *"Well, sir, Chipley's a fur piece nawth o' here. And ah guess y'all never heard o' ford hooks. Well, I got a whole cooter hull full of 'em. Well, sir, a cooter hull is a trunk—ya know, the trunk of y'all's car, and ford hooks is uncut strang beans."*

I invited them for supper later that evening if they'd help me string the ford hooks—yes, sir, best ford hooks I ever had. *Who'd a' thunk it?*

Next, a dear friend of ours invited us over for dinner one night. He said he and his family would love to cook for us, and since these were dear Christian friends, I said we'd be eager to join them for dinner. I knew these folks well—great people. They were poor in the things of this world, but rich in spirit. Oh, and one thing most people don't know about when it comes to Southern folk and manners and such is that most of their children are respectful. It's always *"Yes, sir"* or *"Yes, ma'am"* or *"No, sir"* or *"No, ma'am"* to their parents, and there's never any sassing or back talk. And it's not just window dressing—most of these children, countryfolk all, are genuinely respectful of their moms and dads and equally respectful of their elders in general.

So when Saturday night rolled around, we drove out to the country and down a small dirt road, and we pulled up to an old white wooden-frame house that appeared to be about 100 years old. It also looked as though it hadn't been painted in decades, and the planks on the wooden porch were warped, and you could see gaps down through the porch to the dirt below. But these were great people—they were simple people, and they loved the Lord.

That evening one of their boys set the table, and when I asked him about how he was doing in school, he said, *"I'm doin' fine, sir. My grades are pretty good. Thanks fer askin', sir."* It was refreshing to hear young people who showed consideration and respect—refreshing, indeed.

This was in the middle of the summer, and the 93° temperature outside, combined with the oppressing humidity and the fact they didn't have the benefit of air conditioning, made it nearly unbearable, but the company was great, and I was looking forward to an evening of fellowship. But first—*supper.*

"Y'all like turnips?" my friend asked.

Of all the root family the turnips weren't my favorite dish. I'd always thought that eating turnips was a bit like eating some of the flower bulbs, like those of the tulips or geraniums, but I thought I'd give them a try. I instinctively knew that whatever these dear friends fed us was likely the best they had, so I pretended to be eager for my supper—*of turnips.*

When his wife came out with a large bowl of greens, along with a bowl of white rice, I thought, *Hmm, salad too.* But after the blessing a few minutes later, they seemed ready to dig in, so at one point I asked, *"I see the salad, but where's the turnips?"* My friend responded, *"These are the turnips."*

I was a bit confused, so I asked, *"You know, the round bulbs—the turnips? These are greens. Are we having turnips tonight?"*

"Oh, these are the turnips. We throw the root away," he replied.

Ah, the simple pleasures of sitting down for supper with a loving Christian family out in the country. I loved it even though I had to hold my nose for the rest of supper because those turnip greens smelled pretty ripe.

And then there's the grits. You haven't lived 'til you've had grits. It seems every restaurant in the South has grits. Yes, sir, ground-up hominy (grits) usually served with butter and salt and pepper—mmm, mmm, good *(NOT!).*

So let's see—I've had turnips (turnip greens), collard greens, mustard greens, grits, and oh yes, boiled peanuts. In California you have people pushing little carts around, selling burritos and tamales, but in

Florida you have carts and roadside stands selling hot boiled peanuts. I loved 'em, but several years later during one trip back to Florida my wife nearly lost her lunch when she tried a bag full of hot boiled peanuts. She cried out in disgust, saying, *"Yuck, how can you stand these things?"*

Whatever you do, though, don't try the chitlins unless, that is, you like cut-up pieces of hog bowels deep fried in lard—yes, sir, good ol' lip-smackin' Southern-cookin' hog bowels. *Oops, sorry… chitlins.*

Chapter 23

the "accuser"...

Before I came running back to God, it had been so long since I'd felt his presence... felt *anything*. He had been such a presence in my life, and I'd seen him actually work miracles. I'd walked with him, but then I was walking alone. I'd felt like a man crawling through the desert sand, dying of thirst, and yet I was most foolish of all because I'd once tasted of the living water.

I'm not saying that God did any of this to me—the failures, the injuries, and the health concerns. God is not the author of death, disease, or any kind of injuries. He is the God of life, of healing, of love and power, and of a sound mind. But I also know that sometimes God will allow these things to happen as a last resort to allow us to refocus on him. Satan had to get permission from God to do the things he did to Job, and once it was all over, God restored Job and then multiplied his blessings on him. I won't be so presumptuous as to suggest that Satan had to approach God for permission to attack me... I just don't know.

women sometimes use men too...

Remember, much of this story is about my life as a prodigal. I struggled considerably over the details of the next part of my story, particularly because they're things I'm not proud of and about which I'm *actually very much ashamed*. I didn't want to just blurt it out, with some rather sordid details, but I also didn't want to gloss over what happened. Before returning to Christ and rededicating my life to him, during the years without the presence of God in my life, I realized I'd been running from him. I'd been mad at God, and I was running away from him, and the farther I got, it seemed the faster I'd run. I couldn't come to grips with the fact I no longer had God in my life, so I kept running. I'd endured a painful marriage with Karen, and during the last several years of that marriage, the anger and bitterness had taken their toll on me, and I felt totally emasculated. Without realizing it, my ego, my manhood, had been stripped from me.

After the marriage was, for all intents and purposes, over, I discovered that other women found me attractive, and during that time there were women—many women—seemingly everywhere. I didn't seek them out—I didn't have to. They were everywhere, and they seemed to seek me out. Only years later did I realize this was part of the spiritual warfare over my soul.

One young woman simply said to me, *"I don't even want to know your name,"* and then she went on to tell me what she *did* want (you can figure the rest of that one out for yourself).

Another time, the summer before I met Diane, I had been at a Fourth of July party at Mount Baldy, which is a small mountain community in Southern California. There was a crowd that had gathered for a street dance in front of the fire station, and everyone was listening to a local band play some soft rock oldies music. About that time a beautiful and very well-dressed young woman spotted me. She looked like a movie star. She might as well have stepped off the pages of some high-class fashion magazine. Without saying a word and without ever taking her eyes off me, she walked through the crowd, walked directly up to me, and gave me a passionate kiss. Again, use your imagination what happened next.

One Friday night I met a young woman who invited me to spend the weekend with her at her place in San Diego, but when she learned I'd had a vasectomy, she suddenly began screaming and calling me names.

It appeared she had chosen me, and she was angry because all she wanted me for was for me to father a child for her. *To her, I was a likely seed donor.*

Most of us grow up with the impression that men often use women, and I'm sure that's true, but I found that women sometimes use men just as easily, and I felt used and shallow. It was as though I had been drinking saltwater. I was thirsty, but when I drank, it only made me thirstier. I'd almost completely forgotten about the living water. I was, indeed, living the life of the prodigal son.

The only reason I'm telling you this is, I'd much rather you hear it from me here and now instead of later from one of those "gotcha" journalists. I'm not proud of it, and it's certainly nothing I'd want to boast about, but it happened. If I'm ever confronted with my past, I won't lie about it or try to cover it up. There might even come a day when some stranger approaches me with, *"You don't know me, but you're my father."* Who knows?

For many years I carried around a great deal of guilt over this. Even after I came back to the Lord and rededicated my life to him, I still couldn't shake the feeling of just how unworthy I was because I had been a man of God, and I'd walked with the presence of God in my life, complete with miracles, and yet I had fallen so far. I just couldn't reconcile myself with who I once was and what I allowed myself to become. Sometimes during prayer, long after I had repented and turned from those ways, I would sometimes try to remind God of my past sins and how guilty I'd been.

It'd been so long since I'd heard the voice of God. I don't mean a booming voice from a cloud, but his voice nonetheless. Then one day in particular after I'd been carrying this guilt around for so long, I entered into prayer, and I began rattling off a list of all those sins that continued to haunt me, sins about which I'd long since confessed and repented. I'd felt that if I continued to remind God of my list of sins, then I might eventually have the shame and guilt I knew I deserved. It was then that deep in my soul I began to hear God speak to me again, and this time I heard him in a very faint whisper. He said, *"I don't remember."*

A little surprised, I began again with, *"Lord, don't you remember?"* as I started to list the things about which I was so guilty and ashamed, and again he whispered, *"I don't remember."*

Then I heard God's whisper just a little louder in my ear…

"Didn't I tell you that when you confessed your sins I would no longer remember them, and that I'd cast them from me as far as east is from west and remember them no more?" (See Jeremiah 31:34, Psalms 103:12.)

So even trying to drag up the past for this, my story, is painful for me especially when I know that God has forgotten my sins. I just didn't want you to hear it from anyone else or to think I'd simply glossed over it. I never stopped believing during this time—I just stopped following the Lord. It was never a matter of hypocrisy because I never claimed to be living the Christian life during those years. I also knew there was a level of idiocy in being mad at God.

being faithful in the little things…

So when I began seeking God in earnest once again, I started by asking him to give me some sign, some indication, that he still had a purpose and plan for my life. After an endless and unbroken string of failures, failures that would have sent most people over the edge, I pleaded, *"Please, God, give me something to do, something that even slightly resembles success. God, you know how I've handled failure… I've been an absolute success at that. Please, God, let me succeed at something… anything."*

I've never tried to bargain with God… that was not it at all. It's just that after such a convincing string of failures stretching some twenty years, it's pretty easy to begin thinking of yourself as a failure.

My prayers have constantly been, *"Father, please grant me a broken and contrite spirit. Please give me a heart that hungers and thirsts after righteousness. Heal my conscience so that it actually hurts if I sin, and put within me a desire to be obedient to you."*

Chapter 24

The last time I saw Max Rapoport was in 1972 when I brought him to Lakeland for a series of meetings in which he preached at the First Assembly of God Church back in the early seventies. Late in the summer of 1997 I tried to locate Max. I wanted to be back in touch with some of the people I'd worked with earlier in my ministry. I located an old address book, which was at least 25 years old, that contained an address and phone number for Max and Sandee, but I was sure that these listings were outdated. So in May or June of that year I decided to try calling him, and sure enough, the numbers were no longer valid. I also attempted to locate him, using a locating service on the Internet called *Who Where,* but I came up blank.

A few months later I tried again, and sure enough, Max and Sandee's names popped up on that Web site, and they were living in Corona, California, and it was just about two miles from where we'd been living, also in Corona, for the past five years. Max and I were in constant fellowship over the next several years.

In addition to wanting to locate Max, I had also wanted to renew my fellowship with Christians who had been involved with me earlier in the ministry in Florida. I especially wanted to locate Bill Davis because I had led him to the Lord all those years ago, and I had wondered for many years about the results and if he'd still be serving God. In 1972 I'd attended Bill's wedding in Tampa when he married a lovely young woman named Darlene. After that I last saw Bill when he was the pastor of a large and thriving church in Tampa, but since that time I had completely lost track of him. Many times, over the years, I had attempted to find a telephone number or address for Bill, but without success.

However, I recently managed to locate Bill's number by locating Wayne Friedt. At the time, I had no idea that Wayne had been the pastor at the Believer's Fellowship in Lakeland. You may recall in an earlier chapter when Wayne had been part of my team going into the schools in Central Florida. He and I had a great time recalling when God did such great things with and through us, and we had a renewing of our fellowship that blessed me tremendously. About ten years earlier Bill Davis had given Wayne his phone number, and he still had it.

I called and left a message for Bill, and when he returned my call, it was one of the most moving telephone calls I'd ever received. I explained to him that I hoped to return to Florida soon to renew acquaintances and to do what I could to make amends to some of the young Christians I had felt I'd let down. Bill interrupted me, saying, *"Ken, I want to make it absolutely clear. You never let me down in any way. In fact, I praise God every day for you, and I've been praying for you every day for more than twenty years. If it weren't for you being there and being willing to pay the price, I'd be dead. You saved my life."*

He went on to say, *"In fact, I feel I let you down because when you came to me for help, when you were going through some difficult times, I wasn't there for you, and I ask your forgiveness. I wouldn't normally say this because it sounds as if I'm boasting, but somehow I feel God wants you to hear this. If it weren't for you, being there and being willing to pay the price, none of this would have happened, but God has given me a worldwide ministry, and I've been able to lead thousands of people to the Lord over these years. You have no idea how many times I've given my testimony all over the world, telling about that night in Florida when I came into a Christian coffeehouse, and you were there to tell me about the love of Jesus, and you prayed for me, and God set me free and filled me with the Holy Spirit."*

Bill went on to tell me how that one night on the *700 Club* television program they had featured his story and reenacted the night I'd led him to the Lord. The broadcast was seen in some thirty countries all over the world. This confirmed to me that not all my efforts had been in vain.

By this time we were both in tears, and later that evening I experienced such joy from those words that I laughed and praised God for hours. For the first time in a long while I was once again experiencing *"joy unspeakable and full of glory"* (1 Peter 1:8). You see, for so many years I had wondered if all those years of ministry had been in vain. I'd wondered if any of those I'd led to Christ were still serving him or if they'd all fallen away.

But I was learning that the effects of my ministry were still being felt all over the world. Youth Challenge (the name was changed to the Anchor House) is still continuing, more than forty years after God called me to begin that work. Sometimes I can't contain all the joy… *praise God!*

locked up for murder…

During the late 1990s I had been volunteering at Heman G. Stark prison in Chino, California. This prison was part of the California Youth Authority because the inmates there were all between the ages of 18 to 24, but by the time an inmate reached his 25th birthday, either he had to be transferred to another prison, or he had to be released. The warden at the prison had explained to me that 80 percent of the inmates had been locked up for murder, but because of their ages or the circumstances of their cases, it had been determined that these young men had a higher probability for rehabilitation, so they were sentenced to serve their time at Stark.

The chaplain at that prison was a man named Leonard Banks. Rev. Banks was a big, tall black fellow (I thought he was in his forties, but it turned out he was in his sixties), and I soon learned why so many of the young men at the prison loved Chaplain Banks. You didn't have to be around Leonard very long before you knew he knew Jesus. He was firm with them, but he also loved them, and they knew it. In fact there had been quite a move of God at the prison during Banks's tenure as chaplain. Often the chapel services were packed.

Max Rapoport had met Chaplain Banks at a local Kinko's when he went in to have some prints made of a newsletter I'd written. The two struck up a conversation, and that was the beginning of our invitation to begin ministering at Stark prison. Max and I often spoke there at the chapel, and it was always well received. Most of those in attendance had already been led to the Lord by Chaplain Banks, but occasionally, there were decisions for Christ.

One night while preaching at the chapel, I sensed something very troubling in my spirit. As I spoke to these young inmates about choosing which God they would serve, the god of this world or God, the Creator of the universe, I began to sense something in a very strong way, something the scriptures describe as discernment of spirits—there were serious demonic forces present, and suddenly I knew many of them were tormented with a spirit of murder. As I was speaking, I told them that the Lord had let me know that many of them were obsessed with the thought of murdering someone. Before we concluded that evening, there were six young men who asked for prayer, saying they wanted to be set free, confessing the same obsession—they'd been tormented by a spirit of murder, and they wanted to be set free.

In addition to preaching and some one-on-one counseling, I was also asked to teach some of the inmates once a week at cell block C and D. Many of the young men had made a commitment to serve Jesus, and some of them showed a real hunger for God's word.

After a few months teaching at that particular cell block, I learned that Ineasie Baker, a woman volunteer chaplain at the prison, had been murdered in the same cell block, C and D, and her body had been put in a Dumpster, and she ended up in a landfill up in the high desert near Victorville, which was about an hour's drive to the north of Chino.

The chapel services were always exciting because many of the young men gave their testimony about how Jesus had set them free, free on the inside, and soon the word was out, and more and more were attending the services at what was known as the Protestant Chapel. The excitement wasn't over the attendance, which had been steadily growing, but it was over the changed lives.

So many, many lives had been miraculously changed—so many that it set off a conflict, a conflict with the Catholic chaplain at the prison. It seemed that so many of the young men had committed their lives to Jesus, and at the same time attendance at the Catholic services dwindled to an all-time low, and the Catholic chaplain was not happy about it. More than once he filed official complaints with the prison officials, but the numbers at the Catholic chapel still continued to fall. Several times the priest had claimed that Banks was proselytizing, but the truth was that the young inmates saw the changes in their fellow prisoners, and they were drawn to Banks and to the move of God in his services.

The Catholic priest eventually filed a formal complaint in Sacramento, still claiming that Banks was proselytizing, and it eventually resulted in Banks losing his position as chaplain, and as I understood it, the Catholic priest was either fired or transferred. Banks soon took a position as chaplain at a prison in Arkansas.

into the dungeon...

I had been working as a volunteer at that prison for more than two years when one of the guards offered to take me to a section they called the dungeon, which was a maximum-security ward for their most violent offenders. I hadn't been expecting them to offer to take me there at that time, so when they did ask me if I wanted to visit that cell block, I remembered that I'd left my Bible back at the prison's chapel. The guard was impatient and insisted, if I wanted to go to the dungeon, I had to come now and that he didn't want to wait for me to go back to retrieve my Bible.

I was led down a set of stairs that, in turn, led to an area of the prison that was underground. Then the guard unlocked the heavy steel doors that led into the part they called the dungeon, and immediately,

I knew why it was called by that name. Even before I stepped into the corridor, which had a large bank of cells on each side, I could see that each cell was without bars, but instead had a solid steel door and solid walls so that the only way to see into that cell was through a small glass slit that was about 1" × 5" set at eye level. This meant that the inmates couldn't see out, and no one else could see in unless they stood directly in front of that small slit. The glass was tempered and had what looked like chicken wire pressed between two plates of glass.

As I walked through the steel barred gate, somehow these young men sensed something, and there was a spontaneous agitation that gradually spread and began to build. It was something of a crescendo building throughout the unit. One after another they began to scream out, shouting obscenities. The guards hadn't announced my presence, and none of the inmates could see me unless I was standing directly in front of the tiny glass slit or if they were looking through it and I was standing directly in front of their cell, and yet they all seemed to erupt in anger at my presence. I looked through the slit into one of the cells, and I saw that these cells were only about 6 ft. × 8 ft., and then I saw that the prisoner inside was jumping up and down on his bunk, and then he began literally bouncing off the walls and screaming at the top of his voice, *"Get out of here with that bleep--ing Jesus. We don't want any bleep--ing Jesus in here."*

It became such a chorus of rage, screaming and howling and banging on their cell doors—a crescendo that reverberated throughout the cell block—that two guards soon rushed over to me, grabbed me by the arms, and physically pushed me out the door.

"You've got to leave now. I've never seen them so riled up. What the hell did you do? What did you say to them?" one of the guards shouted in my face.

I hadn't done anything. They didn't understand that it was the presence of the Holy Spirit within me that had them so agitated. It wasn't because they had seen me, which they hadn't—they didn't need to. They could sense God's presence, and they were violently agitated.

This type of thing had happened to me before, during my time in Florida. My very presence would stir up the demonic spirits in people, and they were unable to ignore it—they were compelled to respond.

I know this happened to Jesus quite often. I'm not comparing myself to him, but I know I have the same Holy Spirit in me that he had. Even when they saw him from far away, they sensed the Spirit of God in him, and they reacted. They always did. Jesus agitated the spirits in them, and people couldn't be neutral in his presence.

And this is an indictment on all of us today—you, me, all of us. How is it that we can enter into a room or a crowd with many people present, many who may have evil, demonic forces active in their lives, and they're not the least bit uncomfortable in our presence? *Wow!* I yearn to always be walking in the Spirit—so much so that the enemies of our soul are agitated just by my presence. I've only been in that place occasionally. I'm tired of playing patty-cake with the devil and his minions. I want that back in my life all the time.

A new chaplain was soon hired at the prison, and this young man had a particular denominational slant on things, some of which did not line up with ours. That meant with Banks now gone, so went my invitation as a volunteer chaplain at the prison. The reason I have detailed the events was in no way an attempt to diminish the work of anyone else—not the new Protestant chaplain or the Catholic chaplaincy, but those were the events as they happened, and you can draw your own conclusions.

mom flatlined for 90 minutes...

Just after the turn of the century and the horrible events of 9/11 my mother's health began to slip away. She'd had type 2 diabetes for many years without knowing she had it, and the disease had taken its toll on many of her organs, primarily on her heart. During that time, they discovered she had poor blood circulation in her legs, and the determination had been made to clean out her femoral artery. The doctor described it to me, using medical terms, and when I asked him to explain it to me in layman's terms, he said, *"It's a Roto-Rooter' job on her artery."*

Following the surgery, my mother contracted a deadly E. Coli infection that nearly took her life, and she was in a touch-and-go battle for her life for weeks afterward. That infection also further compromised her heart.

Then in 2004 I got a call from my younger brother, Les, that Mom was in critical condition in the Kaiser hospital in Fontana. Her cardiologist said we needed to gather the family around, and someone needed to perform her last rights. Diane and I were living in Corona at that time, which was a little more than half an hour drive from Fontana.

When we arrived at the intensive care unit, many of our family had gathered, and Diane and I noticed fearful looks on everyone's faces. When I spoke to Les, he explained that our mother had flatlined for the better part of ninety minutes, with the doctors using the defibrillator to restart her heart several times, each time only to have it stop again, and this happened over and over. The cardiac specialist explained to me that she'd endured such lengthy periods without oxygen that if she were to survive, she would likely have suffered so much brain damage from the oxygen deprivation she'd most likely exist only in a vegetative state, but he went on to say that it was unlikely she'd survive the night.

Mom's face had the pallor of death over it—there was no movement, and according to the doctors, she was as good as dead. She was in a deep coma, and there were no signs of life except for the rhythmic *clunk, clunk, clunk* of her breathing machine. Mom had never signed a DNR (do not resuscitate) order, and since I had Mom's power of attorney, I wasn't about to let them pull the plug on her.

It's very seldom that God is in the business of taking someone—taking their life, that is. When a believer comes home, that person is welcomed into heaven, but not because God took him or her. I've always believed that God is not the author of death (that's a subject for discussion later). So as my mother was lying there as though dead, I quickly cleared the room of family members, and I pulled the privacy curtains closed, and then I began to pray over Mom and rebuke Satan and the spirit of death. I began to exercise faith—faith to the pulling down of strongholds, praying in the Spirit over Mom and laying hands on her. After about ten or fifteen minutes with her, praying and taking hold of spiritual forces, I was confident I'd done all I could, and Diane and I started the thirty-five-minute drive home.

When I pulled my GMC Suburban into the garage, I immediately began to hear the phone ring. I hurried through the door into the kitchen and dining room area, and when I reached the phone, it was my brother Les, and he was screaming into the phone, *"Ken, you're not going to believe this. You're not going to believe this. Mom's alive—she's sitting up, she's well, and she's going home tomorrow!"*

Mom did go home the next day, and she lived for two more years, finally passing away at the age of eighty-five.

I spoke at Mom's funeral in Garden Grove, and family and friends had come from far and wide to bid her farewell. This was in the same chapel I'd preached at my father's funeral thirty-four years earlier, and many of the same friends and family were there both times.

Then in September of 2007 my older brother Reg died from complications with congestive heart failure. Diane and I flew to Houston to attend his funeral, and I was now hit with the realization that I was the oldest remaining Simmons. First Dad died, followed by all his brothers and sisters, then Mom passed away, but not before all her brothers and sisters had died, and now Reg. Except for my children and Reg's children all still living, I was the elder of the Simmons clan, and I'd been left with the responsibility of holding what's left of the Simmons family together, and I wasn't sure I was up to the challenge.

"Heavenly Father, above all, I want to know you once again, to walk with you, and to talk with you as I once did. Father, I want to learn to praise you again. My flesh hates to praise you, but my spirit cries out, Abba,

Father. Please complete the work you started in me so long ago... please don't give up on me."

I had drawn a line in the sand. From that point on I committed my life to serving the Lord. If I sin, I will repent. If I fall down, I'll get back up and keep on getting back up. My course is set. Jesus is my Lord, and he is my master.

I was like the prodigal who had left his father's house and went off to do his own thing. He lived fast and loose, and after he'd finally squandered his inheritance and everything he tried failed, he decided he'd try to come back. He thought, *Even my father's servants live better than I'm living. Even the scraps from his table would be better than this.* So he began making his way back. Then one day his father saw him from afar, and he shouted to the rest of the family, *"We're going to have a great feast. My son who was dead is now alive,"* and he killed the fatted calf and put a robe on his son and a ring on his finger—no judgment, no questions about why he'd squandered his inheritance; his son was alive!

I'm not going to pretend the road back was easy. There were times I grumbled the whole way. Yet he still loved me and forgave me.

That's the way God is—when we come back to him.

Chapter 25

perilous times...

Ever since the tragic events of September 11, 2001, during which 2,996 people were killed when Muslim terrorists flew passenger jets into the World Trade Center towers and the Pentagon and would have crashed another plane into the US Capitol Building or the White House if not for brave passengers who stormed the cockpit, causing the plane to crash into a field near Shanksville, Pennsylvania, the world has realized that we are in the midst of frightening and perilous times. Subsequent Muslim jihadist attacks in London, Paris, San Bernardino, and Belgium have made it clear that we may be rushing headlong into what many now believe are the End Times.

In 2004 an earthquake in the Indian Ocean caused a massive tsunami that took the lives of 283,000 people, and in the 2011 Tohoku earthquake and tsunami in Japan, the death toll exceeded 16,000. Between 2010 and 2012 it is estimated that more than 260,000 people have died in Somalia due to one of the deadliest famines in history.

The Islamic State in Syria (ISIS) has declared holy war and established what they call a caliphate, which has plunged the Middle East into a killing field, where genocide is being carried out on Christians and ethnic minorities on a scale not seen since the Nazis in World War II. Christian women, including girls, some as young as six, are routinely kidnapped, raped, and murdered because as one terrorist told his young victim who survived, it *"brings me closer to Allah."* Christian children are being buried alive, beheaded, and crucified, and there seems to be no limits on their barbarity. Just in the past few years there are now more Christian martyrs than at any time in history.

And yet when all hell seems to have broken out, we may be entering the greatest time for the Christian Church in history, a great outpouring of the Holy Spirit.

a great outpouring...

As the world seems to be turning its back on God in record and unprecedented numbers, a move of God that is unimaginable in scale has begun.

In China, officially a Communist-atheist country, there are estimates of more than two hundred million Christians, and that country is on a course to become the world's most Christian nation.

The nation of Iran is the world's largest sponsor of terrorism, but despite a crackdown on Christians in the land formerly known as Persia, the growth of Christianity is nothing short of explosive. The growth of house churches and secret meetings is staggering, and it's now conservatively estimated that there are more than three hundred thousand believers at last count and growing daily.

Argentina is experiencing a revival that it is soon to become the greatest Christian nation in South America. The charismatic move in that country is earmarked by a huge number of cases of signs and wonders, including miraculous healings and casting out of demons.

millions at a prayer meeting...

Lagos, Nigeria, now has what many consider to be the largest church in the world, the Redeemed Christian Church of God, where it is not uncommon to find more than a million Christians gathered together for a Friday night prayer meeting, and they are still there when the sun comes up on Saturday morning. A few years ago CNN sent reporters to investigate this phenomenon (who knows, to debunk it?), and there were more than ten million believers gathered together at a regional conference. True miracles happen at these meetings, so much so that they are considered commonplace. These miracles include many people being raised from the dead (verified and documented); in fact, this happens so often that they no longer make a big deal out of it.

Bill Davis, the former heroin addict whom I led to the Lord in 1972 and who has since then led more than five hundred thousand people to the Lord all over the world, recently traveled to Lagos and gave me a firsthand report of the huge numbers of people in attendance at these meetings—*"in the millions,"* he said.

Bill told me that he personally saw, close-up, numerous miracles that were beyond imagination. He told me, *"This is real, Ken... this is real."*

Filled with worshippers, this building seems to have no end—*amazing!*

The number of Muslim jihadists who have been converted is reaching epic proportions. And most of these are not being converted by some great evangelist, but by personal visions and, in some cases, visitations by Jesus Christ.

A close friend of mine, former US Congressman Mark Siljander, who works extensively with Muslim nations and who has written many books including *A Deadly Misunderstanding*, outlining how many Muslims are being reached for Christ, recently told me about an incident that occurred in late 2015 when two hundred Muslim men inside a mosque just outside Addis Ababa, Ethiopia, who all had a *simultaneous vision of Jesus*, were converted, and they are now going about spreading the word in spite of numerous death threats. These events have now been confirmed by three other independent sources.

Here is what God had to say about this great movement of his Spirit:

"In the last days, God says, I will pour out my Spirit on all people. Your sons and daughters will prophesy, your young men will see visions, your old men will dream dreams." (Joel 2:28; Acts 2:17, NIV)

To me, this says that when all hell breaks loose, God will begin a move of his Spirit that will be unprecedented on the earth, complete with *signs and wonders*.

This prodigal has been restored and has come back at the most exciting time for Christians in history. *Praise Jesus!*

I've led such a boring life…

Several times, while either at The Dove Coffee House, or at the Jesus House, I'd had young men threaten to kill me, twice pulling knives on me. Each time I simply told them, *"Sure, you can cut me and even kill me, but one thing I know for certain, I'll just be with Jesus a little sooner than I thought. But if you don't repent, you'll be in hell forever."*

My life had been threatened on several occasions while I was in the news business and also while I was hauling goods across the country in my Peterbilt tractor-trailer.

In addition to all the close calls I'd had, following all the injuries I suffered, I've had two total hip replacements and two total knee replacements, and when the right hip and the left knee replacements were completed, it was only about six weeks apart. I've also recently undergone a painful elbow surgery due to the many injuries I sustained back in 1992. I was like that proverbial horse I'd mentioned earlier: *"I'd been rode hard and put away wet."*

So let's see. I've been up to my neck in quicksand, attacked by a big tiger shark, chased by an alligator, was face-to-face with an angry mama mountain lion, met the world's oldest man, had lunch with a future US president, became friends with a governor, and had my life threatened by a chief of police and told if I didn't shut up about what I knew, I'd end up in the bottom of a lake, wearing a pair of cement boots. Two guys tried to rob me at gunpoint in my truck, and two more tried to hijack me and chased me down the highway, shooting at me. I was interviewing a man in a car when this crazy guy set the world's speed record for a car while driving it up on its side on two wheels (72 mph). I had a rattlesnake crawl over my bare feet.

And I've been upside down in an open-cockpit airplane, holding on for dear life because my seat belt wouldn't fasten; been bullied and manhandled by a US senator's bodyguard; was in the middle of a riot with bullets flying everywhere, with the bikers shooting at the cops and the cops shooting back; and was attacked by six or eight strikes of lightning while driving my car. I've seen God answer a cursing, mocking rock 'n' roller with a bolt of lightning and ball of fire less than ten feet from him; saw my mother snatched from the jaws of death and alive again; saw an auditorium full of high school students repent and come running to God; and saw a group of Presbyterian teenagers all miraculously touched by God, all breaking out in praise, and all singing in a heavenly language. I've seen drug addicts touched by God and healed with no withdrawals. *And I've personally lived the prodigal's story. I came running back to my Father, and he welcomed me with open arms!*

Yup, I've led a really boring and uneventful life.

Recently, I was reading about the life of Ronald Reagan, fortieth president of the United States, and his departing letter to America in which he told us of the honor he felt for the level of trust given him by the American people allowing him to serve as our president. The letter was written nearly ten years prior to his death as he succumbed to Alzheimer's.

Well, I want you to know about the greatest honor of *my* life—prior to a speech I made many years ago as I was announced as someone who had *"led thousands to the Lord."* Never quite comfortable with statements such as that, as I recall, my comment at the time was, *"I don't know about thousands, but I do know this—it was never enough."*

Then there were others who, when they greeted me for the first time, asked, "Are you *the* Ken Simmons?" Yes, I was honored to find a wife who loves me unconditionally and who loved all my children as though her own, and I was also honored to bring children and grandchildren into the world, but when the time comes for me to depart, I believe it fitting to state without reservations that my greatest honor has been to lead people into the loving arms of Jesus, the Christ, the Son of the living God. For when this happens, they truly pass from death to life (see John 5:24). There are no words to describe how humbling is that honor.

Chapter 26

**Deeper Waters
(The End of the Autobiography)**

The Christian life is, in many ways, like a swimming pool. When we're young beginners, we stay in the wading pool and gradually work our way to the shallow end. Our moms and dads are there to watch out for us, with warnings, *"Stay in the shallow end."* In an earlier chapter, I told you of the incident when my father pushed me into the pool at the New Mexico Institute of Mining and Technology in Socorro, New Mexico, and for years after that I was deathly afraid of the water. It took me many years of determined effort to overcome that fear. Unfortunately, many Christians never make it to the deep end of the pool, instead settling for splashing around in shallow water. The story I've just related to you for the past couple of hundred pages has chronicled my struggles and painful resistance to allowing God to lead me into deeper water. A great deal of those struggles were handled very poorly, and as I look back at it, I can see I was afraid of the deep end too. The shallow water is comfortable. You're not going to drown there, and the chances of getting hurt are slim. I only hope that after reading this, you too will see that God wants us to go deeper—in Him.

I've never claimed to be an expert on anything, but in this chapter, I've written my thoughts on a few issues that I believe to be true, and I try to answer some questions that we all ask at one time or another. This part of my book is not autobiographical. Here are a few of those questions:

why does a good God send people to hell?...

Well, the simple short answer is that He doesn't. In fact, there is no act you can commit that will send you to hell, nor is there an act, any deed, or anything you can do that is so good it will get you into heaven. That'll begin to make sense as you read on. And if you'll read my section still further on down entitled *"Heaven Is for Butterflies,"* you'll see that God never created hell for us, but for Satan and His rebellious angels. But because we are spiritual beings, we, in our natural (carnal) and unredeemed state, couldn't exist in heaven—at all. It would destroy us.

When man fell from grace, he changed from spirit, soul, and body to body, soul, and spirit. Let that sink in for a minute.

Why did Adam and Eve not even know they were naked until after they sinned? They were transformed and not for the better, but for the worse. With the caterpillar as an example, we must be changed or transformed (See 2 Cor. 5:17). When we repent and are transformed, God sees us as perfect as though He's looking through the blood of Jesus, and that's the only way to escape hell and the only way to go to heaven—because Jesus paid the blood penalty: "Without the shedding of blood there is no (sin) remission..." (See Heb. 9:22). He took our sin and shame to the cross and conquered death, hell, and the grave for us once and for all so that we'll never have to hear the verdict, "Guilty."

I want to reiterate. There is nothing you or I or anyone can do, no act so terrible you can commit, that will send you to hell. Nor is there anything you or I or anyone can do that will make us good enough to get us into heaven. You can never be bad enough, and you can never be good enough—to send you to hell or earn your way to heaven. If we could ever be good enough, then why did God send His Son to take our punishment for us?

My son Jeff has some real trouble with that one. One day he asked me, *"Do you mean that Adolf Hitler could get to heaven? That's crazy."*

I tried explaining to him that it was nothing that Hitler did nor any of his heinous and barbaric deeds he committed that sent him to hell, but it's the rejection of the saving power of Jesus that makes that determination. Even though Hitler's murderous acts indirectly caused at least fifty million people to die and he was the very embodiment of evil on earth, that didn't send him to hell. It was his ignoring and choosing not to accept the sacrifice Jesus made, and that alone would mean Hitler couldn't avoid that "guilty" verdict. That's why those who don't repent and come to Him cannot enter heaven, but have to face the judgment without Jesus standing in for us, taking our punishment on Himself. Had Adolf Hitler ever come to the end of himself, repented of his wickedness, and asked God for forgiveness, then received Christ as the sacrifice for his (Hitler's) sins, he could have been saved.

"Jesus said… 'I am the way, the truth, and the life. No one comes to the Father except through Me.'" (John 14:6, NKJV) Jesus went on further to say, *"He who believes in Him is not condemned; but he who does not believe is condemned already, because he has not believed in the name of the only begotten Son of God"* (John 3:18, NKJV).

Let's use another example to further illustrate this point. After the fall of mankind in the garden, the only person who has ever seen God and lived was Moses, and he only caught a brief glimpse of the backside of God. When Moses came down from the mountain, he was physically changed—so much so that the children of Israel couldn't even look at him because his countenance was glowing and radiating, and they had to cover their faces. Something happened to Moses. He experienced a transformation or, in the original language of the Bible, a metamorphosis. We'll go into this in more detail later in the section on butterflies.

why isn't everyone healed?…

That's a great question. Many today wonder why God doesn't just heal everybody. Why are some healed and the rest of the world go on suffering? Couldn't God just say the word and everybody would be healed?

Sure. Put in the larger text of the world with its billions of people, why does evil even exist?

I know that early in my Christian walk I struggled with some of these same questions. Before moving to Florida, I took my father to a Kathryn Kuhlman meeting at the Shriners Auditorium in Los Angeles sometime during the late 1960s. Kathryn Kuhlman (1907–1976) was a controversial figure who many called a faith healer, and she had a television program called *I Believe in Miracles* in the 1960s and '70s, and she became world-renowned for the miraculous healings that surrounded her ministry. I say *controversial* because many claimed she was a hoax and that some of the healings were staged, and I suppose some of that could have been true, but I personally witnessed one miracle I'd never forget when a young blind woman saw again.

During that meeting, I made my way to the center of the auditorium as Dad was making his way toward the stage, and I saw a young woman who was obviously blind. I know because I saw her up close, close enough to see the cloudy covering over her eyes and close enough to see that someone led her by the hand through the crowd. The young woman never made it up on the stage. But when Kathryn Kuhlman prayed for healing for the blind that night, she was praying for anyone in the audience who suffered without sight. I was only a few feet away from this young lady when I saw God heal her—God healed her, and He *healed her instantly and completely*. There are no words to describe the joy that came over her. She was ecstatic as tears of joy streamed down her face, and her rejoicing could not be contained. Earlier in my ministry, while in Florida, I had prayed for one young woman who was technically, legally blind, and she was healed and had to throw away her glasses because they no longer worked for her, but this woman was totally without sight, and God healed her instantly and miraculously.

Soon afterward Dad made it to a long line of people who were on the stage, and when Ms. Kuhlman prayed for my father, he dramatically fell to the floor, and some men on the stage had to catch him to break his fall. And yet when we returned home that night, Dad still had the cancer. Why did God heal this young woman of her blindness, and yet my father still had cancer—cancer that would later take his life? I don't have the answer.

But I do know that for reasons only God Himself knows, He has chosen to work through people. All throughout human history God has chosen people as His vessel and His conduit. And the Father has chosen to honor faith, and that's the key. He honors faith. Over and over, Jesus told people that it was their faith that healed them.

Sometimes you hear someone make a comment that goes something like this, *"Well, if it was God's will, then he'd have been healed"* or *"If it's God's will, your son will be saved,"* etc. The word of God tells us that God is *"longsuffering toward us, not willing that any should perish but that all should come to repentance"* (2 Peter 3:9, NKJV).

And yet we know that thousands of people die (perish) every day without knowing the Lord, and we know how that will turn out for them. If it's God's will that no one should perish and that all should come to repentance (and be saved) and yet so many die without salvation, which is it? Was it God's will they die and face an eternity without God? No, God honors and acts on faith.

I've had some miraculous healings in my own life, such as the broken rib healing within a week after it (the fact that it was broken) served its purpose in enabling the doctors to find a life-threatening cancerous thyroid tumor and remove it. I've survived a deadly form of skin cancer, and yet I'd still had to undergo two total hip replacements and two total knee replacements. I always hoped I'd be healed, but when I wasn't, I didn't turn down the wonderful work that doctors performed. God works through people. He works through believers, and God honors faith. If I or someone else praying for me ever has faith as that proverbial grain of mustard seed, I'll be healed.

God could have healed a woman named Tabitha before she died, and He could have also done so after she died, without any involvement from Peter, but God chose to honor faith by having Peter pray for her to raise her from the dead (see Acts 9:32–42).

So if you figure out why God has chosen to use people and He's chosen to honor the faith of believers (people), let me know. Until then we'll just have to accept it.

why do we have to be "born again"?...

Today it's likely that everyone in the modern world has heard the phrase "born-again Christian." Today the secular world seems to bristle at this label, and unfortunately, many Christians use it as a badge, indicating some sort of superiority to any other kind of Christian (although in here we will soon see there is no other kind of Christian). When someone says, *"I'm a born-again Christian,"* it seems almost rhetorical as if what we're really asking is, *"What kind of Christian are you?"* Although usually not said in that spirit, the world has, indeed, taken it as a sign of self-righteousness and spiritual superiority.

And others in the secular world have seen this as a requirement, if you will, that you must be "born again"... as some kind of harsh commands from a tough, iron-fisted God who is saying to the world, "It's my way or the highway," demanding, *"You must be born again, or I won't let you into heaven."* If the world only knew who God is. If they only knew the truth that God is not some mean-spirited taskmaster who has placed before us an impossible obstacle course through which, if successful, we might gain entry to heaven—if we're lucky enough to make it through his torturous life tests.

And if only the world knew that it was not some religious catch-phrase invented by evangelical Christians, but was a basic spiritual truth that Jesus revealed, saying, *"I tell you the truth, unless you are born again, you cannot see the Kingdom of God"* (John 3:3, NLT).

If you're a speed-reader, please turn off the turbo, and read the following slow enough to let it penetrate deep into your thoughts, because it answers so many of our most profound questions.

Adam was created in the image of God and, as such, had a fellowship with God that none has known since, except for Christ, who was God's only begotten Son. God created Adam that he might fellowship with man (mankind) and that man would share in His glory. Adam and Eve walked in the cool of the evening in the garden with God. Imagine actually walking and talking with God, strolling through the garden with Him in paradise. In the previous section when I addressed why some people ended up going to hell, man was made in His image, which was *spirit* first, then *soul*, and then *body*.

This was a *race of beings* in whom God breathed the breath of life (literally, the breath of lives), and this race of beings was *spiritual*. God created spiritual beings who could fellowship with Him and share in His glory. God wanted—*He desired*—this fellowship with man.

God's intention from the beginning was to create, in His image, a *spiritual* race that originated from Him and with whom He could fellowship and with whom He could share His glory. You should underline that last sentence, for it is on that basis and that understanding that you will begin to have the foundation for knowing God's purpose for mankind.

It was only after the fall of man that *another race came into being*, and that was the *natural* man, and the natural man completely reversed God's order, from being one of *spirit, soul, and body* to becoming that of *body, soul, and spirit*. This was a different race—or a different species, if you will—and this race had as its origin the fallen Adam, who had yielded to Lucifer, the fallen one, who tempted first Eve, then Adam to eat of the tree of the knowledge of good and evil. This was only half truth... *for man already knew good;* now he would know *evil*. Now man had the choice to exercise his free will, to choose between good and evil, but since being *introduced to evil,* God's mold for man had been reversed. Man was now body (flesh), then soul (mind, emotions), and lastly, spirit (spiritual, or the consciousness of God).

Just as man's seed cannot produce apes or monkeys and the seed of apes cannot give birth to man... *the natural man cannot give birth to spiritual man.* Or put differently, monkeys will always breed monkeys, dogs will always breed dogs, and natural (fallen) man will always breed natural (fallen) man. The natural man, which is the seed of Adam, who had fallen (due to the temptation followed by his disobedience), can only produce natural man.

This bears repeating. The natural man, which is the human species that resulted from the fall of Adam, from that which was once *spirit, soul, and body...* to one of *body, soul, and spirit...* can only give birth to the same species. Carnal man will always father carnal children, for this is the natural state of things. If man had remained spirit (then soul, then body), he would always father spiritual children, and there would never have been the need for Jesus to take our place and our punishment for sin.

This is not a rule laid down by a harsh God, but merely a fact of natural law. Once you see this principle, then you can see that is not a punishment meted out by a harsh God. Hell is where Satan will ultimately end up, and for the *natural man,* hell is the natural place where natural man will naturally end up.

Once man was changed from the image of God, which was spiritual, mankind was now a different race... a race made of up *natural* beings who were a reverse image of His original creation, and the only way for God to restore man to that fellowship and to restore man to His glory was to send His Son to walk among us and to be sacrificed for our sins that the *natural* man could die, *"I am crucified with Christ"* (Gal. 2:20), and that the *spiritual* man could be resurrected or *"raised us up together; and made us sit together in heavenly places in Christ Jesus"* (Eph. 2:6).

"And be not conformed to this world: but be ye transformed by the renewing of your mind, that ye may prove what [is] that good, and acceptable, and perfect, will of God" (Rom.12:2, KJV).

So back to the issue of being born again. People may want to argue the point, but other than the undeniable fact that Jesus said, *"I tell you the truth, unless you are born again, you cannot see the Kingdom of God"* (John 3:3) *(it's kinda hard to find any wiggle room and get past this one)*—was this just another rule from a demanding God? Here's another way to help understand it.

heaven is for butterflies...

This illustration, in the form of an analogy, is that of the butterfly. Imagine, if you will, that caterpillars wanted desperately to fly like butterflies and that flying was the only way to reach high enough to enter heaven. *But not only could caterpillars not fly, but also the very nature of heaven was foreign to them, and to be in heaven and in the presence of God would destroy them.* They simply could not survive in heaven's environment. The caterpillar, in spite of all its attempts to fly, can never take to the skies. If you imagine man or mankind as the caterpillar, this becomes even clearer.

So regardless of all its attempts to live a good life and to live honestly among all the other caterpillars, it simply could not (fly) enter into heaven. This was not a *rule*, but a *law* much like the *law of gravity...* a stone cannot rise up and float away like a puff of smoke, but always falls to the earth because the laws of gravity are absolute here on earth. The caterpillar is doomed to its natural existence. In order for the caterpillar to enter into the kingdom of heaven (fly), it must undergo a change... a *metamorphosis*, if you will. Many times this word is found in the scriptures, and it originates from the Greek word *metamorphoo*, which means "to be transformed." "And be not conformed to this world: but be ye *transformed* (metamorpho) by the renewing of your mind..." (See Romans 12:2).

The caterpillar must be transformed—period. It has no wings, and unless it undergoes this *metamorphosis* and miraculously becomes a butterfly, it will never fly—that is, it will never enter into the kingdom of heaven. For heaven is a spiritual place, and caterpillars are of *natural* origin. Heaven is for butterflies... and only for butterflies, which are symbolically *spiritual* beings and can survive only in heaven, for in heaven is the presence of God. The caterpillar must first die. It must die (to itself) before it can ever experience that transformation into a butterfly, just as we must die (to ourselves) and then become transformed into spiritual beings. If you read this one hundred times, it won't be too many. This is incredible spiritual truth.

Jesus described it this way: "Most assuredly, I say to you, unless a grain of wheat falls into the ground and dies, it remains alone; but if it dies, it produces much grain" (John 12:24, NKJV). Every farmer knows this. They know that seeds must be put in the ground and, in effect, die (and undergo a transformation) for new life to spring up.

As I mentioned earlier, maybe you recall the story of Moses, who, after leading the Israelites through the desert for so many years, saw the burning bush on the mountain and sought to meet with God. After Moses's fasting and praying, God finally revealed himself to Moses, but he instructed Moses to hide himself in the cleft of the rock and to look only at God's backside or *"hindered parts,"* for no man could look directly upon God and survive. Even after this brief glimpse at the backside of God, Moses was temporarily *transformed* (metamorpho), and when he came down from the mountain, the children of Israel *"could not steadfastly behold his face"* because Moses was shining so brightly after having looked upon *just the backside of God* that the people had to cover their eyes… he had been in the presence of God, and he literally glowed with a radiance that natural man could not look upon.

If Moses, who, centuries later, returned with the prophet Elijah to meet with Jesus on the Mount of Transfiguration (see Matt: 17), could not bear to look upon God, how could *natural* man, in his *natural* state, bear to look upon God and be in His presence in the kingdom of heaven? It would destroy natural man. Only the *spiritual* man, who has been born again *(transformed),* can enter into the kingdom and be in the presence of a holy God.

I cannot overemphasize that hell is not a punishment invented by a cruel God. Hell is the natural end for natural man, which was the only place in which Lucifer and his fallen angels could exist after his fall as one of the archangels of God.

The caterpillars must go to the place for caterpillars, and the butterflies must go to the place for butterflies. Natural man is going to go to the place for natural man, and his body will return to the dust of the ground, but his spirit will live forever, either in the place created for Satan and his fallen angels or in the heaven that was created for the transformed man or woman. For *natural man* to enter into the kingdom of heaven, he must first be spiritually reborn or *transformed* by having his sins removed, which was accomplished by the blood of Jesus. Then he must die, which was accomplished by the cross of Jesus, and the natural man must then be born again, a new man: "*Therefore, if any man be in Christ, he is a new creature: old things are passed away; behold, all things are become new*" (2 Cor. 5:17, KJV).

So we, in our unredeemed (natural) state, are not condemned to hell by a demanding God… *in our natural, fallen state, there is no other place for us.* God's original plan before the fall of mankind was for us to fellowship with Him and share in His glory. The only way we can possibly do this now is for us to undergo a transformation… *back to our original, spiritual state.* We are like that caterpillar, and in our natural, unredeemed state, being in heaven and in the presence of God would actually destroy us. We would physically burn up—ignite in the atmosphere of heaven.

can someone lose their salvation?…

The sad truth of the matter is that some evangelical Christians have, for so long, taught us that salvation through Jesus Christ is a *"get out of jail free"* card or an *"escape from hell"* ticket to heaven. And it's true that the first benefits we realize from submitting our lives to the Savior is that we, through the beginnings of this transformation we call *salvation*, are not condemned to the place where the natural man must (as illustrated earlier) naturally end up and that heaven is our eternal resting place. This is certainly not meant to even hint a minimizing of salvation. How could anyone minimize such a glorious gift of God's grace and mercy? *It is the greatest gift of all!*

But if that were God's only eternal purpose, for us to escape hell and make it to heaven, then He could simply cut our lives short the moment we surrender to Christ to accomplish that goal.

But what if I sin? This is a centuries-old dilemma that theologians have struggled with for centuries. On one hand, you have the extreme that says, every time you sin, you have to get saved all over again. Then at the other end of that argument is one that says, *"Once saved, always saved,"* and nothing you could ever do could cause you to lose your salvation.

We do know that Jesus Himself said that He is the good shepherd and that if one of his sheep is lost, He will leave the ninety-nine and go after that one lost sheep. Here He's saying that He'll go to extreme measures to make sure that no one is lost. He further strengthens that argument with statements such as this: *"I give them eternal life, and they will never perish. No one can snatch them away from me, for my Father has given them to me, and he is more powerful than anyone else. No one can snatch them from the Father's hand"* (John 10:28–29, NLT).

This brings us back to the issue of free will, which is a principle God will never violate. Years ago Pastor Karl Strader taught me a valuable lesson, and that was to always interpret scripture with scripture. Scripture should always be measured against other scriptures so as to minimize the chance for personal interpretation.

If "once saved, always saved" were an absolute truth and that nothing we could ever do could cause us to be lost, that in itself implies that when a name is written in the book of life, it can never be removed, and yet, in the Book of Revelation the scriptures are very clear that there are circumstances in which God will remove (blot out) their name from the book of life (see Rev. 22:19, NKJV).

Even during the years I was running from God, I never forgot any of the scriptures I'd memorized, and some of them were on this very subject, my backslidden condition:

"For if we sin willfully after that we have received the knowledge of the truth, there remains no more sacrifice for sins, but a certain fearful looking for of judgment and fiery indignation, which shall devour the adversaries." (Heb. 10:26, KJV)

"For if after they have escaped the pollutions of the world through the knowledge of the Lord and Savior Jesus Christ, they are again entangled therein, and overcome, the latter end is worse with them than the beginning. For it had been better for them not to have known the way of righteousness, than, after they have known it, to turn from the holy commandment delivered unto them. But it is happened unto them according to the true proverb, the dog is turned to his own vomit again; and the sow that was washed to her wallowing in the mire." (2 Peter 2:20, KJV)

why is the world in such a mess – isn't God in control?...

This is a question people everywhere ask. Terrible earthquakes and tsunamis happen, and hundreds of thousands are killed, and even millions, left homeless. A famine occurs, and millions starve. Hurricanes and tornadoes devastate cities and states every year. It seems that wars and rumors of war are happening everywhere, and the tragedies seem endless. Why did God let this happen?

A beautiful young girl is kidnapped and raped, and other innocent children, brutally murdered. What's going on? Why did God let this happen?

Hitler came to power, and because of him, more than fifty million people died. Where's God in all this?

Shortly before the terrible events that occurred on 9/11, I was preaching at the California Institution for Women in Chino, California. I asked the women inmates, *"How long will you continue to listen to the god of this world? Without knowing it, some of you have been following him all your lives. He whispers in your ear, 'Why not? Everyone's doing it.' And so you end up overdosing, or you end up pregnant with some really bad guy's baby, or you end up killing someone. How's that been working out for you—listening to the god of this world?"*

Jesus called him the prince of this world, and the apostle Paul frequently referred to him as the god of this world.

Shortly after Jesus was baptized by John in the River Jordan, Jesus fasted in the wilderness for forty days, and He was tempted by the devil, during which he told Satan that *"man shall not live by bread alone, but by every word that comes from the mouth of God.* Scriptures go on to say, "Again, the devil took Him up on an exceedingly high mountain, and showed Him all the kingdoms of the world and their glory. And he said to Him, 'All these things I will give You if You will fall down and worship me' (Matt. 4:8, NKJV).

Something very profound happened at that time, and many people pass right over it and never catch the significance of that passage. Jesus never rebuked Satan when he said he'd give him all the kingdoms of the world. He never said to Satan, *"No, it's not yours to give"* or *"you don't have the right to do that."* Jesus knew that Satan was the god of this world, and all these things were actually his to give. Wow! Let that sink in for a minute. Here was Satan telling Jesus, the Christ, the Son of the living God, that he (Satan) could give him all the kingdoms of the world and all the worldly glory that went with it. Jesus knew that it was within Satan's authority to give him all these things. That's right—Jesus knew that Satan wasn't just blowing smoke, but that he actually could do what he said: give him everything.

Let's go to another passage—one that many of us also pass over, not quite grasping the significance of it.

Jesus had gotten into the boat with his disciples, and during that time a great storm arose, and the disciples were afraid for their lives, but Jesus was calmly sleeping in the boat. The scriptures tell us, *"And they came to Him and awoke Him, saying, 'Master, Master, we are perishing!' Then He arose and rebuked the wind and the raging of the water. And they ceased, and there was a calm"* (Luke 8:24, NKJV).

Many teach that the significance of these passages was that Jesus had the faith, and the disciples didn't, which was true, but there is something else that is of equal importance. Jesus *rebuked the storm!* Why did Jesus rebuke it? *Why didn't he just wave His hand, and it became calm?* Big question—why did Jesus have to *rebuke it?*

We know that Jesus acknowledged that Satan had the power to grant Him all the kingdoms of this world if He'd only bow down and worship Satan. Here we see that Jesus further acknowledged that this was Satan's world—even the weather was within his domain. Yes, you read that correctly. Even the weather was within Satan's domain. Remember, he is the god of this world. *And only through faith, exercised by believers, will these things ever be subject to us.*

This is a broken and cursed world, and we're living in *enemy-occupied territory.* Calamities and catastrophes of every sort occur. Even the principalities and powers of this world are corrupt and under the evil influence of Satan, and it's only when believers exercise faith is any of it ever subject to us. Wars, earthquakes, and rampant crimes—all signal that until Jesus returns and defeats Satan, this world will be in turmoil and under the devil's curse. That bears repeating. It's only when believers exercise faith is your wife healed or your child saved or any other of the devil's evil works undone in this wicked world. That's why the apostle John said, *"Do not love the world or anything in the world. If anyone loves the world, love for the Father is not in them. For everything in the world—the lust of the flesh, the lust of the eyes, and the pride of life—comes not from the Father but from the world. The world and its desires pass away, but whoever does the will of God lives forever.* (1 John 2:16–17, NIV). Wow! Now you may be beginning to see why this world is in such a mess.

The old nature, our old nature (yours and mine), is carnal. The old nature prefers the flesh and its pleasures rather than the things of God. It is my nature, and every man and woman's, to sin and to take pleasure in sin. The natural man would rather lust than pray, would prefer adultery than remaining faithful, and would much prefer the pleasures of this world than that which is spiritual. And yet the old man can never know the kind of *"peace of God which passes all understanding"* (Phil. 4:7), and he can never know the *"joy unspeakable and full of glory"* (1 Peter 1:8) until he is surrendered to the Lord and makes him Lord of his life. This world can never offer and can never know this kind of life.

like drinking saltwater...

During the years when I was in a backslidden state and running from God, I learned firsthand that tasting of this world's pleasures, the lusts of the flesh, was a lot like drinking saltwater. It's somewhat like sailors during World War II, adrift for sometimes weeks, dying of thirst with water all around them. The irony of it doesn't go unnoticed. When you crave something, hoping it will satisfy you, sometimes you find yourself craving and lusting for anything to quench your thirst, and in desperation you, in effect, drink the saltwater. It satisfies briefly, but soon you realize it never sated your thirst. Instead you are now thirstier than ever. The more you drink, the thirstier you become until finally you realize that nothing of this world can quench the thirst.

To have Christ revealed in us means more than just going around, talking about Jesus and being nice to people. Christ was motivated, compelled, by compassion for the people. He didn't live and die and rise again so that he could promote a doctrine or a group or an agenda. Jesus came to earth to touch peoples' lives and to touch them infinitely and completely. That same compassion welled up in Peter when he told the crippled beggar, *"Silver and gold have I none, but such as I have, give I thee. In the name of Jesus, rise up and walk"* (Acts 3:6, KJV), and the same man was seen *"walking, and leaping, and praising God"* (Acts 3:8, KJV). This was Christ revealed, and He was revealed in Peter that day.

After Jesus returned from the wilderness where he spent forty days fasting and enduring temptations by Satan, he then went into the city of Jerusalem and entered the temple. When he stood up, he was handed the book of the prophet Isaiah and read aloud, *"The Spirit of the Lord is upon me because He has anointed me to preach the gospel to the poor; He has sent me to heal the brokenhearted, to proclaim liberty to the captives and recovery of sight to the blind, to set at liberty those who are oppressed; to proclaim the acceptable year of the Lord"* (Luke 4:18, NKJV), and then he said to them, *"Today this Scripture is fulfilled in your hearing"* (Luke 4:21, NKJV).

From that point on, everywhere Jesus went He touched lives. He preached on the kingdom of God, and then He healed the sick, He brought deliverance to those who were oppressed by demons, and He preached the good news of salvation. And every time He touched lives, He again fulfilled that scripture, *"The Spirit of the Lord is upon Me."* When He fed the crowd of about five thousand and when He healed the sick, cast out demons, and even raised the dead, that scripture, *"The Spirit of the Lord is upon Me"* was fulfilled for everyone to see and hear.

In fact *every time a man or woman of God today* reaches out to touch someone, to bring them salvation, or to ease the pain of a broken heart or to bring about deliverance to those who are oppressed, they are fulfilling that same scripture. This is Christ being revealed—manifested, if you will—in us, for He came to touch peoples' lives, and when we touch others, we too learn we have the authority to stand up and say, *"The Spirit of the Lord is upon me because He has anointed me to preach the gospel to the poor; He has sent me to heal the brokenhearted, to proclaim liberty to the captives and recovery of sight to the blind, to set at liberty those who are oppressed; to proclaim the acceptable year of the Lord"* (Luke 4:18, NKJV).

All of mankind, everywhere, cries out for some evidence that God is real and that God's people are real. The apostle Paul said, in his letter to the Christians in Rome, that the *"earnest expectation of creation eagerly waits for the revealing* [or the *manifestation*], *of the sons of God"* (Rom. 8:19). God wants to reveal His Son in me and in you so that when the world sees us, we are the manifestations to the world that God is real and that His Son lives in us. If we bring food and clothing to the poor, if we bring healing to the sick, and if we bring comfort to those who are brokenhearted or deliverance to those who are in bondage… we are revealing or manifesting to the world the Son of God.

with God all things are possible...

It was quite impossible for Bill Davis to be completely and instantly healed of bleeding ulcers and set free from his heroin habit the night he came to the coffeehouse. And in the natural it was impossible for God to answer the scoffer, the one at the rock festival who had an upraised fist, cursing God, with a bolt of lightning from the skies. It was impossible for those who were tormented by unclean spirits to be set free and delivered. It's not possible for revival—true Spirit-led, God-blessed revival—to break out in a prison where most of the men are in there for murder... or for revival to break out in some of the Middle Eastern Muslim nations where Christians are put to death for their faith... but with God all things are possible.

As I said in the beginning chapters of this book, this is no game... this is not playing church. This is not Sunday religion... we are the *Church*, made up of "living stones," and the Church, when going forward in the whole truth of God, is the manifestation of Jesus Christ on the earth to a lost, dying world.

The apostle Paul said that even us, who were dead in trespasses and sins, who once walked according to the prince of the power of the air (Satan), have been quickened, have been made alive, and have been raised up together and made to sit together in the heavenly places in Christ Jesus (see Eph. 2:1–6).

"For God has not given us a spirit of fear, but of power and of love and of a sound mind." (2 Tim. 1:7).

When we go into an area where evil seems to have been turned loose, we need to believe God... believe that it is the *demons* who fear and tremble and *not us*, not the children of God. (See James 2:19.)

If we step out on faith and we fail, what will happen to us? We might look pretty foolish if we start to believe God for these kinds of things and they don't happen, and yet that's often the trigger setting off the miraculous.

I came literally within seconds of ignoring that still small voice when I was standing alone on that stage at that high school auditorium in Dade City, Florida. For a brief moment I asked myself how foolish I'd look if nothing happened, and I wasn't sure I was hearing from God or if it was my imagination, and in a split-second decision I decided I'd better obey what I thought was the voice of God and pray. That's when God honored my faith and my obedience, and there was a miracle at the high school when so many students came running down to the front to surrender to Jesus. Many times I've wondered how things might have turned out differently if I ignored what I thought I was hearing and just ended the assembly as usual. Sometimes split-second decisions can have effects that last a lifetime.

So what if we fail? Aren't we all failures anyway, and for years was I not the poster child for failure? And if it's the signs and wonders we seek, we're bound to fail anyway. But if it's the love and compassion that compel us to reach out and touch others in need, whether we fail or succeed, it is God's doing anyway.

Some would say, *"I've seen so many phonies and so many abuses in these areas. You've got people knocking people down and calling it being slain in the Spirit, and you've got all these people trying to turn it into a showbiz performance."*

True, but do we stop sharing the truth because some abuse it? Are the poor no longer with us? Are the brokenhearted no longer hurting? Do the tormented no longer need deliverance? Are the lost now found?

I once saw a well-known evangelist who called a young man from the audience to come forward to the stage. This young man was a crack addict, and without even looking at the young man, the evangelist brought the audience to a fever pitch with a countdown... *five... four... three... two... one...* and then without so much as looking at the man, he smacked him on the forehead with the palm of his hand, and the young man fell over backward... supposedly being *slain in the Spirit*.

I thought about what I had seen, and I wondered where Christ was in any of this. Where were the compassion, the words of comfort, and the power to heal and set free? All this demonstration accomplished was to put the spotlight on that evangelist. If all that was being revealed in him was himself and not the character of Christ, then all that was accomplished was a performance that demonstrated only the preacher's character and not the character of the Lord, who was compelled by love and compassion.

On those occasions when God has used me to reach out and touch others, sometimes with miraculous results, it is an overwhelming and, at the same time, humbling, experience. For I know that within me—that is, within myself—there is no power to save, to heal, or to set free… and so when these things do happen, you know it is all God, and no one but God can take credit for it—especially not me.

Not long ago I saw a homeless old woman who seemed to be beaten down by this world and by life itself. She shuffled along, pushing a broken down old cart and carrying plastic bags filled with all her worldly possessions. It was truly a pathetic sight. Hers seemed to be a life of hopelessness. I was troubled in my spirit and I began asking God what to make of it. It was then that I believe God *struck me, hit me,* with the realization that this poor soul was worth more than all of this world's wealth -- all of the worldly possessions, all of the gold, silver, and treasures that this world has to offer. That little, insignificant *nobody* of an old lady was worth more than all the fortunes of the world. Jesus said, "For what profit is it to a man if he gains the whole world, and loses his own soul?" Such is the value of one soul. Yet for most of our lives we strive for this world's treasures, never realizing that if this little old lady has Jesus, the Christ, the Son of the Living God in her heart, *she has it all! She is blessed beyond measure and her reward will be beyond our imagination.* Such is the kingdom of heaven.

On March 17, 1972, I was on my way to commit suicide by overdosing with heroine. The doctors said I had a bleeding ulcer, and if I didn't have surgery, I'd be dead in a matter of hours. I was a heroin addict and a professional thief and robber, and I'd been in and out of prison several times. Since I had nothing to live for, I decided not to have the surgery, so I drove my car down Main Street in Lakeland, Florida, on my way to my parents' home where I planned to OD on some heroin I'd stolen, and as I rounded the corner, I saw a bonfire at what used to be a biker bar, now run by a group called Youth Challenge, and I heard the song, *"Hallelujah."* I pulled my car over and a long-haired young man said to me, *"Jesus is here to set people free."* After leaving 3 times before, thinking I was at a church, I almost turned around to leave again, but instead I decided to go in, and when I did the Director, Ken Simmons, said *"Young man, God's got His hand on your life."* Somehow he knew I was going to commit suicide that night. He then quoted Joel 2:28, saying, *"God said, In the last days I will pour out my Spirit on all flesh."* He then went on to say, *"It doesn't matter what you've done. You could be a thief, drug addict, alcoholic, bank robber, or ex-convict, it didn't matter to Jesus, he still loved you."*

    I fell to my knees and repented, and to my shock I knew I was forgiven. Then they prayed for me to be baptized in the Holy Spirit. I was gloriously baptized, and the rest is history. I've been walking with Jesus ever since, and I have shared my story in Europe, Asia, Africa, and all across America, and countless thousands have been saved since. *March 17 is my new birthday!*—Bill Davis.

In Loving Memory

Lee Simmons

Dad, you never knew the wonderful impact you had on my life. Through all your years of pain and suffering, you never once cried out, *"Why me?"* Your character always came through, and you were an example to all of us in the Simmons family. We've missed you, but we'll see you again.

Myra Simmons

Mom, your nature always came through, and you were loved by everyone. I can't wait to see you again, and I'm so glad you're no longer suffering.

Reginald "Reggie" Simmons

Reg, you and I came through a lot together, and for the longest time you and I weren't on the same page. I'm so grateful that in your later years you finally came to know our Lord and Savior Jesus Christ. Can't wait to see you, big brother.

Bill Green

I hope you have found the peace in him, the peace for which you struggled so hard to find here on earth. I know you loved the Lord, and I hope God has a big grand piano there for you to thrill the angels.

Beverly Barrington

You were one of my first children in the Lord, for I introduced you to him, and when I see you again, you can handle the introductions.

Rev. Wayne Johnson

Never have I known a gentler spirit in a man. God's grace and mercy were so evident in your walk with him.

Al West

Al, you never got to finish writing my story, but thanks for kick-starting it in the right direction. I'll see you in paradise, brother.

Max Rapoport

I have known Max Rapoport since 1967 beginning with our times together sharing Jesus with the hippies in Huntington Beach. Max was greatly used by the Lord and he will be missed, by me and everyone who knew him. Max left for heaven on Jan. 16, 2017.

About the Author

In 1969 he felt the call of God to begin a work in Florida, with no money and without the backing of any church or organization. Those humble beginnings started a movement that would have a ripple effect that would eventually reach many around the world. But in spite of countless miracles and changed lives, turmoil at home eventually found him running from God—a prodigal, whose long journey back to the Father's home would finally lead him to redemption and victory. This is the miraculous and moving story of Ken Simmons.

CPSIA information can be obtained
at www.ICGtesting.com
Printed in the USA
BVHW031758230220
573077BV00001B/29